# Human Flourishing

# Human Flourishing

Economic Wisdom for a Fruitful Christian Vision of the Good Life

Edited by
Greg Forster and Anthony R. Cross

Foreword by Matthew Croasmun

◥PICKWICK *Publications* · Eugene, Oregon

HUMAN FLOURISHING

Economic Wisdom for a Fruitful Christian Vision of the Good Life

Copyright © 2020 Greg Forster and Anthony R. Cross and the contributors. All rights reserved. Except for brief quotations in critical publications or reviews, no part of this book may be reproduced in any manner without prior written permission from the publisher. Write: Permissions, Wipf and Stock Publishers, 199 W. 8th Ave., Suite 3, Eugene, OR 97401.

Pickwick Publications
An Imprint of Wipf and Stock Publishers
199 W. 8th Ave., Suite 3
Eugene, OR 97401

www.wipfandstock.com

PAPERBACK ISBN: 978-1-7252-5943-0

HARDCOVER ISBN: 978-1-7252-5944-7

EBOOK ISBN: 978-1-7252-5945-4

Cataloguing-in-Publication data:

Names: Forster, Greg, editor. | Cross, Anthony R., editor. | Croasmun, Matthew, foreword writer.

Title: Human Flourishing: Economic Wisdom for a Fruitful Christian Vision of the Good Life / Greg Forster and Anthony R. Cross, with a foreword by Matthew Croasmun.

Description: Eugene, OR: Pickwick Publications, 2020 | Includes bibliographical references and index | xxviii + 208 p.; 23 cm

Identifiers: ISBN 978-1-7252-5943-0 (paperback) | ISBN 978-1-7252-5944-7 (hardcover) | ISBN 978-1-7252-5945-4 (ebook)

Subjects: LCSH: Economics—Religious aspects—Christianity | Christianity—Economic aspects | Economics—Moral and ethical aspects

Classification: BR115.E3 C767 2020 (print) | BR115.E3 (ebook)

Typeset by Anthony R. Cross.          Manufactured in the U.S.A.

Endorsements of the Oikonomia Network's new "Collaborative Theology" Project

"There is a widespread concern among seminary leaders these days that theological education must look for new directions. I hope that they will look in the directions where the 'Collaborative Theology' project is pointing. This is precisely the kind of preparation for ministry that we desperately need: equipping church leaders to equip, in turn, a new generation of Christian disciples to be serve God's purposes beyond the walls of the churches. This marvelous Collaborative Theology project shows us how we can take hold of what are often seen as frustrating challenges and transform them into exciting and creative opportunities for new forms of kingdom service!"
*Richard Mouw, Fuller Theological Seminary*

"The vision laid out in 'Collaborative Theology' is exactly what's needed to break through the institutional barriers and silos that are holding us back from forming the vast majority of Christians for whole-life discipleship. After twelve years and hundreds of interviews, conferences and collaborations with theologians both inside and outside the academy, I agree with the assessment that many are aware of the problems and are eager to move forward, but the institutions needed are either absent or, even worse, have proven to be hindrances. At the Theology of Work Project, we have several times come close to trying some of these ideas; they're the right ideas, but the TOW Project has concluded that our organization is not positioned or gifted for this kind of work. The Oikonomia Network is well-positioned and capable to develop this kind of work. I heartily support this initiative and hope the ON will be able to launch it soon!"
*Will Messenger, Theology of Work Project*

"Oikonomia Network's vision for *karam* collaboration speaks to a central missiological need in this cultural moment. The diagnosis of the locus of contemporary ills in the fragmentation of modern praxis and its impact, not simply on the institutions of western cultural life, but also on the church and in particular the theological academy, is insightful and important. A radical new approach to the biblical and theological formation of a new generation of leaders is at the heart of the 'repairing and rebuilding of the broken walls' that is our foundational missional task. The Oikonomia Network are world leaders in this endeavor and deserve all the support we can give. I wholeheartedly support this initiative."
*Paul Williams, British and Foreign Bible Society*

"Education used to be about more than training people for occupations. It used to be about building up men and women for their most important vocations: being human and living wise, flourishing lives with one another, before God, to God's glory. In an age where theological education has become pathologically fragmented, I heartily welcome this new initiative in collaborative theology. Fostering interdisciplinary communities of learning that combine theory and practice, knowing and doing: this is the way to bridge the gap between church and academy for the good of both bodies—and society too."
*Kevin Vanhoozer, Trinity Evangelical Divinity School*

"This vital initiative gets to the heart not just of a US challenge, but of a global challenge. With a few exceptions, our research shows that theological education has indeed failed to offer a compelling vision of what flourishing, everyday, holistic discipleship looks like, and consequently has neither taught it to its students nor taught them to pass it on to others. What is required to address such a systemic, cultural problem is not ranks of 'add-on' modules or specialist centers for 'this, that or the other,' but an entirely new integrative approach to the whole task. And that is precisely what this bold, creative, well-researched, well-structured, well-led collaborative venture is designed to do. I couldn't be more enthusiastic about its potential."
*Mark Greene, London Institute for Contemporary Christianity*

"I love the 'Collaborative Theology' project! This has great potential to bring theological education to a wider audience than the traditional seminary and pastoral preparation. It fits well with the goal of the church to 'seek the welfare of the city' and pursue human and community flourishing, ultimately in the context of a vibrant relationship to God and neighbor. I'm very supportive of the project."
*Scott Rae, Biola University*

"Most of my fifty years since graduating from Berkeley have been dedicated to a pursuit of the integration of my biblical Christian faith with my life, my thinking, my work and my behavior. My forty-year career as a professor and my nine books are all about that mission. What a massive difference it would have made (as I drew all the pieces together) to be helped and sustained by a truly 'Collaborative Theology' as described in this proposal. With the technologically-enabled cultural fragmentation of our world in high gear, the 'Collaborative Theology' project rises to top priority. We have no time to waste."
*David Gill, Gordon-Conwell Theological Seminary*

"The 'Collaborative Theology' project is a tangible means through which theologians can offer a robust corrective to the fragmentation they have had a

significant hand in perpetuating. The project can build on the many recent efforts to reconnect the church and seminary in a way that is mutually fruitful. I am excited about this collaboration because it moves beyond diagnosis toward promising prescriptive alternatives that advance God's redemptive work through his people."
*Donald Guthrie, Trinity Evangelical Divinity School*

"As someone who has both a deep appreciation as well as growing concern for the theological academy, I believe there is a compelling and urgent need for structural reform. While the Sunday-to-Monday gap is greatly crippling the flourishing of the local church, the theory-to-practice gap is fundamentally compromising the mission of the theological academy. I know of no greater need than for theological education to make a decisive turn from silos of specialization to scholarly communities of collaborative integration. The Oikonomia Network is perfectly positioned to be a primary change agent for desperately needed reform. I wholeheartedly believe this is not only a highly strategic opportunity, but an investment with far-reaching impact for generations to come."
*Tom Nelson, Made to Flourish*

# Contents

Contributors ........................................................................................... xi

Acknowledgements ............................................................................... xiii

Foreword
Matthew Croasmun ............................................................................... xv

Introduction
Greg Forster and Anthony R. Cross ..................................................... xxiii

### *Faith*

Chapter 1
Flourishing, Justice, and the Gospel as "Subduing" the Earth
J. Michael Thigpen ................................................................................. 3

Chapter 2
Nations in the Metanarrative of Redemption: A Gospel for Public Life
Greg Forster .......................................................................................... 16

Chapter 3
"Better than a Slave:" Paul and the Economics of Slavery—
A Rejoinder to Ulrike Roth
Lynn H. Cohick and John Anthony Dunne ......................................... 28

Chapter 4
Waiting with Eager Longing: The Inseparability of Human Flourishing
from the Flourishing of All Creation
Suzanne McDonald ............................................................................. 45

### *Hope*

Chapter 5
Lamentable Obligation in Augustine's Political Theology
Greg Forster .......................................................................................... 61

Chapter 6
Paying It Forward: Medieval Monastic Economies of Salvation
Greg Peters ............................................................................................ 74

## Chapter 7
Bankrupting Heaven: The Printing Press and the Collapse of the Indulgence Market
Nathan Hitchcock ................................................................................... 87

## Chapter 8
Godly Non-Profits: Extending the Porterfield Thesis
Robert E. Wright ................................................................................... 102

### *Love*

## Chapter 9
Failure to Thrive in the Lord's Ordered World: Causes for Poverty in the Book of Proverbs
Daniel J. Estes ....................................................................................... 123

## Chapter 10
Paul, Poverty, and Economic Justice
John W. Taylor ..................................................................................... 135

## Chapter 11
Martin Luther on Usury and the Divine Economy
Jonathan Lett ........................................................................................ 155

## Chapter 12
Capitalism, Socialism, and Karl Barth's Pragmatism: Lessons from a Disillusioned Socialist for Christian Economic Engagement
Kimlyn J. Bender .................................................................................. 176

**General Index** ..................................................................................... 201

# Contributors

Kimlyn Bender, Professor of Christian Theology, George Truett Theological Seminary, Baylor University, Waco, Texas, USA

Lynn Cohick, Provost/Dean, Professor of New Testament, Denver Seminary, Littleton, Colorado, USA

Matthew D. Croasmun, Director, Life Worth Living Program, Lecturer, Humanities & Divinity, Associate Research Scholar, Yale Center for Faith & Culture, New Haven, Connecticut, USA

Anthony R. Cross, Adjunct Supervisor, The International Baptist Theological Study Centre, Amsterdam, The Netherlands

John Anthony Dunne, Assistant Professor of New Testament, Bethel Seminary, St Paul, Minnesota, USA

Daniel J. Estes, Distinguished Professor of Old Testament, Cedarville University, Columbus, Ohio, USA

Greg Forster, Director, Oikonomia Network, Trinity International University, Deerfield, Illinois, USA

Nathan Hitchcock, Sevensided Consulting, Brandon, South Dakota, USA

Jonathan Lett, Assistant Professor of Theology, LeTourneau University, Longview, Texas, USA

Suzanne McDonald, Professor of Historical and Systematic Theology, Western Theological Seminary, Holland, Michigan, USA

Greg Peters, Professor of Medieval and Spiritual Theology, Biola University, La Mirada, California, USA

John W. Taylor, Professor of New Testament, and Director of Academic Graduate Studies, Gateway Seminary, Newport Beach, California, USA

J. Michael Thigpen, Executive Vice-President and Provost, Professor of Old Testament, Phoenix Seminary, Phoenix, Arizona, USA

Robert E. Wright, Paul Coverdell Distinguished Visiting Fellow of Policy Studies, Georgia College and State University, Ocean City, New Jersey, USA

# Acknowledgements

"For everything created by God is good, and nothing is to be rejected if it is received with thanksgiving, for it is made holy by the word of God and prayer" (1 Timothy 4.4–5). We receive the gift of this book, all the contributions associated with it, and all the fruit we hope it will bear with thanks to our God, King and Savior for his holiness, and for the holiness of his word, which gives life.

We are joyfully grateful to the authors who contributed these excellent essays. Exploring how theological knowledge can serve human flourishing will be a major task of the church in the coming generation. These essays show that theological scholars have crossed over from merely lamenting the lack of top-quality scholarly investigation of that question to taking first steps in providing it. These authors have invested their time in this endeavor in spite of the fact that there are currently relatively few scholarly publication outlets supporting this vital work. To them, to Matthew Croasmun for contributing a foreword, and to others who contributed papers to the Oikonomia Network colloquia in January 2019 from which this volume originates, we are greatly indebted.

We are also grateful to Wipf & Stock for seeing the potential of this volume. The church does continue to need theological scholarship focused on the old questions. But it also needs scholarship that takes the risk of addressing new—or, rather, newly restored to great urgency—questions about how theological knowledge can serve human flourishing. This requires not only an investment from scholars who have limited time and must work in the hope that their labors will be recognized, but also publishers who must set priorities under similar limitations. We are indebted for the missional vision that the publication of this volume by Wipf & Stock represents.

We owe a debt to the scholars who organized and led the Oikonomia Network's January 2019 colloquia, and served as contributing editors of this volume. David Buschart organized and led the colloquium on theology. Michael Thigpen organized and led the colloquium on biblical studies. Nathan Hitchcock organized and led the colloquium on Christian history. We couldn't have done it without them.

Miroslav Volf gave a plenary address to a joint plenary of all three colloquia, which was also joined by those attending the annual faculty retreat of the Oikonomia Network. Volf unpacked the argument from his book *For the Life of the World*, co-authored by Croasmun, calling upon theology to integrate its disciplines around the mission of helping human beings flourish. The audio of that address is available at the Oikonomia Network's website, oikonomianetwork.org. The following day, Volf shared another argument from *For the Life of the World*, concerning the challenges of a pluralistic society and how Christians can be faithful in that context, at the Karam Forum 2019 event; that address is available on the Oikonomia Network's YouTube channel.

The activities of the Oikonomia Network, including the January 2019 colloquia, have been financially supported by the Kern Family Foundation.

Our warmest gratitude goes out to the members of the Oikonomia Network steering committee. One of the editors of this volume (Greg Forster) has had the privilege of working alongside these wise leaders as chair of the steering committee since it was formally convened in 2013, and informally for years before that. They have tirelessly invested themselves in building up our community, with little reward other than the hopeful knowledge that they are helping build a brighter future for theological education that serves God's people and God's world.

This book is dedicated to them, with friendship and admiration:

- Chris Armstrong, *Christian History*
- Vincent Bacote, Wheaton College
- Gerry Breshears, Western Seminary (member emeritus)
- Deborah Gill, Assemblies of God Theological Seminary
- Donald Guthrie, Trinity Evangelical Divinity School
- P.J. Hill, Wheaton College
- Nathan Hitchcock, Sevensided Consulting
- Tom Nelson, Made to Flourish
- Scott Rae, Biola University
- Charlie Self, Assemblies of God Theological Seminary

# Foreword

The question of the shape of flourishing life is the central question of human existence. It lies at the heart of philosophy. The world's great religions can meaningfully be seen as ways of life and systems of belief oriented around asking this question and discerning and commending particular sets of answers to it. This question has been central for thousands of years because human beings are fundamentally purposive creatures; in all that we say and do, we aim at some desired future.[1] But this question is pressing in a new way right now for a number of reasons.

The question of flourishing life is urgent today in part because of a particular set of obstacles to human flourishing that mark our age. Many of these obstacles are taken up explicitly in this volume: growing income and wealth disparities, the looming climate crisis, the displacement of peoples across the globe. These crises are interconnected. As Pope Francis has noted,[2] the greed that drives the growing divide between rich and poor also pumps carbon into the atmosphere, and the deleterious effects of our ecological crisis fall disproportionately on the poor. As a result of climate change and concomitant ecological collapse, economic opportunity vanishes in places where it once existed, driving macro population shifts. The economic, ecological, and forced migration crises are interconnected and inseparable.

This interconnectedness should not surprise us. Life is a network of structured wholes. As a result, flourishing life is holistic. We see this at many levels. My life only fully flourishes when all aspects of my life flourish. Life on this planet fully flourishes when each ecosystem flourishes. But not just that. Flourishing life is not a mere heap of flourishing lives. Flourishing life is itself a structured whole that is more than the sum of its parts. Flourishing life emerges from interlocking complex interdependencies, because life itself does just this.[3]

The global pandemic in the context of which I write this foreword is disclosing once again the complex nature of these interdependencies. A biological entity so small and parasitic on other forms of life that it is only disputably alive at all (the virus) is bringing the world economic system to its knees. In the process, we witness daily unintended consequences of the interconnectedness of global supply chains.

---

[1] Miroslav Volf and I offer an expanded account of the centrality of this question in *For the Life of the World*, 13–17.

[2] Francis I, *Laudato Si'*.

[3] I have elaborated this emergent account of life in *Emergence of Sin*, 22–101.

Even more, the pandemic is revealing the asymmetry of these dependencies. The newly coined category of "essential workers" makes plain the extent to which the subsistence of many upper- and middle-class folk depends on the (often minimum wage or "gig") labor of others. No doubt, this asymmetry is merely the pandemic manifestation of the parent-child relationship James Baldwin observed between black and white Americans.[4] The strong have long been dependent on the weak in ways the strong often lack the eyes to see (1 Cor. 12.21–25). Even as we note our interdependencies, we must note the asymmetries of the structures on which our lives depend.

At the end of the day, the pandemic has simply shown us again the contours of the economic and ecological crises that we face. Both are challenges of home. This may surprise many. For most of us, home means our domestic home: the people in our household—friends, roommates, a partner, a spouse, parents, children—and the place where that household resides. A home is just this: a set of dynamic relations between people, things (living and inanimate), and place, marked by resonance, attachment, and boundary maintenance. These three marks are adopted from the work of my colleagues, Miroslav Volf and Ryan-McAnnally-Linz.[5] I will refer to them collectively as the ethics of care constitutive of home. A home is a dynamic set of relations marked by a particular ethic of care.

And, indeed, for many, the present ecological and economic crises have brought about visceral crises of home in this most basic, domestic sense. Economic and ecological pressures scatter families across the planet. Shifting population patterns stir up ideologies of blood and soil among those privileged to remain in their places. Let us not be deceived; these false histories deprive of home even those who remain at home, for true home depends on telling the truth about place and about history.

But to say that our economic and ecological crises cause a (separate) crisis of (domestic) home is not quite right. Rather, these crises are themselves crises of home—though homes of different sorts and different scales than we often consider. If we have ears to hear, our crises of economy and ecology should warn us that there is something profoundly narrow about our vision of home—our vision of *oikos*, from which both *eco*-nomics and *eco*-logy are derived. Our whelming *eco*-challenges are particularly challenges of home in the sense of *oikos*—home as a structured whole. In order to discern, articulate, and commend visions of flourishing life, Christian theology needs a constructive *oikology*, to borrow Susannah Ticciati's term,[6] sufficient to the complex economic and ecological crisis of our day.

---

[4] Baldwin, *Fire Next Time*, 101–103.

[5] Volf, "Modern Homelessness."

[6] Ticciati, "Reconceiving the Boundaries of Home."

If home is a dynamic set of relations, then each of these domestic homes is itself set within a broader context of larger homes, larger sets of relations of analogous sorts. Our domestic homes are located within broader socioeconomic and ecological homes.

As modern Westerners, we tend to divide these three homes into two categories, which we call private and public. (If we think at all about our ecological homes, we lump them into the public sphere.) As many feminist thinkers have pointed out, this dichotomy between public and private is fundamentally deceptive and often depends on patriarchal thinking that elevates the public as masculine and denigrates the private as feminine. But it is not just that the public–private distinction is illusory and patriarchal. It also harms our relationships to our socioeconomic and ecological homes in at least two additional ways. First, in this paradigm, the concept of home is equated with, and thereby reduced to, the domestic or private. The result is a dangerously atomistic and reductive picture of home that fails to recognize the interdependencies that exist between our domestic homes and their broader socioeconomic and ecological contexts. Second, the public–private paradigm renders oikological concerns irrelevant within the public—chiefly the economic—domain. Restricting all species of care to the private realm yields a public realm akin to a Hobbesian "state of nature," in which any ethic of care is appropriately disregarded. One can see something similar happening in the way we relate to our ecological home. Instead of seeing the non-human world as continuous with ours and, in fact, constitutive of it, we objectify nature as something distinct from us and treat it as something to tame, to domesticate. That is, we see nature as some*thing* we must *turn into home* (Latin, *domus*), rather than an interconnected network of beings and things whose relationships with one another and with us in large part constitute any home we might ever experience.

Careful attention to the Pauline tradition's treatment of these various different homes—domestic, civic, and ecological—would lead us to a conception of home at once more complex and more unified than the modern public–private dichotomy offers. To be sure, Paul is concerned about all three: our domestic homes, our civic homes, and our ecological homes. But, most often, these three arise as contexts and as metaphors for another home: the ecclesial home. In thinking about church, the Pauline tradition mixes and matches various images of home, suggesting that there is something universal to right *oikonomia*, regardless of the scale.

Beginning at a smaller scale than even the domestic home, Paul offers the internal economy of the individual body (the "physiological home," we might say, if we can stomach the suggestion of dualism such a phrase might suggest) as a model for the church (the ecclesial home) in 1 Corinthians 12 and Romans 12. Here, the main point is to establish the existential interdependency of members of the ecclesial body, the mutuality of the ethic of care within the ecclesial home, and their unity in Christ, whose body they collectively constitute. However, members of the ecclesial body are marked not just by the home-logic of the church, but also by the (potentially distorted) logics of the broader socioeconomic context. There are those marked as strong and those marked weak, those considered wise and those considered foolish. Maintaining the order of the ecclesial home necessarily bleeds into concern for the order of the socioeconomic home in which it is embedded. A holistic understanding of home rules out quietism from the start.

Gazing outward, Paul also takes up language of the democratic political ideals of the Greek city (a vision of the civic home) in his account of the church. The word *ekklēsia* is itself borrowed from Greek political language. It is the word for the voting body of democratic city-state, the deliberative body that seeks the good of the city. (Cf. Acts 19.39 for this generic Greco–Roman usage.) Much of 1 Corinthians is probably best understood as advice about how this body can best perform its duties of spiritual discernment. (One might think especially of chapters 11–14, but this interest is found throughout the letter.) And we see the *ecclesia* functioning as exactly this sort of body beyond the Pauline corpus in a place like Acts 15. Here, the decision of the Jerusalem Council begins with an adaptation of a stock phrase from Greco–Roman political language: "it has seemed good to the Holy Spirit and to us" (Acts 15.28, cf. Josephus, *Antiquities* 16.163). The church in its legislative role functions as a democratic deliberative body. Obviously, as it is applied to church, the oikology of the democratic state is expanded. As Paul is at great pains to say and to defend in 1 Corinthians, the *ekklēsia* of Christ is more inclusive than the *ekklēsia* of the polis. (Membership, for example, is not limited to propertied men.) And, as we see in Acts, the deliberative body, crucially, includes the Holy Spirit, whose presence suffuses the entire ecclesial body politic. God's activity and presence are pivotal in the dynamic relations that constitute the ecclesial home. God's cruciform definitions of genuine power and wisdom (1 Cor. 1–2)—fundamental categories for the discernment work of the ecclesia as deliberative body—lie at the heart, then, of the politico-ecclesial oikology.

Later in the Pauline tradition, the domestic household is taken as a model for the ecclesial home. Many have reflected on the problems caused by these invocations of the ancient domestic model—particularly in the so-called household codes. Doubtless, these domestic accounts of the ecclesial home have to be squared theologically with the older (and, I take it, more fundamental) oikologies of somatic solidarity and pneumatic democratic deliberation. In any case, the rhetorical emphasis seems to be in arguing *from* a particular domestic oikology rather than *for* it—and the problematic hierarchies are often invoked precisely in order to be subverted christologically into modes of mutuality. The flagship case would seem to be the much-debated extended marriage metaphor in the household code of Ephesians (Eph. 5.21–33). Here, the insistence that the author is "speaking about Christ and the church" (v. 32) makes clear that the primary rhetorical goal is not a teaching about marriage, but about the oikology of the ecclesial home. Christ, in a position of authority vis-à-vis the church, gives himself up for her, setting a model for how power is to be exercised. This, I take it, is a key aspect of the christological ethic of care at the heart of the Pauline tradition's logic of home. It is applicable to the household, to the church, to the city, to the creation, and everywhere in between. By virtue of the primacy of this ethic, we can read these texts as transforming their own conception of the domestic household, calling into question the very paradigms of authority and power the standard household code itself invokes.

Finally, it is also clear that, for Paul, there is an ecological, or even more broadly, cosmological home in light of which the church's own oikology is shaped and which is itself illuminated through an understanding of the church. The proper ordering of creation (its oikology) is sufficient to reveal God's very nature (Rom. 1.20). While this order has been distorted through "subjection to futility," the whole creation (the ecological home) groans and waits for the unveiling of the children of God (the ecclesial home) (Rom. 8.18–23). This obscure locution in Romans perhaps finds elucidation in 2 Corinthians. In as much as there is a new creation coming to be "in Christ" (2 Cor. 5.17), God's reconciling work in the church is nothing less than a redemption and a drawing-to-eschatological-fulfillment of the ecological home. As in every other home, the ecological/cosmological home comes to full flourishing as it is united with God, when, in the end, God is "all in all" (1 Cor. 15.20–28). It is this unity of God and God's people at home with one another and at home with the entirety of the creation, that is the model of the renewed creation. If the creation is a model for the ecclesial home, the church in turn becomes also the model of the ecological home.

In every case, the exchange of meaning in the analogy flows both directions. Surely, we learn something about the church-as-home from consideration of somatic, domestic, civic, and cosmological homes. But, even more significantly, we learn something about these other homes, as the analogies inevitably run backwards as well. Why? Because the Christian conviction is that all homes, as dynamic relations, are intertwined and all ought to be governed by a unified oikology that enables a christological ethic of care. The Pauline tradition, in thinking about church, demonstrates again and again this confidence that good *oikonomia* is good *oikonomia*, transferable *mutatis mutandis* from one sort of home to another.

The church is that place in which Paul works out the unifying oikology of creation—the logic of home. For Paul, the church becomes the site of *oikological* reformation, the place where the very concept of home is repaired as its eschatological fulfillment draws near. But the point is not that we withdraw from our civic or ecological homes any more than it would be that we should withdraw from our domestic homes. The ecclesial home is to serve as a site for the renewal of home *as such* for the sake of the renewal of all of creation—the domestic, civic, and ecological homes—in the presence of God. In the case of the civic home, this renewal precipitates a renewal of the logics of the spheres of the civic realm, including, crucially in our world dominated by economic reasoning, the economic sphere.

Paul's unifying oikology is a theology of the kingdom of God, an understanding of God at home with the world and the world at home in having become the home of God. It is an account of care within the dynamic relation of persons, things, and place that rightly structures our homes of various scales. This account is hardly limited to Paul. Canonically, the account of home as a dynamic relation of God and God's creation runs from Genesis' strolls in the cool of the evening in the Garden of Eden (Gen. 3.8) to Revelation's declaration that "the home of God is among mortals" (Rev. 21.3). As Miroslav Volf and I have argued, this story of the kingdom of God as the story of God's home can be seen as a unifying narrative of scripture and the heart of the Christian tradition's account of flourishing life.[7] Such an account points us again and again to our particularity, our locatedness, and our interdependence within complex networks of relatedness in which we are embedded. It points us again and again to our relatedness to God, to one another, and to the entirety of God's creation.

To be clear, I don't take this brief foreword to have offered the oikology we need. At best, I hope I have gestured toward the sorts of concerns a theological account of home sufficient to our economic and ecological challenges might take up and some of the biblical paradigms that might be relevant to such an undertaking. In the end, I suppose all of this merely adds up to an affirmation of the importance of the questions this volume takes up. To the extent to which the question of flourishing life is fundamentally shaped in our moment by a multi-level crisis of home, then asking the question of flourishing life in terms of economics and ecology has never been more important.

But I hope it is also clear that the fact of the unity of this oikology—a unified theory of home that runs from Eden to the New Jerusalem—itself speaks to the specific domestic, socioeconomic, and ecological challenges we face today. It will, for example, warn us off false conceptions of self in which we imagine ourselves as atomistic individuals who, in having transcended space, time, and body, have transcended or conquered (they often amount to the same thing) our civic and ecological homes—that is, it will warn us against whiteness and its ascendance as a global ideal.[8] It will demand that we consider our responsibilities to one another as democratic citizens in an economic sphere no longer divorced from the care ethic of home. That is, in applying ancient biblical texts to modern economic challenges, it will demand we take seriously the fact that, unlike our ancient forebears, we do not act

---

[7] Volf and Croasmun, *For the Life of the World*, 66–78.

[8] Yancy, *Look, A White!*, 161. See also Birt, "Bad Faith of Whiteness."

merely as disempowered subjects of empire, but rather as political agents—all too often, as agents of empire. We cannot claim biblical warrant to reserve our charity to the domestic or ecclesial spheres. It will require that we apply whatever we have learned in the church about the so-called strong and weak to our posture within the natural world by which we are constituted.

This is where flourishing life is found: in learning to function as members of a living, interconnected creation being drawn to eschatological fulfilment as the home of God. Only if we can be captured by this vision can we begin to meet the modern crisis of home. Come, Holy Spirit.

Matthew Croasmun
*June 2020*

### Bibliography

Baldwin, James. *The Fire Next Time*. New York, NY: Vintage, 1993.
Birt, Robert. "The Bad Faith of Whiteness." In *What White Looks Like: African–American Philosophers on the Whiteness Question*, edited by George Yancy, 55–64. London: Routledge, 2004.
Croasmun, Matthew. *The Emergence of Sin: The Cosmic Tyrant in Romans*. New York, NY: Oxford University Press, 2017.
Francis I. *Encyclical Letter Laudato Si' of the Holy Father Francis. On Care for Our Common Home*. 2015. http://www.vatican.va/content/francesco/en/encyclicals/documents/papa-francesco_20150524_enciclica-laudato-si.html
Ticciati, Susannah. "Reconceiving the Boundaries of Home: The 'Oikology' of Ephesians." *International Journal of Systematic Theology* 21.4 (2019) 408–30.
Volf, Miroslav, and Matthew Croasmun. *For the Life of the World*. Grand Rapids: Brazos, 2019.
Volf, Miroslav. "Modern Homelessness." *The World as God's Home*. The Cadbury Lectures, 28 May 2019.
Yancy, George/*Look, A White! Philosophical Essays on Whiteness*. Philadelphia, PA: Temple University Press, 2012.

# Introduction

This book is a step forward for an urgent conversation in theology. In our time, there is a growing consensus that theological knowledge ought to help cultivate authentic human flourishing in the church and, through the church's participation in the cultural structures of the nations, in the world as well. The natural next step is for theological scholars to explore how their knowledge in its particularity—knowledge about such topics as what Proverbs and Paul say about poverty, Karl Barth's encounters with capitalism and socialism, or how the gospel relates theologically to the cultural mandate—could contribute to the real-life flourishing of truck drivers, administrative assistants, stay-at-home parents or leaders in business and government as each of these carries out their daily tasks in a pluralistic and fragmented world.

In the past generation, the theological disciplines have been struggling to overcome the dismissive perception that they are just historical and technical studies. To do this, they must show that they provide knowledge—real insight—into the deep structures of reality. Through the works of Mirsolav Volf and Matthew Croasmun, Kevin Vanhoozer, Jonathan Pennington and many others, theological scholars are increasingly recognizing that in order to show that theology is knowledge, they must show how it can help cultivate human flourishing. That is the tangible test of whether the ideas produced by the theological disciplines really provide knowledge about reality. If theological knowledge is knowledge at all, it must be useful—though of course it has other value as well.

Moreover, in addition to this external imperative, there is a powerful internal imperative to deploy theological scholarship for human flourishing. While we can in principle pursue theological knowledge for its own sake, the knowledge about reality that we actually discover through theology demands that it be pursued for more than its own sake. We can ask, "What does God's word say?" without intending to put the answer to use. But if it turns out that one of the things God's word says is that you should put God's word into action, that discovery has consequences. If theological knowledge is knowledge at all, it must inspire the people who know it to make it useful.

These recent realizations, naturally, build on older theological thought. Indeed, concern for how theological knowledge can serve human flourishing has always been part of the church's reflection on God's word, as some of the historical essays in this volume explore. More recently, the current interest in human flourishing grows out of prior work done by such figures as Richard Mouw, Dallas Willard and Lesslie Newbigin on the theological side, and Oliver O'Donovan, Graeme Goldsworthy and Christopher Wright on the biblical side. Even figures like John Howard Yoder and Walter Wink, who take a more unambiguously oppositional stance toward existing cultural structures, or contemporary "two kingdoms" theologians like David

VanDrunen, who emphasize the distinctiveness of church institutions from civil institutions, incorporate a profound concern for authentic human flourishing at the center of their theologies. The disputed questions between Mouw, O'Donovan, Yoder and VanDrunen are not about whether theological knowledge should serve human flourishing, but about what theology tells us about human flourishing, and how theology can cultivate it.

### Economic Wisdom against Fragmentation and Resentment

The background of all these developments is the fragmentation of cultures under conditions of advanced modernity, and the growth of polarized resentments that this fragmentation naturally creates. Cultures become fragmented in advanced modernity largely as a byproduct of developments that are in themselves good and necessary. Religious freedom and increased concern for human rights make it difficult to maintain a morally coherent culture in a way that is not felt to be unjust and oppressive; economic and technological development increase our power to isolate ourselves and to minimize negative consequences from bad behavior.

While the deepest causes of fragmentation are developments that in themselves we neither can nor should regret, this fragmentation constitutes a major challenge to human flourishing. Incoherent cultures lack the normal social conditions to support moral formation and ethical standards—the overcoming of our congenital tendencies toward materialism, complacency, narcissism and injustice. The breakdown of institutions that are essential to human flourishing is both a cause and an effect of fragmentation.

One problem of special importance is the division of cultures into mutually hostile groups locked in perpetual conflict. By far the easiest strategy for a social group to maintain a coherent sense of its identity and purpose under conditions of fragmentation is to identify an enemy who has hurt the group, and focus the energies of personal and social formation on the battle to "defend ourselves" (i.e., aggressively attack the other) and "take back what is rightfully ours" (i.e., forcibly seize resources and status symbols). Fragmentation also makes it easy to construct a plausibility structure for such resentments, as the loss of coherence, stability and power that every group experiences because of fragmentation can be blamed on the enemy. And, of course, resentment-driven conflict puts money and power into the hands of people who are skilled at cultivating resentment, and is thus a self-perpetuating enterprise.

However, advanced modernity also opens a path to a potential solution. While the old loci of social coherence are in decline, there is a new openness to action in a different social sector—a sector that is also less susceptible to takeover by resentment-driven conflict. Christian activity in that cultural domain can help coherence reemerge.

*Introduction*

In the ancient world, political structures were the source of social coherence. As the advanced religions (the "Axial" or "world" religions) grew, a shift occurred. Religious structures joined with—or even supplanted—political structures as the locus of social coherence. Both these types of institutions are unable to create cultural coherence in a social world where people have the right (as a result of religious freedom and respect for human rights) and the power (as a result of economic and technological development) to believe whatever seems right to them about ultimate reality. Where people choose their own beliefs, religion is the subject of social conflict, and politics is the primary platform where that conflict is carried out—through proxy battles over the moral foundations of public policy, and sometimes more openly, through competition to seize political status symbols.

In the advanced modern world, to the extent that we have a common public life at all, it is mainly lived out in the domains of work and commerce. This phenomenon has a variety of causes. At the simplest level, among those whose primary vocations take them into the public square, the overwhelming majority do their work in the commercial world; political, religious, artistic and other kinds of non-commercial professionals are numerically small. In the frankly inegalitarian social world of premodernity, the non-commercial class could comfortably maintain itself as a social elite in spite of its small size. But the moral egalitarianism of the modern world demands that whatever the overwhelming majority of people in the public square are doing is the real center of public life. In other words, democracy in politics and the priesthood of all believers in theology not only reinforce each other, but work together to elevate commerce over both politics and the church as the locus of shared life. Another cause is the transformative power of wealth creation and technological development, for good and ill, unleashed by the modern economic regime of property and contract rights.

The new power of commerce over social life is an opportunity for Christians. It means that a Christian view of economic life is essential to a modern Christian view of human flourishing. But it also means that Christians have the power to pursue human flourishing in a domain where openness to the creation of new structures is greatest, and the incentive structures that maintain conflict-driven resentment are relatively weak. There is, admittedly, a growing penetration of the "culture war" into commerce—but this is relatively recent and peripheral compared to the near-total multigenerational captivity of our political and religious structures. Commerce is to some extent colonized by the culture war, but the colonizers are not primarily economic actors; they are political and religious resentment machines.

## Seeking Coherence across Disciplines

Theological scholarship can provide coherence in a fragmented world because it is a knowledge tradition with a supernatural source. Two thousand years of accumulated wisdom in understanding the Bible's testimony have produced a living body of insight we can draw on today. Ancient and yet always new, grounded in eternity but capable of informing practical life, the accumulated theological wisdom of God's people is the storehouse of the "big story" within which leaders can find truth, coherence and stability as they craft solutions to specific problems.

A key obstacle to coherence in the theological knowledge tradition—and hence to its contribution to human flourishing—is the separation of the theological disciplines from one another. There is nothing inherently wrong with the existence of multiple theological disciplines. However, when the different disciplines operate using deeply dissimilar conceptual categories and methods, integration will not occur for most people, and it will not come easily to the few who do pursue it. Under these conditions, theological knowledge has become as fragmented as the advanced modern world itself.

This is not a coincidence. The current structure of the theological disciplines does not create fragmentation by accident, but by design. It is fragmented, and fragmenting, on purpose. Advocates of an aggressive and uncritical embrace of modernization—Friedrich Schleiermacher foremost among them—designed the fourfold disciplinary structure (systematic, biblical, historical, practical) that now dominates the theological academy. It did not grow organically out of the two-thousand year theological knowledge tradition, but was invented in the nineteenth century by radical modernizers who saw the theological tradition as an outdated legacy the church needed to overcome to be relevant.

Thus, interdisciplinary work—as difficult and frustrating as it often is—is the only path to a theology that cultivates human flourishing. However, such work does not begin with immediate interdisciplinary interaction. It begins with each discipline considering the question of human flourishing for itself, and then bringing the results of those inquiries into interdisciplinary dialogue.

This book had its origin in three colloquia held by the Oikonomia Network in January 2019: theology, biblical studies and history. However, the chapters in this volume are not grouped by discipline. Rather, they are arranged in cross-disciplinary sections according to the three traditional "theological virtues" of faith, hope and love. Our hope is that this will stimulate the reader to see connections across disciplinary divisions—as, for example, between a biblical paper on the meaning of the mandate to "subdue the earth" in Genesis 1.27–28 and a theological paper on how the pursuit of human flourishing must be in harmony with the pursuit of flourishing for the nonhuman creation; or a biblical paper on poverty in Paul and a historical paper on Barth's wrestling with the capitalism/socialism dilemma.

*Introduction*

The first section, "Faith," contains papers whose most immediate implications are doctrinal—or, in one case, apologetic. J. Michael Thigpen considers how pursuit of human flourishing, justice and even proclamation of the gospel can be seen as fulfilling the Genesis mandate to "subdue" the earth. Greg Forster traces the role of "the nations" in the Bible's gospel metanarrative, and why this implies a need for a theology of public life. Lynn H. Cohick and John Anthony Dunne respond to the claim that Paul profited from slavery in his missionary work. Suzanne McDonald makes a theological case that flourishing must include all of creation, not just humans.

The second section, "Hope," contains papers that trace the development of Christian thought and practice over time. Greg Forster examines a key theological claim in Augustine's *City of God* that set the stage for much of both medieval and early modern Christian approaches to public life. Greg Peters reviews medieval thought and practice on the subject of "economies of salvation." Nathan Hitchcock traces the interdependence of technology, economics and theology in the indulgences crisis of the early sixteenth century. Robert E. Wright holds up the enormous social role of nonprofit companies, many of which were religious, in the eighteenth and nineteenth centuries.

The third section, "Love," contains papers that focus on applied social ethics—including some historical cases where the focus is on ethical issues of enduring importance rather than on historical development. Daniel J. Estes looks at poverty in Proverbs, while John W. Taylor looks at poverty and justice in Paul. Jonathan Lett walks us through the challenging but provocative subject of Martin Luther's writings on trade and usury, while Kimlyn J. Bender looks at Barth's capitalism/socialism dilemma, which is also our own.

There is much more work still to be done. Reconnecting theological knowledge to the way people actually live their daily lives and do their daily work will be a generational endeavor. In the long run, deep reforms in the structure of the theological academy may be required. The next step toward this exciting and challenging future for theological scholarship is to go beyond the generic claim that theology should cultivate human flourishing, and show how it can do so in detail. The essays in this volume do this with wisdom, skill, faithfulness and compassion.

Greg Forster and Anthony R. Cross
*June 2020.*

# Faith

CHAPTER 1

# Flourishing, Justice, and the Gospel as "Subduing" the Earth

## J. Michael Thigpen

### Introduction

As I have argued elsewhere, the account of humanity's creation in the image of God in Genesis 1.26–28 is specifically crafted to lead the reader to conclude that God's intended outcome, his purpose for creating humanity in his image, was to create flourishing communities, not just flourishing individuals.[1] The cultural or creation mandate as it has been called—God's command to be fruitful, multiply, fill and subdue the earth, and to rule over the living things on the earth—is rightly seen as a command to fulfill God's intention. Humanity is to fill the earth and bring about flourishing. God created us in his image for this very purpose.

But how are we to flourish in the presence of sin? What role, if any, does the mandate which flows from our creation in God's image, play in our flourishing in the presence of sin? Traditionally, the creation mandate has been mined for flourishing with regard to stewarding the world's resources, and with regard to culture and the structures of civilization. When issues related to sin are dealt with in this traditional approach, the role of the mandate is to remind us that God's world is still good, and that we can direct our stewardship of natural resources and cultural structures towards God in worship. That the world will be redeemed and our relationship with creation will be restored as part of God's unfolding plan of redemption is also typically included, but only from the larger narrative arc of scripture, not from the mandate itself.[2]

These are fine approaches which are very valuable, and which serve as trustworthy guides to our interaction with God's creation. Yet, it seems that this approach has potentially misunderstood one element of the creation mandate, the command to subdue the earth.

---

[1] Thigpen, "In Our Image."

[2] Two excellent examples of this approach are Wolters, *Creation Regained*; and Wilson, *God's Good World*.

## Trouble in Paradise?

This command, along with the command to rule over the creation, has been perceived as problematic for some time now. Some even question whether flourishing is really the intention of the creation mandate. The presence of the terms רדה (exercise dominion, reign, rule) and כבש (subdue) have caused great concern that the mandate in Genesis 1 is a license for humanity to exploit the earth and abuse others.[3] Far from being a mandate to flourish it is seen as an authorization for selfishness and brutality.

This view does not fit the literary context of the command, nor subsequent uses of כבש in the Old Testament. Humanity is not given "absolute or independent power; he was to govern as the viceroy and regent of the One in whose image he was created."[4] It is clear from Genesis 1 that God's intention in creation was to provide for the needs of the creatures he made. He designed creation to flourish and he blessed it.[5] In light of this account of creation, if humanity is to represent God, then they must represent his care for creation. Further, if they are to reign as God's representative then they exercise a beneficent reign like his.

Like many aspects of the creation story in Genesis 1–2 the mandate is told twice. The first instance in Genesis 1.26, preceding the creation of humanity, uses only the royal term רדה, to rule. In the second instance, the mandate is expanded. In Genesis 1.28, the giving of the mandate is preceded by the act of blessing and the mandate is given in greater detail. Not only is humanity to rule (רדה) all living things and the earth itself, but humanity is also to subdue (כבש) the earth. If we explore the term רדה, which seems to be the more general category for humanity's prescribed role, we find strong evidence to support the contention that humanity's representational reign should be caring and constructive, not domineering and destructive.[6] Leviticus 25.43 specifically contrasts harsh rule over another with the character of YHWH. Furthermore, the "reigning king of Psalm 72 is also the champion of the poor and the disadvantaged. What is expected of the king is responsible care over that which he rules . . . Man is created to rule. But this rule is to be compassionate and not exploitative."[7]

---

[3] So White, "Historical Roots," 1203–7.

[4] Block, "Eden: A Temple?," 5.

[5] Although this is easily seen in the text, it is crystalized when comparing the biblical account of creation to various ancient near Eastern accounts where mankind is an afterthought and creation is made to service the needs of the gods. So Hamilton, *Genesis 1–17*, 140.

[6] For more on the quality and character of humanity's representational reign, see Thigpen, "Our Representational Reign," 125–40, and "In Our Image."

[7] Hamilton, *Genesis 1–17*, 138.

The question of כבשׁ (subdue) is more difficult, as this term denotes more force than רדה and it assumes some level of hostility between the subduer and the one subdued.[8] It can used for subjugating someone in war, into slavery or for assaulting someone.[9] This is the harder term as it seems to assume conflict and conquest. So how would this fit in the idyllic world of the creation mandate and how does it relate to ability to flourish in the midst of sin?

## The Meaning of Subdue

Although it is possible to read כבשׁ in light of the beneficent nature of רדה, or to see it as subduing the land agriculturally as Hamilton does, it seems more likely that "subdue" is added in light of the conflict in the garden that will come in Genesis 3.[10] As I will demonstrate in the survey below, there is no lexical evidence to soften the force of "subdue," and the idea of subjugating the land agriculturally does not fit with the usage of כבשׁ in the Hebrew text or extra-biblical texts. So what does it mean to subdue the earth? The textual and theological usage of subdue in the Old Testament suggests that rather than subduing the earth, through use of its resources or agriculture, the intended meaning of this portion of the mandate is the subduing of the inhabitants of the earth. As we shall, see this makes perfect sense in the pre-curse garden where the serpent comes to tempt Adam and Eve to rebel against God. The conflict intimated by כבשׁ is needed even in the garden once sin is present. This is not license for harshness or violence, but rather the just force needed to protect the earth and its inhabitants, and to exercise the representative reign for which humanity was created.[11]

## A Lexical Survey of כבשׁ

### The Occurrences

The verb כבשׁ occurs fifteen times: Genesis 1.28; Numbers 32.22, 29; Joshua 18.1; 2 Samuel 8.11; Jeremiah 34.11, 16; Micah 7.19; Zechariah 9.15; Esther 7.8; Nehemiah 5.5 (x2); 1 Chronicles 22.18; and 2 Chronicles 28.10. Outside of Genesis 1.28, in every occurrence where כבשׁ is used with ארץ, earth, it refers to subduing the inhabitants of the land and not the land itself as a

---

[8] Hamilton, *Genesis 1–17*, 139.

[9] Koehler and Baumgartner, *Hebrew and Aramaic Lexicon*, 4:260 (hereafter *HALOT*).

[10] Hamilton, *Genesis 1–17*, 139–40.

[11] Although a third term, משׁל, is used, the concept of ruling over or subduing sin is found in Gen. 4.7, which would seem to indicate that this reading of "subdue" in Gen. 1.28 is plausible.

resource (Num. 32.22, 29; Josh. 18.1; 1 Chr. 22.18). Additionally, where כבש is used with a term synonymous with land גוי, nation, in 2 Samuel 8.11, or with other designators for inhabitants like בְּנֵי־יְהוּדָה וִירוּשָׁלַם, the sons of Judah and Jerusalem, in 2 Chronicles 28.10, the usage is the same. It is the inhabitants who are subdued.

Exploring the remaining uses, with the exception of Micah 7.19 where subduing sin is in view, all other uses of כבש refer to the subduing of people, not resources. This includes subduing into slavery (Jer. 34.11, 16; Neh. 5.5; 2 Chr. 28.10) and sexual assault (Esth. 7.8).[12] Other than Genesis 1.28, every use of "subdue" refers to subduing people or inhabitants, not resources. Despite the clarity of the other usages of כבש this interpretation is rarely encountered.

In Aramaic and Syriac the range of meaning for כבש includes capturing or conquering a city.[13] In Akkadian, *kabāsu* can mean: to step on something (unclean) accidentally, to step upon something on purpose, to trample, to crush, to defeat an enemy, to bother, to make people do work, to press people.[14]

*Attempts to Understand Subdue*

The most common way of understanding the conflict inherent in כבש is to view the object, ארץ, earth, in agricultural terms. Nothing "more is intended here than the basic needs of settlement and agriculture: man is to fill up the earth, take possession of it, and take control of it. Basically what is intended is tilling; it corresponds with the 'working' or 'tilling' of the ground in . . . Gen ii.5, 15."[15]

Goldingay suggests, "Perhaps it recognizes that the earth will have to be treated harshly if it is to realize the destiny that God immediately goes on to describe, of producing food. To this end humanity has to attack the earth, break it up and thus make it usable." Yet Goldingay goes on to say that "the way humanity is to go about subjugating the world is by procreation, not by

---

[12] With regard to Zech. 9.15 I read this text with Klein. The term "Slingstones" "functions as a metonymy for the warriors who wielded the weaponry. The text then focuses not on the destruction of the weapons, but rather on the warriors whose evil impulses the Lord would blunt." Klein, *Zechariah*, 283.

[13] BT San 109a(14); P Dt2:34; P Ju9:45. There is one agricultural use in the fourth century AD, but this is so far past our context as to be of no use in the study.

[14] Oppenheim, Reiner and Biggs, eds, *Assyrian Dictionary*, 5 (hereafter *CAD* K). It can also be used in its most basic physical sense to walk off (measure), stamp down, or to walk on. In an extended meaning it can be used similarly to Mic. 7 for forgiving sin, for the pardoning of an offense by a king.

[15] Barr, "Man and Nature," 22.

*Flourishing, Justice, and the Gospel as "Subduing" the Earth*  7

violence—which Genesis abhors."[16] His approach leaves the reader with a bit of hermeneutical whiplash going back and forth between the peaceful subduing of procreation and the violent agricultural attack of food production.

Richard Middleton suggests that although many of the כבש texts have to do with an exercise of power over persons with some connotation of violence, "texts having to do with subduing land/earth (which are probably the most relevant to Genesis 1), there is no implication of a violent or adversarial relationship to the land or earth per se. Indeed, Deuteronomy 3.20 and 31.3, and Joshua 1.15, . . . which are parallel to Numbers 32.22 and 32.29 . . . do not utilize kabas but yaras which means simply to 'take possession of' in a neutral sense."[17]

This approach simply does not work. Although it is true that there is no adversarial relationship in these texts between the land itself and the people of Israel, the physical land is not what is in view when the verb כבש is used, nor when ירש (to possess or dispossess) is used in these texts. The context in Deuteronomy 3.20; 31.3 and Joshua 1.15 is the Israelite defeat of the *people* of the land. They inherit or possess the land after the defeat of their enemies! The land is not possessed until its current inhabitants are driven out of the land through the conquest and subsequent campaigns. Contrary to Middleton's claim, these are inherently adversarial texts. He is certainly correct that the adversary is not the land per se, but based on the usage of the verb, there is a clearly stated adversary—the current inhabitants of the land. The Israelites possess the land by dispossessing the people. Subduing the land is not an act upon the land, but upon the inhabitants of the land.

### Genesis 1.28 in its Narrative Context

*Translation and Textual Details*

At this point, we need to return to Genesis 1.28 in its narrative context with the lexical survey in mind.[18] Here is my translation of Genesis 1.26–28.

> [26]The God said, "Let us make humanity in our image, according to our likeness, so that they may rule over the fish of the sea, and over the birds of the heavens, and over the beasts, and over all the earth, and over all of the crawling things that crawl upon the earth." [27]So God created man in his image. In the image of God he created him. Male and female he created them. [28]Then God blessed them. And God said to them, "Be fruitful, and multiply, and fill the earth, and

---

[16] Goldingay, *Old Testament Theology*, 1:113.

[17] Middleton, *Liberating Image*, 52.

[18] I have previously commented Gen. 1.26–27 and the relationship of those verses to Gen. 1.28. Due to space restrictions, I will not be able to fully integrate that material here. See, Thigpen, "In Our Image."

subdue it. And rule over the fish of the sea, and over the birds of the heavens, and over all the living things which move upon the earth."

Mark D. Vander Hart in his article "Creation and Covenant" notes that "According to the Masoretic accenting, the verse 'division' comes on the verb" subdue in Genesis 1.28. Although the five imperatives seem to break down into two sets (be fruitful–multiply–fill and subdue–rule), the Masoretes indicate we should see the division after the command to subdue, linking it with the three prior commands. According to Vander Hart there is a clear progression. "Multiplying presupposes fruitfulness, and filling the earth presupposes the multiplication of human beings. This logically leads to the idea of the fourth verb." Vander Hart goes on from these insights to assert that

> God intends that they subdue it and hold it in subjection. The objects (sic) on the verb כִּבְשֻׁהָ refer to the nearest feminine noun in the previous sub-clause, with "the earth" understood "as mankind's realm for living, without territorial or geographical boundaries, his whole world."[19]

I agree with Vander Hart that the context for the command to subdue is the multiplication of humanity and that the Masoretic accentuation encourages us to read the text this way. Yet, subdue in every other text where it occurs with earth means the subduing of people. What if the same is true here and "the earth" refers to its inhabitants?

*Other Options for Subdue in Context*

Some have suggested options along this line, but only in passing and without fleshing out the implications of a revised understanding of the task of subduing. Perhaps the closest readings to mine are those of Mark Saucy and Greg Beale. Saucy asks of Genesis 1.28,

> But why the strong language if ruling and subduing is just about extending the food supply and making more sacred space, which is where most versions of the "culture mandate" leave it? The answer suggested by the text itself as well as the rest of the canonical narrative is that the commission for human beings from God aimed at something more, namely, *human domination of the spirit world*.[20]

---

[19] Vander Hart, "Creation and Covenant Part One," 5. The quoted material is Vander Hart's translation of S. Wagner, כבש, *Theologische Wörterbuch zum Alten Testament:* Band IV; ed. by G.J. Botterweck and H. Ringgren; Stuttgart: Verlag W. Kohlhammer, 1984, 46.

[20] Saucy, "Storied Work," 144 (emphasis original).

He views the presence of the serpent in the garden to be "a failure of the image of God to keep the sacred space of Eden according to the charge of Gen 2:15."[21]

Beale suggests similarly that Adam and Eve should have subdued the serpent, in line with the command to subdue in Genesis 1.28.[22] When treating the mandate, Beale comments, "In particular, Adam was to begin to subdue and rule the over the creation by cultivating the garden (2:15), by naming the created animals (2:19–20) . . . and by 'guarding' the garden from the entrance of unclean things, such as serpents."[23]

Both Saucy and Beale recognize that subdue in Genesis 1.28 represents conflict with the serpent in Genesis 3. I would suggest, however, that there is much more to this command. Genesis 3 certainly presents a scenario in which Adam and Eve should have acted in line with their mandate to rule and subdue. They were to reign in the garden, as royal representatives. They should have ruled over and subdued the serpent. I think most biblical interpreters would agree with this, even if they still embrace a primarily agricultural or technological approach to subdue. It just fits the overall narrative too well not to see this as a missed opportunity to fulfill their mandate. But is the serpent the only option? What about Adam and Eve themselves?

### Cain, Adam, and Eve

The next major failure in the storyline is Cain's failure to rule over sin. Although neither רדה nor כבש is used, the synonymous verb משל makes its first appearance. As Goldingay has observed, Cain's story is parallel to Adam and Eve's story in significant ways.[24] Sin personified in the actions of the snake in Genesis 3 give way to sin as a metaphorical lion lying in wait to spring upon Cain. In both circumstances humanity, here Cain, must act. He must rule over and subdue sin. If Cain will not subdue sin, sin will rule over him. Here in Genesis 4, it becomes even clearer his failure is not a failure to subdue some external part of creation. He has failed to subdue himself. Control of self is lost. Rulership is lost. The mandate is subverted.

Returning to Genesis 3, might not the first proper targets of subduing be Adam and Eve themselves? What if Eve had chosen to rule over sin, to subdue herself? What if Adam had subdued the serpent? What if he had intervened and subdued Eve instead of merely standing with her? What if

---

[21] Saucy, "Storied Work," 145.

[22] Beale, *New Testament Biblical Theology*, 34–39.

[23] Beale, *New Testament Biblical Theology*, 383.

[24] Goldingay, *Old Testament Theology*, 1:150.

Adam had subdued himself when offered the fruit? Yes, the serpent needed to be subdued, but so much more so did Adam and Eve. They failed to love God and to love each other by failing to rule over their own sin in the first place, and by failing to intervene lovingly with one another. We see this more clearly with Cain, but the parallels of Cain's story press us to see it now in the garden.[25]

### Repetition and Change with Noah

Moving along through the narrative we encounter the mandate language of Genesis 1.26–28 again in Genesis 9. The use of the language of blessing and the threefold imperative to be fruitful, multiply, and fill serves to "transport the reader back to the world of Gen 1."[26] This refrain from Genesis 1 serves as an inclusio marking off Genesis 9.1–7 as a distinct unit which focuses on restarting the mandate in the post-flood family.[27]

If we read the story carefully, however, we see that one key element is missing. Blessing is present. God speaking to humanity is present. The command to rule is present in the new food laws even though the term רדה is not found. But where is the command to subdue? Is it not found in the institution of the death penalty? Society is now charged with subduing the rogue one among them.[28] The hostile element, the one who works against God's creation of man in his image, is to be subdued.

If this reading is accepted, we now have the mandate to subdue the earth functioning fully from the individual to the society. As the stories of Adam, Eve, and Cain show, we must first and foremost subdue ourselves. If we do not, then sin will subdue and rule over us. We must subdue one another. Adam and Eve failed one another. Finally, in the post-flood re-initiation of the mandate, we must subdue on a societal level. Humanity united must subdue the evildoer in their midst.

---

[25] Goldingay summarizes the parallels as "There is a gift from God, a circumstance that tests, a divine warning and a creature that threatens. There is then an act that ignores the divine word, yields to the creature and fails the test. The act stimulates another searching divine question that receives a chilling response, an anguished 'what have you done' and a terrible curse, an experience of expulsion, but also an act of mercy." Goldingay, *Old Testament Theology*, 1:151.

[26] Hamilton, *Genesis 1–17*, 313.

[27] Wenham, *Genesis 1–15*, 192.

[28] On the various issues in the interpretation of Gen. 9.6, see Zehnder, "Cause or Value?"

## The Creation Mandate, Flourishing, and Justice

*Elements in the Definitions*

If the reading I have suggested above is accepted, it would entail that flourishing and justice are part and parcel of the creation mandate. Humanity's rule is designed to facilitate flourishing and to enact justice. Any attempt to separate the two will fail as it will not fully reflect humanity's mandate, abandoning humanity's creation in the image of God as the basis for both flourishing and justice.

As I attempted to move from this reading of the creation mandate to our contemporary context, it seemed clear that there are several elements of the narrative we must attend to if we want to arrive at valid definitions of flourishing and justice that are truly reflective God's design and are operative in our post-Genesis 3 world.

From Genesis 1–2 we must maintain the priority of the image of God and we must maintain that our creation in the image is just that, our creation. We must apply the dignity and honor of being created in the image both to ourselves and to others. It must apply to me *and* to you if we are *both* to flourish and if there is to be justice for *both* of us. It is the image which most fundamentally binds us together as humans.[29]

Following on from our creation in the image of God, we must recognize that flourishing and justice must both be communal and cooperative. Humanity is designed to function communally and cooperatively.[30] This means that conceptions of flourishing or justice that are individualistic either in origin or implementation are not aligned with our creation mandate.

Flourishing and justice inherently involve economics. True human flourishing is more than economics and advancement. It includes a right relationship with God, healthy relationships with others, and a God-honoring relationship with the creation itself. Without each of these there may be glimpses of flourishing, an echo of the goodness seen in God's intent for humanity, but not true flourishing. Yet, human flourishing is not less than economics.

If you will permit a brief foray into the New Testament, notice how Jesus weaves together these ideas in the Sermon on the Mount. "Do not be anxious

---

[29] I should note that I have specifically constructed this study to address humanity as a whole. As such I am not yet exploring the communal nature of the church and our connection to the broader community of humanity. This work should be done, but the first step in this study is to look at humanity in general since we seek flourishing and justice for all, not just those in the church. It is surely true that genuine flourishing at the deepest levels will not occur outside the kingdom, but the influence and impact of the kingdom surely does include a level of flourishing for those outside akin to Jeremiah's seeking the welfare of the city.

[30] For an exploration of these ideas see Thigpen, "In Our Image."

... but seek first the kingdom of God, and his righteousness, and all these things will be added to you" (Matt. 6.25–33). What are "these things" to which he refers?—our lives, what we eat, what we drink, what we wear. It is not the case that these are unimportant things, that they are excluded from the flourishing life of the kingdom. Far from that, we ought not worry about them because our Father knows our needs, and just as he cares about the intimate details of the animal world we are to oversee, so, too, he cares for us. Yet, the most important thing is to pursue our relationship with him, the kingdom and his righteousness. To put it in Genesis terms, we need to realize he is our creator and we are made in his image, and now we are recreated, born again in Christ. That is foundational to the activities and needs of flourishing that are found in the mandate's commands. So flourishing in both the Old and New Testaments is more than economics, but it is not less than that.

Justice clearly involves economics, though it, too, cannot be reduced simply to economics. It must include the rule of law and a just society as exemplified in the instruction God gave to Israel. It must also involve the protection of the most vulnerable as seen in the laws against unjust judges, false witnesses, and favoritism. Justice must be pursued and maintained personally, interpersonally, and societally. In each of these contexts, sin must be subdued. Ultimately justice involves both judgment and salvation, though intermediate forms of both salvation and judgment may often fall far short of what we rightly expect in the fullness of the coming kingdom.

*Defining Flourishing and Justice*

God created humanity in his image so that we might be enabled to carry out his mandate to rule over and to subdue the earth. These two commands represent his express intention for humanity to flourish, to live in and rule the world as his royal representatives. In our own small ways we are to create and order the world for the benefits of its inhabitants in line with the example we have from God. Rightly related to him and to each other we flourish communally and cooperatively as we live out the mandate in our personal lives, in our interactions with those closest to us, and societally as our communities work in complementary and cooperative fashion to build God's good world.

Where sin threatens, we are mandated to subdue it. We are to subdue it in ourselves, lest it rule over us. We are called to subdue it in one another lest we fail to love our neighbors as ourselves. We are called to subdue it communally as society confronts the lawbreaker, protects the vulnerable, and ensures a truly just system that is founded on the very person of God as we see in the law's refrain "because I am YHWH."

## The Gospel and Subduing

It is fitting to ask here at the conclusion of this study, where is the gospel in all of this? To begin to answer this we again return to the text of Genesis 1. We must note there that the mandate to rule and subdue is founded on God's blessing. As traditionally held, it is God's blessing that enables humanity properly to care for, utilize, and rule over the earth and its resources. The importance of his blessing for the fulfillment of the mandate is seen in its prominence in the return of both blessing and mandate language in Genesis 9.

Now we must also take into account that the task of subduing sin individually, interpersonally, and communally is also an enactment of God's blessing and of his mandate to humanity. Subduing sin is not an act of self-justification or human-centered quest for justice. It is a gospel act that begins and ultimately ends with God. Our work in it is cooperative and obedient, but it is not final or ultimate. Our subduing of sin will not deal with sin with finality. It is an intermediate step in all that God is doing with regard to sin in the world.

At this point we need to return to our one outlying text, Micah 7.19. There we read in the ESV, "He will again have compassion on us; he will tread our iniquities underfoot. You will cast all our sins into the depths of the sea." Here the ESV has chosen not to translate כבש as "subdue," but rather by its most basic physical sense which was seen in some of the Akkadian uses. However, there is an Akkadian usage that I think fits far better here.

In Oppenheim, Reiner and Biggs' article on the cognate *kabāsu*, definition 4d indicates uses with the meaning "to forgive, pardon a sin." One such occurrence is translated as, "if the king wants to pardon PN for his offense, let him do so."[31] Not only can כבש mean to forgive sin, it is attested in such circumstances to be a royal act! So we might well translate Micah 7.19 as "He will again have compassion on us. He will forgive our iniquities. And he will cast all of our sins into the depths of the sea."

The ultimate subduing of sin comes in the gospel. God's free act to forgive sin and his corollary act of final judgment together provide the final solution to sin.[32] As such, I would suggest that part of the mandate is the proclamation of the gospel—to ourselves, to each other, and to the world. True flourishing requires it, for it is the only means by which we can rightly relate to God, to each other, and to the creation. All of our justice is at best flawed, but his acts can provide both true salvation and true judgment. Thus, God alone can provide true justice. Our part is representative. Our acts of justice as we subdue sin in ourselves, with one another, and in our communities point back to the one who created us in his image. We can truly flourish in the presence

---

[31] *CAD K*, 9.

[32] For an exploration of the relationship between salvation and judgment, see Thigpen, "Storm of YHWH."

of sin, but only where sin is subdued and only when our mandated acts are fueled by his blessing, then brought to consummation in his great acts of salvation and justice.

## Bibliography

Barr, James. "Man and Nature The Ecological Controversy and the Old Testament." *Bulletin of the John Rylands University Library of Manchester* 55 (1972) 9–32.

Beale, G.K. *A New Testament Biblical Theology: The Unfolding of the Old Testament in the New*. Grand Rapids: Baker Academic, 2011.

Block, Daniel I. "Eden: A Temple? A Reassessment of the Biblical Evidence." In *From Creation to New Creation: Biblical Theology and Exegesis*, edited by Daniel M. Gurtner and Benjamin L. Gladd, 3–20. Peabody, MA: Hendrickson, 2013.

Goldingay, John. *Old Testament Theology: Volume 1. Israel's Gospel*. Downers Grove, IL: InterVarsity, 2003.

Hamilton, Victor P. *The Book of Genesis: Chapters 1–17*. New International Commentary on the Old Testament. Grand Rapids: Eerdmans, 1990.

Klein, George L. *Zechariah*. New American Commentary 21B. Nashville, TN: B&H, 2008.

Koehler, Ludwig, and Walter Baumgartner. *The Hebrew and Aramaic Lexicon of the Old Testament*. 3$^{rd}$ ed. Leiden: Brill, 1994.

Middleton, J. Richard. *The Liberating Image: The Imago Dei in Genesis 1*. Grand Rapids: Brazos, 2005.

Oppenheim, A. Leo, Erica Reiner, and Robert D. Biggs, eds. *The Assyrian Dictionary of the Oriental Institute of the University of Chicago: Volume 8. K*. Chicago: Oriental Institute, 1971.

Saucy, Mark. "Storied Work: The Eschatology Turn and the Meaning of Our Work." *Journal of the Evangelical Theological Society* 60.1 (2017) 139–62.

Thigpen, J. Michael. "'In Our Image': Our Creational Identity and Economic Conflict." In *The Bible and Money*, edited by Hallvard Hegalia and Markus Zehnder. Sheffield: Sheffield Phoenix, forthcoming.

———. "Our Representational Reign: Royal Leadership in the United Monarchy." In *Biblical Leadership: Theology for the Everyday Leader*, edited by Benjamin K. Forrest and Chet Roden, 125–40. Biblical Theology for the Church. Grand Rapids: Kregel, 2017.

———. "The Storm of YHWH: Jeremiah's Theology of God's Heart and Motives." *Bibliotheca Sacra* 176 (2019) 418–28.

Vander Hart, Mark D. "Creation and Covenant Part One: A Survey of the Dominion Mandate in the Noahic and Abrahamic Covenants." *Mid-America Journal of Theology* 6.1 (1990) 3–18.

Wenham, Gordon J. *Genesis 1–15*. Word Biblical Commentary 1. Waco, TX: Word, 1987.

White, Lynn. "The Historical Roots of the Ecological Crisis." *Science* 155 (1967) 1203–7.
Wilson, Jonathan R. *God's Good World: Reclaiming the Doctrine of Creation*. Grand Rapids: Baker, 2013.
Wolters, Albert M. *Creation Regained: Biblical Basics for a Reformational Worldview*. 2nd ed. Grand Rapids: Eerdmans, 2005.
Zehnder, Markus. "Cause or Value? Problems in the Understanding of Gen 9,6a." *Zeitschrift für die alttestamentliche Wissenschaft* 122 (2010) 81–89.

CHAPTER 2

# Nations in the Metanarrative of Redemption: A Gospel for Public Life

## Greg Forster

Nations, which are a key element in forming our identity and culture, play a central role in the Bible's metanarrative of redemption. While the modern "nation-state" is not identical with the biblical "nation," and theologians have not yet developed adequate frameworks for relating the social categories of the Bible to the social categories of advanced modernity, there is a more basic point that we can and must start putting at the center of our theological ethics: our public life—living as members of our nations in the daily life that takes place in our homes, workplaces and communities—must be rooted in the gospel that goes out to the nations.

The role of the nations in the gospel metanarrative challenges nationalism (the idolatry of nations) while also challenging purely individualistic and ecclesial conceptions of discipleship that exclude public life from the scope of Christian concern. It challenges disciples of Jesus to think of themselves as members of our nations, and thus as implicated in and responsible for the lives of our nations (in cooperation with our non-Christian neighbors, giving rise to much conflict and tension that cannot be fully resolved until Jesus returns). This metanarrative also gives a new impetus to evangelism, as the spread of the gospel to all nations advances the gospel mission of reconciling the nations, and reveals the glory of God in new ways through the discipleship of diverse peoples.

### Nations are Central to the Metanarrative of Redemption

The nations come to the fore with particular clarity in the stories of Babel (Genesis 11), Pentecost (Acts 2) and the New Jerusalem (Revelation 21–22). While the nations are a key part of the gospel story throughout, these incidents provide an especially clear window into the essential place of the nations in God's plan of redemption. In light of the role the nations play in the gospel metanarrative, an understanding of the metanarrative that does not include God's intentions for the nations and his redemptive action regarding them will result in an anemic understanding of redemption and provide insufficient theological grounding for Christian life in the present age.

Nations are depicted in the Bible as people-groups that are typically marked off from one another by differences including, but not limited to ethnic cohesion, covenants with their gods, royal offices, and shared history.[1] These differences occur in widely varying modes and degrees; the identity and boundaries of a nation are socially constructed and historically contingent, giving rise to complexity and ambiguity (for example, the ambiguous relationship between the Jews and the Samaritans in the New Testament era). Because of this ambiguity and contingency, scripture should not be taken as providing a universally valid account of what is or is not a "nation" and how nations relate to such categories as "ethnicity." Even the distinction between nationality and ethnicity as we now understand those terms is largely of modern origin, and thus not a subject of conscious reflection by the biblical authors.

Distinct nations are not present in God's original creation, but as the consequences of the fall unfold, they are introduced as—and remain consistently—a central part of the gospel metanarrative. God introduces nations into history at Babel (Genesis 11) as a way of controlling the negative effects of sin. But even as he does so, he also creates a separate nation for himself—Israel (Genesis 12)—whose role will be redemptive rather than merely remedial; this nation's redemptive work will serve the other nations. Conflict between this special nation (which carries God's redemptive plan on behalf of all nations) and the other nations (which remain in rebellion against God and resist the redemptive plan) is a consistent theme of the Old Testament.

An especially important juncture in God's plans for the nations arrives with the transition from the Old Testament to the New Testament. God reveals the inadequacy of the Mosaic covenant (by itself) for salvation, and transfers the special redemptive role of his people from a separate nation to a church that is explicitly sent out to all nations. This church is given an outpouring of the Holy Spirit at Pentecost (Acts 2) unprecedented not only in degree but in kind, permanently breaking the special association of the redemptive community with the cultural structures of a particular nation. The church community lives into this new reality, with many strains and conflicts along the way.

This new trans-national community culminates in the climax of the biblical narrative, not (as we might expect) with the removal of the national differences imposed at Babel but with the redemption of the nations as nations. The account of the New Jerusalem (Revelation 21–22) emphasizes that the redeemed people are God's people, but also that they are "the nations." The contrast between Israel, which is God's people, and the nations

---

[1] Köstenberger, "Nations," 676–77.

of the world, which are not, has been transformed. Now, all the nations are God's peoples, plural (Rev. 21.3).

### Babel: God Divides Sinful Humanity into Nations

God created the human race as a single family speaking a single language, but these conditions gradually changed as a result of the fall. The Cainite and Sethite lines of descent take starkly different spiritual directions, but remain a single people-group with a single language. Some of the markers of distinct nationhood (separate histories, for example) are present to a degree between the Cainite and Sethite lines, but the text does not describe them as distinct nations. Divisions into distinct people-groups ("clans," "languages," "lands," and "nations") are introduced in Genesis 10. However, the focal point of this division into people-groups is the Babel account in Genesis 11.1–9; the divisions noted in Genesis 10 appear to have occurred after the Babel events, as their consequence.[2] The placement of the Genesis 10 account of the nations before the Genesis 11 account of their division stresses a unity underneath the diversity; in contrast to pagan myths, which often depicted separate origins for the nations, it points to a common ancestry for all nations in the narrative of Genesis 1–9.[3] All nations ultimately come from God's original creation (just as Israel did) and are part of his story.

An important theological point follows from this history. If we are to see ethnic diversity as constructive and glorious rather than merely a restraining or negative condition, we must discover this constructive glory soteriologically and eschatologically. Protologically, looking back toward creation, we find only that ethnic diversity is a mark of the fall. The "Cape Town Commitment" errs in asserting that "ethnic diversity is the gift and plan of God in creation."[4] Ethnic diversity is God's gift and plan, but not in creation; he introduces it to restrain the effects of the fall. The passages cited by the "Commitment" (Deut. 32.8 and Acts 17.26) establish that God ordained ethnic diversity, but not that it was present before the fall or that it would have naturally developed in an unfallen world. In fact, by noting that God

---

[2] There are three indications that Genesis 10 and 11 are not in chronological order, and thus that the Babel account is the pivotal moment for the emergence of nations: the references to diverse "languages" in Genesis 10 followed by the statement at Gen. 11.1 that "the whole earth had one language and the same words;" the occurrence of an additional Shemite genealogy after the Babel account in Gen. 11.1-9; and the statement that humanity spread out over the earth (as described in Genesis 10) after the events at Babel (Gen. 11.8-9).

[3] Hays, *From Every People and Nation*, 59–60.

[4] "Cape Town Commitment," I.7.B and II.B.2. Note also the statement at II.B.2 that the Bible "values" ethnic diversity "in creation and redemption."

originally made humanity in ethnic unity and then divided it, they reinforce the connection between ethnic diversity and the fall. J. Daniel Hays is correct: "Adam and Eve, as well as Noah, are non-ethnic and non-national. They represent all people, not some people."[5]

Genesis 11.1–9 emphasizes human depravity as the motive force in the Babel events, indicating that Babel and the consequent division of humanity into nations is an unfolding effect of the fall. God originally made human beings to fill, cultivate and protect his world (Gen. 1.28 and 2.15). They were made to cooperate in this task rather than do it as isolated individuals; hence it is "not good that the man should be alone" because he needs "a helper fit for him" to cooperate in this work (Gen. 2.18). The Babel account echoes the creation design in its focus on the work of filling (Gen. 11.2) and cultivating (Gen. 11.3–4) the world, as well as the power of cooperation (Gen. 11.6).

The abilities to do these things have been turned against God after the fall, in at least three ways. First, they are used in the service of pride ("a name," verse 4). Second, the illusion of independence from God—the futile quest for security in our own power—leads humanity to abandon the mandate to fill the world, preferring to gather and stay put to maximize their defenses (verse 5). And third, the original mandate of protecting or guarding the material world, placed alongside the mandate to cultivate the world in Genesis 2.15, has dropped from view; the world has become mere raw material to be consumed by human desires (verse 3).

Verse 6 observes that so long as the fallen human race is able to cooperate, it gains greater and greater power to do evil as it grows more numerous. Shockingly, God declares that "nothing that they propose to do will now be impossible for them." Even allowing for hyperbole, this is a striking statement of the great power God has given his image-bearing creatures when they cooperate. However, the need for cooperation in order to exercise this power, which God wove into his original design of human nature, provides a weak point in humanity's evil designs.

God divides humanity into nations in order to limit the scope of its potential cooperation in wickedness. By confusing speech, God divides humanity at what is probably the most basic and fundamental level. Every area of human culture—and therefore human activity—is deeply dependent upon speech. The central role of language in structuring all human activity, and even thought, is not only familiar from everyone's experience; it is indicated in the biblical text in Adam's ability to invent language *de novo* (a power that we have since lost, either in the fall or at Babel). Genesis 2.19 associates Adam's linguistic power with his dominion over the nonhuman creation.

Having confused their language, God then disperses humanity over the face of the earth (verses 8–9). This forces humanity out of its sinful tendency to huddle together in one place for a false sense of security. It pushes the newly

---

[5] Hays, *From Every People and Nation*, 48.

divided nations back outward, to restore the original plan of humanity filling the world.

### Israel and the Nations after Babel

God's creation of a new nation for himself through the call of Abram (Gen. 12.1–3) takes place against the backdrop of the division of humanity into nations at Babel, and its meaning is importantly shaped by that context.[6] In this first call to Abram, God stresses not only Israel's special relationship with himself, the land he will give it and the large number of people it will produce, but also the promise that all nations will be blessed by Israel. God creates this special nation as part of his ongoing work to restore the original created pattern, which was "God's people living in God's place ruling under God's rule."[7] While the immediate people and place will be Israel living in the holy land, the long-term purpose of calling out Abram is to restore the whole human race—the peoples of all the nations of the earth—as God's people, and the whole earth itself—the lands of all the nations of the earth—as God's place.

After a narrative taking place in the future holy land, emphasizing the land and the descendants (Gen. 12.4–9), Abram and Sarai go to Egypt, where the contrast between God's new nation and the other nations is emphasized (Gen. 12.10–20). The contrast between Israel and the other nations will remain a theme throughout the Old Testament. But the promise of blessing to all nations, given in the moment of its creation, also remains a theme.[8] Israel is called to be set apart (holy) to God from all other nations. God uses the opposition between Israel and its enemies to emphasize his own holiness through that of his people. At the same time, God not only shows steadfast covenant love toward his own people, but also reiterates his promise that all nations will be blessed through that people.

This history culminates in the exile to Babylon—that is, to Babel—and the return. The location of the exile emphasizes once again the role of the nations in the metanarrative. As a result of the Genesis 11 events, Babel/Babylon is a paradigm of the nations' enmity to God.[9] Just as Babel was followed by the founding of Israel, Israel's failure is followed by exile to Babel. "Exile [in Babylon] was a defining experience for the nation of Israel . . . The impact of

---

[6] Millar, "People of God," 684–85.

[7] Millar, "People of God," 684.

[8] Köstenberger, "Nations," 676–77.

[9] Arnold, "Babylon," 394.

this experience plays a highly formative role in the national life of Israel even to this day."[10]

The exile and return set the stage, in negative and positive ways respectively, for the coming of the Messiah. The exile shows, negatively, the insufficiency of the Mosaic covenant (by itself) to achieve redemption. God punishes the disobedience of his people by taking away their possession of the holy land and putting them under the rule of a foreign nation. But God, faithful to his promises of redemption, also promises a return from exile. This return is associated, positively, with a new covenant between God and his people: their sin will be forgiven, they will be given new hearts, and God's glory will dwell with them (Jeremiah 31; Ezekiel 36, 39, and 43).

### Pentecost: God Makes Disciples of Many Nations

The cross and resurrection of Christ are, of course, the pivot on which the story turns. The story of the nations, like the story of everything else, is transformed. The revolutionary consequences of the cross and the empty tomb for the world's nations are most clearly seen in the story of Pentecost.

After accomplishing his earthly mission, Jesus ascends to heaven and promises an outpouring of the Holy Spirit (Acts 1). This begins the transition to a new age in history, during which Jesus will exercise "all authority in heaven and on earth" and send his people in the power of the Spirit to "make disciples of all nations" (Matt. 28.18–19). Following the revelation that the Mosaic covenant was insufficient by itself, the other nations are grafted into the Abrahamic covenant so the restoration of the creation design—God's people in God's place ruling under his rule—can be carried forward in a new way (Rom. 9–11). The church, which ultimately will be made up of the peoples of all nations, is God's people; the whole world, the lands of all nations, is God's place; faith in and discipleship to Christ is how we rule under his rule. This faith in and discipleship to Christ are how we are grafted into the Abrahamic covenant; the new covenant not only commands us but makes us able to obey, which the Mosaic covenant by itself could not do.

The transition is completed with the outpouring of the Spirit at Pentecost. Given that the new, transformative role of the Spirit is so important to making the new covenant effective where the old covenant was insufficient, the narrative of his outpouring provides a key window into how the new covenant will differ from the old.

A change in the role of the nations in God's plan is at the very center of Pentecost, indicating that a changed role for the nations is at the center of what makes the new covenant new (Acts 2.5–13). As the Holy Spirit descends, it becomes clear that a miraculous event is occurring (verses 2–3). When the disciples are filled with the Spirit, they being to speak languages

---

[10] Beach, *Church in Exile*, 49.

they don't know (verse 4). People of many nations, gathered in Jerusalem for the feast of Pentecost, miraculously understand one another across language barriers (verses 5–11).

With this outpouring of the Holy Spirit, God dramatically removes the confusion of languages—the restraint on human cooperation—imposed at Babel. That restraint was imposed to limit the effect of sin. But those on whom the Holy Spirit has been poured out in this new way are able to overcome sin. That's the whole point of the Spirit's outpouring, and the key respect in which the new covenant is superior to the old.

The contrast between Babel and Pentecost suggests that believers, transformed in a new way by the Spirit, are now being trusted with the power that was taken away at Babel. This extreme power ("nothing that they propose to do will now be impossible for them," Gen. 11.6) is made possible by cooperation across boundaries. Within the church, God appears to be restoring the full power that he gave to all humanity at creation. Once the Holy Spirit is poured out, the division of the nations imposed at Babel is no longer necessary. God's people will cooperate for good, not for evil, so their ability to cooperate need not be limited!

With the need for this limitation removed, the division between nations is (within the church) relativized. Where God had originally followed up the division of the nations because of their sin by calling Abram to become a separate nation, he now follows up the healing of that sin (among his people) by calling his people to go out among all the nations.

Given the deep significance of language to our sense of identity and meaning, we may well sympathize with the disciples who were bewildered at this miraculous transcendence of language boundaries, and didn't know how to make sense of it (Acts 2.12). Peter's inaugural sermon explains that the risen Christ is now bringing all the promises of the old covenant to their fulfillment (Acts 2.14–36). People gathered from many nations respond in mass numbers to this challenging gospel sermon (Acts 2.37–41). Then, in spite of national differences, they enter into a fellowship so intimate that even ownership of property is relativized (Acts 2.42–47). Such peace, reconciliation and generosity is almost as miraculous as the speaking with tongues itself!

## God Heals the Nations after Pentecost

In light of this new state of affairs, national and ethnic reconciliation must become a central priority for God's people. It cannot be one item among many on the list of things we must do to love our neighbors, but an existential imperative for the church. And that is exactly what we find in the remainder of the New Testament. Like other nations, Israel had been held together by such factors as ethnic cohesion, its covenant with its God, its royal office and its shared history—all of which become problematic with the unexpected transition to the church as people of God in the New Testament.[11]

The issues raised by this transition became central struggles in the early church, as the New Testament amply shows.[12] We see this in everything from tensions among different nations within the church (e.g., Acts 6.1–6; Ephesians 2), to debates over the status of the Mosaic law (e.g., Acts 15; Gal. 2.11–14), to the need for evangelistic methods of explaining the God of Israel to pagan nations with few cultural resources for understanding him (e.g., Acts 14 and 17), to questions about how to relate to authorities outside the church (e.g., Acts 4 and 5; Romans 12–13; 1 Peter 2), and much more.

Jesus' focus was not the "people of God" but the "kingdom of God," primarily meaning God's activity of rule. It is God's rule that creates the "people of God," and he can do so in any social/cultural context—among all nations.[13] Understanding what it means to advance the kingdom of God in this new situation, where God's people are in every nation rather than forming a distinct nation of their own, is one of the main challenges of the church after Pentecost. Bringing the gospel to the nations and wrestling with the conflicts and questions created by this mission is a key theme throughout Acts; developing a theology of faithful living that transcends the Mosaic covenant is a regular theme of the apostolic epistles.

National identity becomes relativized for disciples, but it does not disappear; rather, it becomes a platform or arena within which discipleship can be enacted, as the comments about civil authority in Paul and Peter's epistles attest (Rom. 12.14—13.10; 1 Pet. 2.13–25). What it means to be a "nation" is implicitly called into question, as traditional markers of nationhood (e.g., ethnic cohesion, divine-national covenant, royal office, shared history) are challenged, problematized and/or relativized. However, "national identity matters because it is part of the riches of the kingdom of God. It is precisely because the proper worship of God has been removed from the political sphere that national diversity is—if anything—more valued in the New Testament than seen as problematic."[14]

God introduced nations into human history as a restraint upon sin. However, in creating Israel he took this element of our fallen condition and transformed it into an instrument of salvation. This movement is redoubled at Pentecost, where God no longer enacts redemption within a single nation, but now enters into all of them.

---

[11] Köstenberger, "Nations," 676.

[12] Köstenberger, "Nations," 677–78.

[13] Millar, "People of God," 685–87.

[14] Rivers, "Nationhood," 132.

## The New Jerusalem: Nations Redeemed

The narrative of God's redemptive action entering into all the nations reaches its culmination at the end of history, where the New Jerusalem descends into the midst of all the nations. The nations of the world clearly remain "nations" in eternity (Rev. 21.22—22.5).

The nations are so distinct as nations that they even retain distinctive political offices: "the kings of the earth will bring their glory into" the New Jerusalem (Rev. 21.24). In eternity, the nations will not only be nations but live as nations. They will have public authority structures and an institutional life that shapes the unique identity and story of each nation, distinct from all others. These structures may, of course, be altered by the return of Jesus to almost any extent, and in ways we cannot predict, but that they will be present is clear from the text.

Richard Mouw interprets this verse almost exclusively in backward-looking terms. He interprets the "kings" as individuals who were kings in history, before Jesus' return, coming to give an account of their rule and surrender authority to Jesus.[15] This interpretation neutralizes the vision of nations continuing to live as nations, suggesting instead that the distinct public structures of each nation do not continue in eternity. However, the emphasis in Revelation 21–22 is not backward-looking but forward-looking. The transition from the old world to the new world is now complete; Revelation 21–22 is not about the settling of old accounts but a description of the eternal state of humanity and the earth after all the old accounts are settled. The nations will engage in ruling ("they will reign forever and ever," Rev. 22.5), which implies a need for authority structures.

The eschatological vision of Isaiah 60 also points to continuing public structures among the nations in eternity. In Isaiah 60, the kings of the nations do not come to Israel primarily to surrender and give an account. Verses 11 and 14 may suggest this as one element of the scene, depending on how they are interpreted. But the emphasis in Isaiah 60 is on the kings of the earth serving God and Israel (verses 10, 12, and 16). This implies that the kings remain kings, serving in this capacity on an ongoing basis.

The very diversity of the nations, introduced as a remedy for sin, is transformed into a vehicle God uses to manifest the splendor of his glory in many diverse modes. Like the five wounds Jesus carries in his resurrection body, the nations are transformed from a mark of the fall into a manifestation of the glory and majesty of God's redemptive work. God uses the diversity of the nations to manifest his glory in diverse ways, as they each walk by the light of the Lamb (Rev. 21.24) and reverently bring their glory and honor before him as their gift and service to him (Rev. 21.26).

---

[15] Mouw, *When the Kings Come Marching In*, 43–69.

The worship of God modeled in Israel has now been expanded to include all nations. God has finally established "a house of prayer for all peoples" (Isa. 56.7; see also Mark 11.17). Just as the description of the redeemed world as the New Earth draws on Edenic imagery (tree of life, rivers) to suggest the restoration of the earth, the description of the redeemed community as the New Jerusalem draws on imagery from Israel to suggest that God's redemptive plan in history has reached its fulfillment.

However, crucially, there is "no temple in the city" (Rev. 21.22). In contrast with the temple of Israel, the final house of prayer for all nations is "not made with hands" (Mark 14.58). The temple in Israel, while it was constructed in response to divine instructions, was also a product of Israel's culture and historical situation. The extensive description of the temple's craftsmanship and use of imagery in the Old Testament suggests how contingent it was upon culturally bound symbolic meanings. Pomegranates, gourds and oxen (1 Kings 7) would not provide an edifying liturgical environment for worship today, as they did in ancient Israel.

Without a temple made by hands, the nations are free to remain themselves. Even in their religious observance, they retain their distinctive character. They are, so to speak, "Jesus-ized" but not "Israelized." And "they will be his *peoples* [*laoi* is plural] and God himself will be with them as their God" (Rev. 21.3). This designation, which had been unique to Israel (Gen. 17.7–8; Jer. 32.38; Ezek. 37.27) now applies to every nation on earth.

### Reflections

"In past generations he allowed all the nations to walk in their own ways" (Acts 14.16). But now God is changing the ways of the nations, by sending out the church in the power of the Spirit. Distinguishing our religious affiliation as Christians from national affiliations is imperative. But we cannot do this at the expense of privatizing our faith. If we suppress our faith whenever we participate in the daily activities that make up national life, we are not wholly disciples.[16]

The gospel is a gospel for and to the nations, as well as for and to individuals.[17] The above survey of the biblical metanarrative is sufficient to show that we ought to challenge the assumption that "the gospel" properly understood includes only the redemption of individuals, while the redemption of social groups is an implication or effect of the gospel. As the "Cape Town Commitment" says, "the gospel is God's good news, through the cross and

---

[16] See Volf, *Flourishing*, esp. 59–93.

[17] It is also for and to the physical creation, as Rom. 8.18–24 establishes ("in this hope we were saved" entails that the gospel of individual and cosmic salvation is one gospel).

resurrection of Jesus Christ, for individual persons, and for society, and for creation."[18]

While the difference between saying the gospel is for the nations and saying the gospel has implications for the nations may seem like hair-splitting, it is not. As Dallas Willard has observed, one of the key challenges to building mature discipleship today is that on our understanding of what the gospel is, the gospel is not directly connected to our daily way of life.[19] Willard challenges us to ask three questions:

- Does the gospel I preach and teach have a natural tendency to cause people who hear it to become full-time students of Jesus?
- Would those who believe it become his apprentices as a natural "next step"?
- What can we reasonably expect would result from people actually believing the substance of my message?[20]

Without a gospel that is for and to the nations, our answers to these questions will never be fully satisfactory.

The gospel metanarrative challenges nationalism (the idolatry of nations) in at least three ways. Centrally, it demands the submission of all nations to God, casting down the use of nations as *loci* of ultimate meaning and allegiance. It places love, peace and reconciliation among nations at the center of the church's mission and the life of discipleship. And by reminding us that national differences ultimately originated as a result of sin, it rebukes the pride of nationalistic historical narratives, by which nations create high and heroic origin stories.

Yet we cannot retreat from public and national life; disciple-making is a sociological as well as ecclesial and individual activity. Some parts of the church today—particularly in the United States—are dominated by purely individualistic conceptions of discipleship. One needed corrective to this deficiency is ecclesial models of discipleship, looking to the church as a social *locus* for following Christ. But the biblical metanarrative of the nations compels us also to wrestle with the deep challenges of public discipleship, in harmony with (not to the exclusion of) individual and ecclesial discipleship. We are implicated in, and must cooperate with our neighbors in responsibility for, the lives of our nations.

Recognizing the central place of nations in redemptive history also gives a new impetus to evangelism. The spreading of the gospel to new nations (and to new semi-national or quasi-national people groups) is not only valuable

---

[18] Anon., "Cape Town Commitment," I.7.A.

[19] Willard, *Divine Conspiracy*, 35–59.

[20] Willard, *Divine Conspiracy*, 58.

because it increases the number of saved individuals. It also carries forward God's redemptive plan to reconcile all the nations to himself. And it opens the door for God to reveal and glorify himself in new ways. In church history, whenever the gospel has gone forth in a new cultural setting—or been revived in an old one—God has used that movement to add new dimensions to his people's understanding of his character and purposes. What new manifestations of his glory will God reveal, unimaginable to us now, as the gospel goes forth in new ways in nations around the world?

Bibliography

Alexander, T. Desmond, and Brian S. Rosner, eds. *New Dictionary of Biblical Theology*. Downers Grove, IL: InterVarsity Press, 2000.
Anon. "Cape Town Commitment." Lausanne Movement, 2011, I.7.B and II.B.2. Accessed online at https://www.lausanne.org/content/ctc/ct commitment on December 9, 2016.
Arnold, B.T. "Babylon." In *New Dictionary of Biblical Theology*, edited by Alexander, and Rosner, 393–94.
Beach, Lee. *The Church in Exile*. Downers Grove, IL: InterVarsity Press, 2015.
Hays, J. Daniel. *From Every People and Nation: A Biblical Theology of Race*. New Studies in Biblical Theology. Downers Grove, IL: InterVarsity Press, 2003.
Köstenberger, A.J. "Nations." In *New Dictionary of Biblical Theology*, edited by Alexander and Rosner, 676–78.
Millar, J.G. "People of God." In *New Dictionary of Biblical*, edited by Alexander and Rosner, 684–87.
Mouw, Richard. *When the Kings Come Marching In: Isaiah and the New Jerusalem*. Grand Rapids: Eerdmans, 2002.
Rivers, Julian. "Nationhood." In *Jubilee Manifesto: A Framework, Agenda and Strategy for Christian Social Reform*, edited by Michael Schluter and John Ashcroft, 122–37. Leicester: Inter-Varsity Press, 2005.
Volf, Miroslav. *Flourishing: Why We Need Religion in a Globalized World*. New Haven, CT: Yale University Press, 2015.
Willard, Dallas. *The Divine Conspiracy: Rediscovering Our Hidden Life in God*. New York: HarperCollins, 1998.

CHAPTER 3

# "Better than a Slave:" Paul and the Economics of Slavery—A Rejoinder to Ulrike Roth

Lynn H. Cohick and John Anthony Dunne

Did Paul directly benefit economically from slave labor? Ulrike Roth, currently Reader in Ancient History at the University of Edinburgh, raises this provocative question, taking us to the heart of Paul's shortest letter.[1] Additionally, she asks whether Paul included slave labor in his calculations about growing the church, such that he used "free" labor in supporting the ministry of the gospel. We know that slavery fueled the Greco-Roman economy, and permeated the social order.[2] Slaves made up about twenty percent of the population, and created economic surplus that benefited their owners, and at times, the wider community. Roth concludes that "it is high time to accept that the Christian mission ... was economically underpinned by slavery,"[3] and claims that Paul used a "hybrid approach to slave exploitation."[4] This amounts to Christian slavery, the use of slave labor to increase the social reach of the church. Although Roth speaks of "exploitation," it should be stated that her argument centers on non-sexual, economic use of slaves, not sexual use of slaves.[5]

---

[1] Roth, "Paul, Philemon, and Onesimus," 102–30, and "Paul and Slavery," 155–82.

[2] The literature on this question is immense. Harrill, "Paul and Slavery," 576, notes that Aristotle's definition of slave as a "living tool" was modified in the Roman period, which viewed slavery as "an institution of the law of nations (*ius gentium*) by which, contrary to nature (*contra naturam*), one person is subjected to the power (*dominium*) of another." See also Hollander, "Roman Economy in the Early Empire," 17–19, who observes that scholars estimate 10–20% slaves in the population, who often competed with free labor for work. Patterson, *Slavery and Social Death*, has described slavery as "social death." For an excellent discussion of American slavery, see Noll, *Civil War as a Theological Crisis*.

[3] Roth, "Paul and Slavery," 176.

[4] Roth, "Paul and Slavery," 156.

[5] In Roth's overall contention, "Paul and Slavery," 173, Paul benefits from the controlling narrative of slavery, and does not question it nor struggle with its ethical

Roth contends that slaves did tasks, such as carrying letters or meeting daily household needs, that directly and indirectly supported the financial stability of the apostles, church evangelists and house churches. Roth's theory moves a step or two beyond earlier arguments, such as that of John Barclay, who suggested that Paul and the early church were in a dilemma over slave ownership, as they recognized the tension between the claims of the gospel, and society's evaluation of the slave.[6] Roth erases the tension, and instead declares that church members ordered their slaves to do tasks that specifically promoted the well-being and growth of the Christian community. Moreover, she claims that Paul devised his ministry approach to exploit slave labor and thus increase the growth of the church. Finally, she puts forward that Paul co-owned Onesimus with Philemon.

Roth uses a "maximizing" approach to the New Testament text,[7] which inserts slaves into the text when they are not specifically listed as such. This approach reminds us that slaves, and women, were present in ways that the text does not capture for us. For example, she suggests that we include the presence of slaves whenever the text mentions "household." One can quibble with her suggestion that Epaphroditus was a slave, because he took care of Paul's daily needs, or that Tertius was a slave because so many scribes were, but her point that we visualize slaves within the Christian community is a fair and important one. Part of her critique is certainly valid—scholars might (inadvertently) diminish the importance of slaves within the economic life of the church by stressing the overall poverty of the early Christian community. However, it is another thing altogether to claim that the early leaders strategized about how to maximize their evangelistic efforts by exploiting slave labor.

At the heart of her argument is the determined use of surplus production based on slave labor, which is uncompensated and thus "free" to the church. This type of contribution to the overall growth of the church takes advantage of immoral or unjust practices. This assessment plays out in four ways by Roth. First, she argues that Paul strategized his ministry's growth based on taking advantage of slave labor. This includes the tactics of travel and letter writing. Second, Roth creates the curious and historically improbable category

---

implications. "Exploitation" for Roth is an all-encompassing term, and includes mundane tasks. Any benefit from slave labor, therefore, is exploitation. To name but one example, when Paul requests for Philemon to prepare a guest room for him in v. 22, this is a seen by Roth as an example of slave exploitation, since this preparation of a guest room would be accomplished by means of slaves.

[6] Barclay, "Paul, Philemon and the Dilemma," 161–86. See also Blanton IV, "Economic Functions of Gift Exchange," 290, who suggests that Philemon "may have put a slave at Paul's disposal."

[7] Roth, "Paul and Slavery," 162.

of "secular" as a way to divide certain slave tasks from "religious" tasks, and thus ignores the leadership roles assumed by some slaves in Paul's churches. Third, she seeks to demonstrate that Paul co-owned the slave Onesimus, and benefited from his services directly. Fourth, she contends that there was a pronounced rise in slave exploitation that was coordinated with a decline in Paul's imminent expectation of the *parousia*. Each of these four components will be addressed in turn in the following four sections.

### Paul's Use of Slave Labor in his Ministry-Growth Strategy

Roth argues that in the course of his ministry, Paul discovers the advantages of visits and letters, and with this capitalizes (pun intended) on slave labor to grow his mission. But did Paul really consider various options, and then land on a scheme of visits and letters? Did he have other options to getting the word out about Jesus Messiah? Letters were ubiquitous at this time of heightened mobility throughout the Empire. Government officials traveled on business, merchants traded goods across the Mediterranean, troops marched to the frontiers, Gentile pilgrims sought aid at shrines, and diaspora Jews traveled to Jerusalem for festivals. This travel created both the need for correspondence, and the resources to make it happen. It seems Roth puts the cart before the horse when she postulates Paul's letter-writing as the driver of Paul's enterprise, rather than his travel for evangelism and apostolic mission.

Furthermore, Roth relies on a claim by Ekelund and Tollison that Paul was an excellent entrepreneur.[8] A quick study of this work, however, raises several concerns. First, these authors (economics professors from Auburn and Clemson) assume that people in the first century desired much the same as those in the West in the twenty-first century (based in part on rational choice theory). Second, they suggest that Paul had a great product to sell, namely the sure hope of a pleasant afterlife, granted based on holding monotheistic beliefs and ascribing to moral living.[9] Yet there is little evidence in the ancient sources that pagans craved such a "product" or that Jews believed that Jesus was God's Messiah to deliver the promise. Third, they focus on Paul's entrepreneurship, claiming that Paul's success was due to his letter writing,

---

[8] Ekelund and Tollison, *Economic Origins of Roman Christianity*, 75. See the critical review offered by Sessa, "Review of *Economic Origins of Roman Christianity*."

[9] Ekelund and Tollison, *Economic Origins of Roman Christianity*, 72, state, "There is reason to believe that Gentiles and pagans, facing a far lower relative price and even higher benefits (in the form of social welfare interactions as well as a lower full price due to monotheism and a well-defined afterlife) would not be immune to Christian entrepreneurship." They argue, 56, that "there was but one essential product of the Christian religion at its inception—*the promise of a well-defined, promulgated afterlife* . . . We believe that the *critical* emphasis on it [afterlife] was the fundamental product change that led to its rapid adoption."

which, alongside his visits, created a network of successful churches. It seems unlikely, however, to us that today's Fortune 500 would consider a new venture as a success if it produced a handful of small groups of non-influential, lower status people, led by a man who was repeatedly arrested or driven out of cities! In their own words, "In short, Paul was an immensely successful entrepreneur who helped develop a new product in the marketplace for religion and marketed it brilliantly both door-to-door (travels) and through mail order (epistles). Faith drove Paul; economics drove his methods."[10] Roth accepts Ekelund and Tollison's argument that letters and visits made Paul successful, and links that with her argument that slaves delivered letters and took care of Paul's daily needs, and then concludes that slave labor built Paul's church network and was foundational to its success.

But were his emissaries slaves? Paul's fellow apostles were Jews who had not been enslaved previously. Titus, Timothy, Tychicus, Lydia, Phoebe, these people are not identified as slaves. And it is likely that Paul connected with the Jewish community in the cities he traveled to, as ethnic groups sought out each other for safety and help. Again, we have no way to know if the Jewish couple, Priscilla and Aquila, owned slaves, but they both worked in their trade, so they did not have lots of leisure time. Blanton argues that Paul sold his own labor to Aquila and Priscilla while he lived in Corinth, for he likely had little capital for raw materials needed in his tent making.[11] In fact, Paul declares that he worked to earn his keep (1 Thess. 2.9; cf. 2 Thess. 3.7–8), that at times he did not make use of his apostolic right to compensation (1 Cor. 9.15), and that he received donations, often from those with little surplus (2 Cor. 8–9). Again, if we grant that Tertius was a slave, we have no reason to assume that Paul did not pay him for his services, as educated or skilled slaves could earn money by their trade. Roth reveals a tension within her argument, wanting Paul to be eschatologically focused so that he does not worry about the legal category of slavery, and practically minded so as to build a business model for successful mission and evangelism.

### Slave "Secular" and "Religious" Labor

Moreover, Roth makes a curious divide between "secular" and sacred work. She contends that Paul relied on slave labor for the "secular" job of carrying his mail, thus maintaining links with his network of churches. However, most New Testament scholars argue that these letter carriers were also preachers who explained the arguments of the missives. Phoebe, the letter carrier of Romans, is not presented as a slave; quite the opposite, she is Paul's benefactor (προστάτις in Rom. 16.2). And as such, she could have owned slaves who

---

[10] Ekelund and Tollison, *Economic Origins of Roman Christianity*, 75.

[11] Blanton IV, "Economic Functions of Gift Exchange," 288.

would have served Paul if he had stayed in her home. Roth asks rhetorically that if Phoebe delivered the letter to the Romans, "do we think she travelled alone?"[12] If the answer is "No," which is likely, that simply highlights the embedded nature of the institution of slavery in Paul's day, not the direct and calculated benefit Paul's ministry gained by it.

Roth claims that Paul made a dedicated effort to convert slave owners so as to maximize his resources, "creating the basis for the cult's future position of dominance (even if a worldly future was not envisaged by him)."[13] This claim assumes that once converted, slave owners would offer their slaves' services to Paul, a gesture for which there is little evidence in the broader culture. And it assumes that slaves themselves did not have the opportunity to donate funds or time if they were part of the fledging congregations. For example, the slaves or freedmen of Caesar's household, mentioned in Philippians (Philippians 1), might have relished the opportunity to donate to the community from their wealth, which could have been greater than shop keepers in Philippi. Roth admits as much about Onesimus and others using their *peculium* as an offering, and rightly indicates we need to highlight it today.[14] Roth assumes that masters controlled the churches, but Katherine Shaner argues that the slave, Onesimus, was charged with helping the church directly in a leadership capacity, based on Paul's use of the verb διακονέω in Philemon (Phlm. 13).[15]

Roth argues further that Paul treated legal slavery as unessential so as to stress the importance of spiritual slavery to the Lord, and spiritual freedom within the church. If Paul's Philippian co-workers, Euodia and Syntyche, were slaves or freedwomen, we might have a case here of Paul minimizing their social status while promoting their "spiritual status" as leaders in the church (Phil. 4.2–3).[16] Yet it is not clear that legal slavery was *adiaphora* to Paul. Timothy Brookins rightly points out the fundamental distinction between Seneca's approach to slavery status as *adiaphora*, and Paul's views.[17] Seneca viewed slavery as indifferent based on his strongly negative view of the body as

---

[12] Roth, "Paul and Slavery," 173.

[13] Roth, "Paul and Slavery," 176.

[14] Roth, "Paul and Slavery," 168–69.

[15] Shaner, *Enslaved Leadership in Early Christianity*, 60, explains, "Thus, the purpose clause in verse 13 . . . does not suggest that Onesimus attends to Paul's person during Paul's imprisonment. Rather, Onesimus attends to the practices of an *ekklēsia* in Ephesus, which claims an imprisoned member, Paul."

[16] Marchal, "Slaves as Wo/men and Unmen," 144–45. He continues, 168, that the loyal yokefellow could be the slave owner who is on Paul's side, and together they reinforce slave/freedwomen obedience. Wire, "Response," 178, notes the fragile nature of the evidence.

[17] Brookins, "(Dis)correspondence." See also his "Economic Profiling."

a prison for the mind/soul, and his ambivalence about the possibility of a spiritual afterlife. Paul, by contrast, emphasized the resurrection body in the life to come. Relatedly, early Christians' embrace of asceticism is not a negation of the body, *a la* Seneca, but an anticipation of resurrected life in God's kingdom. Wealthy believers eschewed their money and its social status to better model Christ's lowly estate and social humiliation. Moreover, and more importantly, Paul stressed the owners' debasement to the slaves' level, in accordance with Jesus Christ's own model.[18] Seneca offered only the theoretical notion that slaves and masters were equal in nature; he tries, unsuccessfully, to raise up the slave.[19] Paul lowers the master to the slave's level—based on believers' lives in Christ.

It seems implausible, therefore, that Paul targeted slave owners with the gospel. Surely Paul would not have utilized the rhetoric of becoming a slave of Christ, or of Christ's own humiliation to the point of being a slave (e.g., Philippians 2), if his specific goal was to reach slave owners. Would not Paul have made a more appropriate sales pitch to appeal to slave owners?[20]

## Paul as Co-owner of Onesimus with Philemon

To prove her point further that early Christian leaders, including Paul, took advantage of the economic value of slaves to further their mission, Roth argues that Paul was co-owner of Onesimus.[21] She rests her case on a specific reading of Philemon, and in particular, on the meanings of the term κοινωνία found twice in the epistle (Phlm. 6 and 17). She asserts that in verse 6, the noun signifies fellowship or partnership within the wider Christian community; in verse 17, it refers to the business partnership with Philemon that included the pooling of resources such as Onesimus. The broad definitions used here have ample support in the wider literature.[22] Peter Arzt-Grabner states that the

---

[18] Brookins, "(Dis)correspondence," 198.

[19] Seneca, *Ep.* 47, retains the social hierarchy of master/slave, labeling slaves as inferior relative to their owner. Seneca enjoins the superior, the owner, to treat the slave with empathy because the owner him/herself could at some fateful point also become a slave. And slaves should be able to relate to their owner with respect, not fear. Social hierarchy remains, however, even as does the distinction between a human and a god, 47.16.

[20] If his goal was to win slave owners with this kind of rhetoric, then Paul would have been an even greater salesman than the father of *Tommy Boy*, who was such a remarkable salesman that he could "sell ketchup popsicles to a woman in white gloves."

[21] Roth, "Paul, Philemon, and Onesimus."

[22] Roth, "Paul, Philemon, and Onesimus," 105, remarks that the term "at its most fundamental and practical meaning [describes] a private (voluntary) association of two or more members that aimed at the pooling of resources for a specific goal."

documentary papyri evidence testifies to the business partnership meaning.[23] Roth speculates that Paul wrote to Philemon in part to assert that the partnership is not null and void because Paul is in prison.[24] Yet it seems that Philemon knew enough of Paul's dangerous mission that he was not surprised at another imprisonment. Moreover, Roth argues that Paul drew on Greek law and customs, not Roman law, because Philemon was from Asia Minor and would have operated with the traditional, Attic, customs. The pay-off for Roth is that she can use the centuries' earlier Greek system that included references to co-owning a chattel.[25]

It would have been beneficial for Roth to suggest why Paul got into a partnership of this sort with Philemon. Her point is that Paul needed help with daily activities, and a slave would have suited this purpose well. But why partner with Philemon? Why did Paul need any partner for this? Why did he not simply procure his own slave? This is especially pertinent if Paul accurately reflects Philemon's view that Onesimus is "useless;" why would Paul agree to get involved with a business partner who contributed a "worthless" slave?[26] For Roth, Paul's "exploitation of the services of Onesimus" demonstrates that Paul accepted "worldly slavery."[27] She concludes that once Onesimus became a Christian, Paul had religious duties he wanted him to perform, and wrote to inform Philemon of the new situation. Roth maintains that Paul would have looked to another slave to do the "secular" sorts of tasks that Onesimus was no longer performing.[28]

The weakest aspect of Roth's argument is her claim that Paul empowers Onesimus to act as his agent with Philemon (v. 17), because that seems to contradict earlier statements that business partners shared what they had

---

[23] Arzt-Grabner, "How to Deal with Onesimus?" 136. He adds, 137, that we have no evidence of a slave identified as a κοινωνός by his/her master, nor does Paul use the term to describe Onesimus's future relationship with Philemon. Paul uses the term in Phil. 4.10–20 to thank the Philippians for their financial partnership in his mission.

[24] Roth, "Paul, Philemon, and Onesimus," 114, suggests a corollary that Paul's insistence on his imprisonment is to reinforce the partnership, not promote his authority.

[25] Roth, "Paul, Philemon, and Onesimus," 120 n.68, states, "joint ownership of slaves is one of the most often attested forms of shared ownership over 'things' in our Athenian evidence."

[26] Arzt-Grabner, "How to Deal with Onesimus?" 121, argues that this biographical detail is not related to an allegation that Onesimus ran away.

[27] Roth, "Paul, Philemon, and Onesimus," 124.

[28] Roth, "Paul and Slavery," 171, states, "There is little doubt in my mind that Paul would have resorted to precisely the same supply source that had worked well so far—slave labor."

pooled together. Roth interprets Paul as declaring to Philemon that he, a slave owner, and Onesimus, the slave, are now equals/brothers in the Lord, and that Onesimus is Paul's agent, not beholden to Philemon in the same way he was before baptism. In other words, this business partnership is reworked such that Philemon is no longer to use his "half" of the "chattel," Onesimus, because Paul brought the latter to the Lord. Yet with the statement that Philemon owes him his very life (v. 19), did they ever in fact have a business partnership as Roth describes? The "sacred" and "secular" categories Roth uses fail to adequately resolve this reconstructed situation.

Taking the evidence in a different direction, Artz-Grabner suggests that Paul advocated a business relationship between Philemon and Onesimus. The master and slave will partner together as brothers, as Philemon trusts Onesimus with more responsibilities, and perhaps eventually manumits him.[29] Michael White situates Philemon as the *pater familias* and owner of Onesimus, and as Paul's patron. He argues that Paul takes advantage of the fact that he baptized both men. Paul becomes the spiritual patron of both, thereby "placing Philemon and Onesimus on a more equal footing."[30]

Roth focuses on Paul's declaration that he will pay any of Onesimus's bills, an act which goes beyond typical partnerships that share debts equally. She sees in this statement confirmation that the two are partners.[31] Arriving at a different conclusion, White suggests that Paul was Philemon's client, and, as such, expected gifts from Philemon, his patron. In stating that Paul would pay Onesimus's debts, what he really meant was that Philemon could subtract the debt amount from the total gift he planned to provide to Paul.[32] Regardless of whether Roth or White are ultimately persuasive here, their opposite reconstructions demonstrate the complexity in re-creating the historical backdrop of the letter, and highlight how one's starting point often determines the end result.[33] Why Paul would bring up the issue of debt, if he and

---

[29] Arzt-Grabner, "How to Deal with Onesimus?" 140.

[30] White, "Paul and *Pater Familias*," 188.

[31] Roth, "Paul, Philemon, and Onesimus," 108.

[32] White, "Paul and *Pater Familias*," 188. See also Osiek and Balch, *Families in the New Testament World*, 177.

[33] Roth's position only works if Onesimus is not a runaway slave or an asylum seeker, the former view being the consensus throughout church history going back to Chrysostom. This position is far from uncontested, and the letter is certainly ambiguous enough to be read in a few different ways. A few contend that he was sent to Paul by Philemon; see Cohick, *Ephesians*, 28–30; White, "Paul and *Pater Familias*," 187. Barclay, "Paul, Philemon and the Dilemma," 165 n.16, rightly points out that if Onesimus was a runaway, then Roman authorities, not Paul, would send him back to his owner. Arzt-Grabner, "How to Deal with Onesimus?" 133, distinguishes between

Philemon co-owned the slave? At issue would be the proper tasks Onesimus was to do, or, perhaps, the allotted time each was given for Onesimus's services. In either case, it does not seem that the "debt" would describe Paul's obligation to Philemon. Roth notes that it is the "timing and duration" of Onesimus's absence from Philemon that is at issue;[34] however, she does not consider that Onesimus's elongated stay with Paul is not the former's fault. Since Onesimus was detained because of Paul's circumstances, the slave would not owe Philemon. Instead, Paul would owe Philemon for deciding to change their agreement without his initial consent.

### Slave Exploitation and the Delay of the *Parousia*

One final component of Roth's argument to address in some detail is the proposal regarding Paul's increased exploitation of slave labor coupled with a decrease in his belief in the imminent end of the age. Within Pauline studies, the consensus holds that a delay of the *parousia* impacted the development of Paul's theology, but the connection that slave exploitation develops along the same trajectory is Roth's unique contribution. This aspect of Roth's overall argument begins with the fact that slavery is only mentioned once in 1 Thessalonians, which most believe is Paul's earliest letter.[35] In 1 Thessalonians 1.9, Paul describes the conversion of the Thessalonians as a turning away from idols to serve (δουλεύειν) the living and true God. Given this singular reference, Roth states that at the time of writing 1 Thessalonians "slavery was not yet relevant" for Paul. More fully,

> The fact that a letter regularly regarded as early and concerned with eschatological claims does not mention slavery according to the law reinforces first the early dating and second the proposed interpretation of the later correspondence as providing sustained evidence (however cryptic) for slave exploitation: the changing socioeconomic focus matches the theological evolution (and vice versa).[36]

Roth's observation, in other words, is that, when 1 Thessalonians is juxtaposed with other "later" Pauline texts, we see more references to slavery as

---

a slave who runs away never to return (*fugitivus*) and one who plans to return, but later than expected (*erro*). McKnight, *Philemon*, 3–5, 10, 45, 89, 106–7, articulates the view in his new commentary that Philemon was the owner of the slave, Onesimus, and that Paul did not advocate Onesimus' manumission.

[34] Roth, "Paul, Philemon, and Onesimus," 113.

[35] Roth, "Paul and Slavery," 178, writes, "the time had not yet come for Paul to think ahead and to craft a (temporary) future on earth."

[36] Roth, "Paul and Slavery," 178.

a concept *and* as a real institution of real slaves.[37] Hence, she is claiming that a development in slave *references* implicitly reveals an increasing *use* of slaves, and indeed slave use is ultimately correlated with (and caused by) a waning expectation of the *parousia*. So, as Paul's sense of mission grows and his eschatology allegedly becomes less imminent, slave labor presents itself as the way to fund his regular visits and continual travel.

But what is Paul doing out in the Aegean if he is not concerned with mission already when writing 1 Thessalonians? Even if Roth followed John Knox's approach to Pauline chronology, which dictates that Paul's chronology should be reconstructed from his letters first without the secondary framework of three missionary journeys supplied by Acts,[38] allowing the possibility that 1 Thessalonians was potentially written as early as the late 30s CE,[39] Roth would still need to explain how Paul supported such a trip. If the answer is not slave labor at this early stage, why would it necessarily have to change later on in the way that she proposes?

Furthermore, Roth's argument—that increased slave *references* signify slave *use* along a paired trajectory of increased expressions of realized eschatology—is undermined by 1 Corinthians, which contains futuristic expectation alongside some crucial references to real slaves, such as in 1 Corinthians 7.21–23 (cf. 1 Cor. 12.13), which speaks of the status of free and slave at the time of their calling. This takes place in a context all about the imminent expectation of the end.[40] So the coordination of slave references alongside imminent expectation, in a letter that is regarded as later than 1 Thessalonians, is incongruous with Roth's proposal.

The most serious disruption to the eschatological aspects of Roth's overall argument, however, would be if Galatians is in fact Paul's earliest letter, as some contend. In fact, it seems that Galatians is the fly in the ointment whether it is Paul's earliest letter or not. Galatians contains more references to slavery (both literal and figurative) than any other Pauline text.[41] Indeed this

---

[37] See especially the chart in Roth, "Paul and Slavery," 163.

[38] Knox, *Chapters in a Life of Paul*.

[39] See, e.g., Campbell, *Framing Paul*; Donfried, *Paul, Thessalonica, and Early Christianity*; Lüdemann, *Paul, Apostle to the Gentiles*; Buck and Taylor, *Saint Paul*. Not everyone who follows Knox, however, contends for such an early dating of 1 Thessalonians See, e.g., Jewett, *Chronology of Paul's Life*.

[40] In this chapter, Paul's admonitions come alongside several significant references to imminent expectation. For example, he speaks of an impending crisis in 1 Cor. 7.26 and states that the present form of the world is passing away in v. 31.

[41] Note the following examples. In Gal. 1.10 Paul calls himself a δοῦλος of the Messiah. He speaks of not giving in to compulsion (ἀναγκάζω) and submission (ὑποταγή) in Jerusalem for Titus to be circumcised, which by acquiescing would have been an instance of succumbing to enslavement (καταδουλόω) and a loss of freedom

expands if we include allusions to slave culture, such as, the reference to "bearing one another's burdens" (Gal. 6.2; cf. 6.5) and also τὰ στίγματα τοῦ Ἰησοῦ, which alludes to the practice of branding slaves (Gal. 6.17). A deeper layer to this picture of slavery in Galatians is revealed when considering the influence of the Servant of Isaiah on Galatians.[42] As a summary of some of the Isaianic influence, Paul imagines himself as either the Isaianic Servant of Isaiah 49, or as one who extends the Servant's ministry to be a light to the nations (cf. Isa. 49.6). All of this, of course, adds more nuance to the slave imagery in Galatians and further demonstrates its prominence as a theme in Galatians relative to the other Pauline letters.

Given this observation, if Galatians is early, preceding the Thessalonian correspondence or the Corinthian correspondence, then Roth's argument unravels. In particular, the assumption that Galatians must be regarded as later than 1 Thessalonians on the basis of an alleged development in Paul's eschatology is far from certain. This is because such differences in eschatological emphasis between the letters can be accounted for by *ad hoc* concerns relative to the respective occasions of each letter, rather than by a theological trajectory.[43]

---

(ἐλευθερία in Gal. 2.3–5). Paul refers to the law as a παιδαγωγός, which was often the role of a slave tasked with monitoring and tutoring children before they reached adulthood (Gal. 3.24). The beginning of ch. 4 speaks to the relative status of children vis-à-vis slaves in the ancient world until they reach adulthood (Gal. 4.1), and this analogy serves to inform Paul's understanding of enslavement to τὰ στοιχεῖα τοῦ κόσμου and those that "by nature are not gods" (Gal. 4.3, 8–9). Those under the law were *redeemed* in the fullness of time (Gal. 4.4–5) and have received adoption; by the Spirit former slaves have become children (Gal. 4.6–7). And indeed, as Paul affirms at the end of Gal. 3, there is no longer slave nor free as a result of baptism into the Messiah and putting on the Messiah—the result is oneness in the Messiah which transcends these socioeconomic divides (Gal. 3.28). In the infamous allegory of Galatians 4, we have references to Hagar as the slave woman—παιδίσκη (Gal. 4.22–23, 30–31). Hagar bears children for *slavery* (Gal. 4.24) and corresponds to the present Jerusalem which is *in slavery* (Gal. 4.25). Whatever else may be going on in the allegory, Paul's point in the end comes through in 5.1, you are free so be free; do not submit to a yoke of *slavery* (Gal. 5.1). This freedom does not mean that one can do whatever they want, such as receiving circumcision ("do not use your freedom as an opportunity for the flesh," as it says in 5.13), but rather use this freedom, paradoxically, lovingly to *serve* one another (δουλεύετε), as it says in verse 14 (i.e., "act like slaves towards one another").

[42] On this, see especially, Harmon, *She Must and Shall Go Free*. Cf. also Dunne, *Persecution and Participation in Galatians*, 128–92, and "Cast Out the Aggressive Agitators (Gl 4:29–30)," 255–63.

[43] On this, see Dunne, "Eschatological Emphases in 1 Thessalonians and Galatians."

Even if Galatians is not early, Roth's case still unravels, because she also assumes that *Galatians reflects a more realized eschatology*. This assumption is not compatible with the various futuristic images in the text of Galatians regarding justification and judgment.[44] Although the *parousia* itself is not explicitly mentioned in Galatians, we know from the Thessalonian correspondence that judgment is an event coordinated with the *parousia*.[45] In addition to futurism, there are also connotations of *imminence* in Galatians. In Galatians 6.10, following the use of the judgment trope of harvesting and reaping (Gal. 6.7–9), Paul writes that we are to do good to all "as we have time" (Ἄρα οὖν ὡς καιρὸν ἔχομεν), implying that there is not much left before that harvest judgment occurs. Then, in 6.17, Paul writes, "From now on (τοῦ λοιποῦ) let no one cause me trouble." Τοῦ λοιποῦ is here best taken as a genitive of time, meaning "with the remaining time."[46] In other words, Paul concludes the letter by saying, "*knock it off my friends, we don't have much time left!*" The imminence suggested by Galatians 6.10 and 6.17 is illuminated further by Paul's most explicit reference to time in Galatians 4.4: God sent his Son *in the fullness of time* (τὸ πλήρωμα τοῦ κρόνου).[47] This does not mean in the *middle* of time, or in the *meridian* of time, as if Paul could have anticipated 2,000 plus years of church history. Whether time is the content or the container, the point is the same in Galatians 4.4: *it is full*. This would then also make the other futuristic images of Galatians have a similar *imminent* nuance.

Thus, Galatians seriously disrupts Roth's contention about the umbilical link between eschatological development and slave use regardless of whether it is early or not. Given (1) the references to slavery (both literal and figurative),

---

[44] Justification is fundamentally connected to the future judgment: no flesh "will be justified" (δικαιωθήσεται) by works of the law in 2.16, and "we *await* (ἀπεκδεχόμεθα) the hope of righteousness" in 5.5. Those who produce the works of the flesh "will not inherit" (οὐ κληρονομήσουσιν) the kingdom (5.22). If the Galatians get circumcised Christ *will not be of benefit* to them in 5.2 (ὠφελήσει), presumably on the last day. And there are other allusions to the future judgment in Gal. 5–6, including that "the one troubling you" *will bear* (βαστάσει) the judgment in 5.10, and that each one *will bear* (βαστάσει) his own load in 6.5. The eschatological metaphor of sowing and reaping in 6.7–9 is rooted in a trope of final judgment; *we will reap* (θερίσομεν), Paul says in v. 9, "if we do not give up" (pointing to the need for endurance; note as well there are three uses of θερίσει in vv. 7–8).

[45] 1 Thess. 1.10 speaks of the future *parousia* in terms of "waiting" for the Son who will deliver God's people from the wrath that is coming.

[46] I.e., τοῦ λοιποῦ is not equivalent to the accusative expression τὸ λοιπόν, which means "finally."

[47] It is important to point out that Paul speaks here of χρόνος, the sequence of time, and not καιρός, an appointed time.

and (2) the futuristic and imminent expectations, Roth's argument that Paul's slave-talk is ultimately rooted in a growing exploitation of slaves due to a waning *parousia* falls apart.

## Conclusion: Paul, Slavery, and Social Injustice

In conclusion, at least two paths seem worthy of further exploration. One attends to the concept of social justice, and the critique of slavery as an institution. A second path explores the economic and social ramifications of Paul's convictions about slave labor. Pursuing the first path, we must take care not to read Paul as a defender of our modern notion of social justice, if by that one means an ideology that relies on an Enlightenment view of the individual and on the modern experience of democracy. However, patristic writers spoke of human rights and justice and the common good, even as they also promoted the ascetic life.[48] One can argue whether the apostle Paul was ascetic, but all would agree that he warned against the lure of wealth, and the power of greed (Eph. 5.3–7). The patristic church has much to say on the dangers of wealth. Peter Brown's work in the last two decades highlights the shift in "social imagination" within the Christian Roman Empire as leaders moved from a focus on benefiting the city and growing wealth, to caring for the poor.[49]

The post-Constantine church, no longer the church of the martyrs, expressed devotion through voluntary poverty and asceticism. For example, Ilaria Ramelli argues that a few church fathers, particularly Gregory of Nyssa, linked their views of asceticism with a rejection of the institution of slavery, based on a sense of social justice.[50] One could argue that the ascetic gave up his or her slave as part of giving up all property; however, Ramelli sees a deeper critique, namely the renunciation of oppression.[51] She points to Gregory of Nyssa's sister, Macrina, as one whose ascetic life included manumission of her slaves. Even more, she then lived with those slaves as equals in the spiritual journey, as they "shared the same table and the same

---

[48] Gregory of Nazianzus, *Oration* 14, "On Love for the Poor," *PG* 35.857A–910D; Gregory of Nyssa, *Homily* 4 on Ecclesiastes. See also Gregory of Nazianzus, *Select Orations*, 39–71. An exception is Augustine, who did not promote manumission, see *City of God* 19.15, cf. the discussion in Ramelli, *Social Justice*, 153.

[49] Brown, *Poverty and Leadership*, 1. He remarks, 61, on a glaring omission, namely that bishops focused on the free poor, and not on slaves. It was the owner's responsibility to care for their slaves.

[50] Ramelli, *Social Justice*, 8–10. See also Holman, *Beholden*. For a critical review of Ramelli, see Harrill, "Review of *Social Justice*."

[51] Ramelli, *Social Justice*, 10.

kind of bed."[52] It is popular today to stress that all humans reflect God's image, and thus deserve social and economic dignity. Macrina demonstrates such theology in action, accepting the social shame that went with poverty. In them, we see the fruit of studying the New Testament, including Paul's discussion of slavery within his theology of participation in Christ.

Turning to the economic realities, Paul often talked about himself in terms that stressed humiliation and vulnerability, and to Philemon he identified himself as an old man in chains. Moreover, he spoke of Jesus making himself nothing, taking the nature of a slave (Phil. 2.7). Paul's insight, implicit in his self-description, is that the freedom of slaves is as much an issue for owners, for "free" takes its social worth from the opposite, "slave." The conversation about Onesimus is also a conversation about who Philemon is. Paul touches this when he speaks about "brothers," intending to describe Philemon in a new way (v. 16). There is a parallel to the "women's issues" in church discussions. It is not so much a "women's issue" as it is a "man's issue," because the construction of masculinity is created in opposition to femininity. Said another way, what it means to be a man is defined as the opposite of what it means to be a woman, with the norming virtues attributed to the male.

What could Paul's insight mean in economic terms? For believers in North America, it means that we might focus much more on the wealthy giving up their advantages in creating wealth. Perhaps a story will elucidate this. In 2003, under Bush 43, the President was engaged in free-trade negotiations with Central America, and was considering reducing tariffs on sugar cane coming from there. The Governor of Louisiana, Kathleen Blanco, and her Republican opponent, Bobby Jindal, resisted this move, as it would reduce income from sugar cane produced in her state.[53] What if the local churches in Louisiana had agreed to lower tariffs, even though it would mean much lower pay checks? Instead, sadly, we often preach about donating money to the poor, even as we enjoy legal sanctions that preserve our wealth. Paul understood the Old Testament concept of economic equality, as seen in his exegesis of the story of manna from Exodus 16 preached to the Corinthians (2 Cor. 8.13–15). Here he asks the Corinthians to give their excess to the Judean churches so that the latter will cease to be in want.

Roth misses (or at least underestimates) the impact of this spiritual reality in the lives of believers, both slaves and Paul himself, as she creates "secular" and "sacred" work categories. If she had capitalized more on Paul's eschatology, she could have been more alert to the language of the kingdom of

---

[52] Ramelli, *Social Justice*, 191. Ramelli contrasts Paula's monastic life that included three social levels of women, and refers to Jerome's *Letter* 108. Elm, *"Virgins of God,"* 103, argues, however, that Gregory owned slaves. Ramelli, *Social Justice*, 244, argues that not only Gregory, but Origen, Evagrius, and Chrysostom conclude that "it is impossible to be rich without committing injustice (ἀδικία)."

[53] Bahr and Gaudet, "Blanco, Jindah Listen to Sugar Farmers' Woes."

God within Paul's letters. There Paul speaks of the consequences of our actions today affecting our life in the age to come. The ends do not justify the means. Abuse of wealth, greed, humiliating others—all are condemned in the strongest terms. All believers, as they wait for their inheritance, are given good works to walk in, as all walk according to love, even as our Savior so loved us and gave himself up for us (Eph. 5.2).

## Bibliography

Arzt-Grabner, Peter. "How to Deal with Onesimus? Paul's Solution within the Frame of Ancient Legal and Documentary Sources." In *Philemon in Perspective: Interpreting a Pauline Letter*. Ed. by D. Francois Tolmie, 113–42. Berlin: de Gruyter, 2010.

Bahr, Emilie, and Katina A. Gaudet. "Blanco, Jindal listen to Sugar Farmer Woes." https://www.houmatoday.com/news/20031106/blanco-jindal-listen-to-sugar-farmers-woes

Barclay, John M.G. "Paul, Philemon and the Dilemma of Christian Slave-ownership." *New Testament Studies* 37.2 (1991) 161–86.

Blanton IV, Thomas R. "Economic Functions of Gift Exchange in Pauline Assemblies." In *Paul and Economics: A Handbook*, edited by Raymond Pickett and Thomas R. Blanton IV, 279–306. Minneapolis, MN: Fortress, 2017.

Brookins, Timothy A. "(Dis)correspondence of Paul and Seneca on Slavery." In *Paul and Seneca in Dialogue*, edited by Joseph R. Dodson and David E. Briones, 179–207. Ancient Philosophy and Religion 2. Leiden: Brill, 2017.

———. "Economic Profiling of Early Christian Communities." In *Paul and Economics: A Handbook*, edited by Raymond Pickett and Thomas R. Blanton IV, 57–87. Minneapolis, MN: Fortress, 2017.

Brown, Peter. *Poverty and Leadership in the Later Roman Empire*. The Menahem Stern Jerusalem Lectures. Waltham, MA: Brandeis University Press, 2001.

Buck, Charles, and Greer Taylor. *Saint Paul: A Study of the Development of His Thought*. New York: Schribner, 1969.

Campbell, Douglas A. *Framing Paul: An Epistolary Biography*. Grand Rapids: Eerdmans, 2014.

Cohick, Lynn H. *Ephesians*. New Covenant Commentary Series. Eugene, OR: Cascade, 2010.

Donfried, Karl Paul. *Paul, Thessalonica, and Early Christianity*. Grand Rapids: Eerdmans, 2002.

Dunne, John Anthony. "Cast Out the Aggressive Agitators (Gl 4:29–30): Suffering, Identity, and the Ethics of Expulsion in Paul's Mission to the Galatians." In *Sensitivity to Outsiders: Exploring the Dynamic Relationship between Mission and Ethics in the New Testament and Early Christianity*, edited by Jacobus Kok, Tobias Nicklas, Dieter T. Roth, and Christopher M. Hays, 246–69. Wissenschaftliche Untersuchungen zum Neuen Testament II/364. Tübingen: Mohr Siebeck, 2014.

———. "Eschatological Emphases in 1 Thessalonians and Galatians: Distinct Argumentative Strategies Related to External Conflict and Audience Response." *Journal of Biblical & Theological Studies* 3.2 (2018) 227–48.

———. *Persecution and Participation in Galatians*. Wissenschaftliche Untersuchungen zum Neuen Testament II/454. Tübingen: Mohr Siebeck, 2017.

Ekelund, Robert B., and Robert D. Tollison, eds. *Economic Origins of Roman Christianity*. Chicago: University of Chicago Press, 2011.

Elm, Susanna. *"Virgins of God": The Making of Asceticism in Late Antiquity*. Oxford Classical Monographs. Oxford: Oxford University Press, 1996.

Gregory of Nazianzus. *Select Orations*. Trans. Martha Vinson. The Fathers of the Church. Washington DC: The Catholic University of America Press, 2003.

Gregory of Nyssa. *Homilies on Ecclesiates: An English Version with Supporting Studies*, edited by Stuart George Hall. Berlin: de Gruyter, 1993.

Harmon, Matthew S. *She Must and Shall Go Free: Paul's Isaianic Gospel in Galatians*. Beihefte zur Zeitschrift für die neutestamentliche Wissenschaft 168. Berlin: de Gruyter, 2010.

Harrill, J. Albert. "Paul and Slavery." In *Paul in the Greco-Roman World: A Handbook*, edited by J. Paul Sampley, 575–607. Harrisburg, PA: Trinity, 2003.

———. "Review of *Social Justice and the Legitimacy of Slavery*, by Ilaria L.E. Ramelli." *Journal of Early Christian History* 7.2 (2017) 106–11.

Hollander, David B. "The Roman Economy in the Early Empire: An Overview." In *Paul and Economics: A Handbook*, edited by Raymond Pickett and Thomas R. Blanton IV, 1–22. Minneapolis, MN: Fortress, 2017.

Holman, Susan. *Beholden: Religion, Global Health, and Human Rights*. Oxford: Oxford University Press, 2015.

Jewett, Robert. *A Chronology of Paul's Life*. Philadelphia: Fortress, 1979.

Knox, John. *Chapters in a Life of Paul*. Rev. ed. London: SCM, 1989.

Lüdemann, Gerd. *Paul, Apostle to the Gentiles: Studies in Chronology*. Philadelphia: Fortress, 1984.

Marchal, Joseph A. "Slaves as Wo/men and Unmen: Reflecting upon Euodia, Syntyche, and Epaphroditus in Philippi." In *The People Beside Paul: The Philippian Assembly and History from Below*, edited by Joseph A. Marchal, 141–76. Atlanta, GA: SBL, 2015.

McKnight, Scot. *The Letter to Philemon*. New International Commentary on the New Testament. Grand Rapids: Eerdmans, 2017.

Migne, J.-P., ed. *Patrologia Cursus Completus: Series Graeca*. 162 vols. Paris: Petit-Montrogue, 1857–86 (*PG*).

Noll, Mark A. *The Civil War as a Theological Crisis*. Chapel Hill, NC: University of North Carolina Press, 2006.

Osiek, Carolyn A., and David L. Balch. *Families in the New Testament World: Households and House Churches*. Louisville, KY: Westminster John Knox, 1997.

Patterson, Orlando. *Slavery and Social Death: A Comparative Study*. Cambridge, MA: Harvard University Press, 1982.

Ramelli, Ilaria L.E. *Social Justice and the Legitimacy of Slavery: The Role of Philosophical Asceticism from Ancient Judaism to Late Antiquity*. Oxford Early Christian Studies. Oxford: Oxford University Press, 2016.

Roth, Ulrike. "Paul, Philemon, and Onesimus: A Christian Design for Mastery." *Zeitschrift für die neutestamentliche Wissenschaft* 105.1 (2014) 102–30.

———. "Paul and Slavery: Economic Perspectives." In *Paul and Economics: A Handbook*, edited by Raymond Pickett and Thomas R. Blanton IV, 155–82. Minneapolis, MN: Fortress, 2017.

Sessa, Kristina. "Review of *Economic Origins of Roman Christianity*, by Robert B. Ekelund and Robert D. Tollison (eds.)." *Journal of Religion* 94.1 (2014) 113–14.

Shaner, Katherine A. *Enslaved Leadership in Early Christianity*. Oxford: Oxford University Press, 2018.

White, L. Michael. "Paul and *Pater Familias*." In *Paul in the Greco-Roman World: A Handbook:* Volume 2, edited by J. Paul Sampley, 171–203. London: Bloomsbury/T. & T. Clark, 2016.

Wire, Antoinette Clark. "Response." In *The People Beside Paul: The Philippian Assembly and History from Below*, edited by Joseph A. Marchal, 177–82. Atlanta, GA: SBL, 2015.

CHAPTER 4

# Waiting with Eager Longing: The Inseparability of Human Flourishing from the Flourishing of All Creation

Suzanne McDonald

A fully orbed theological account of what makes for human flourishing has to include at least three sets of relationships as they are made known to us in scripture. Most of the time we only think about two of them. First and foremost, of course, is the relationship that God has established with human beings, and the kind of relationship that we are called to have with him in response. Second, and flowing from that, is what it means to be in right relationship with one another. The third, which is very often marginalized or outright forgotten, is the relationship between human beings and the rest of creation, primarily understood in the context of this paper in terms of the earth on which we are placed.[1]

This third relationship will be the focus of what follows. It is abundantly clear throughout scripture that right relationship between human beings and the rest of creation makes for the flourishing of both, and that the distortion of this relationship as a result of human sin not only damages the rest of God's good creation, it also deeply hinders human flourishing. Our destiny and that of the rest of creation are deeply woven together from the very beginning through to the eschatological consummation.

In the first instance, however, we need to frame the relationship between human beings and the rest of creation by giving a very brief scriptural sketch of the relationship that God establishes with the whole of his creation. It is within the context of God as the one who creates, continues to care for creation, and has a glorious future for what he has made, that God sets human beings in a particular relationship with the rest of his good creation. As we

---

[1] The scope of the term "creation" properly includes everything which is not God. In this paper I will continue to use the term "creation" as the commonly-employed shorthand intended primarily to signify the extraordinary little planet on which we are situated, but I am very sympathetic to using alternative terms such as "earthkeeping" to replace the usual language of "creation care." See, e.g., Bouma-Prediger, *Earthkeeping*, 4.

highlight this handful of themes, we will also draw out preliminary, broad implications for human engagement with the rest of creation, before turning in more detail to some scriptural contours for the nature of our relationship with the wider creation.

First, we need to be reminded that the triune God, who is self-sufficient in his perfect love as Father, Son, and Spirit, had no need to create, but instead freely chose to turn his *ad intra* love outward to make something other than himself. It is the aseity of the triune God that establishes the graciously willed and loving character of God's creating act and ongoing engagement with all that he has made.

The whole of creation is therefore loved into being by the triune God for no other reason than God desires it to exist. It is a delight to God, and by its very existence it resounds with praise of God's glory.[2] This alone should require us to get very personal and practical (and in our current climate—in every sense of that term—very political) very quickly. In what we eat, in how we use energy, in the kind of energy that is available, in how we dispose of waste, in how we travel, in what we buy, to give just a few examples, we need to ask whether we are living in a way that honors the fact that this world has been loved into being by God. We do not like such simple questions, because they make immediate demands upon us and have rippling implications for our lifestyles.

In Genesis 1, God affirms the goodness of each facet of creation, and then surveys all that he has made and proclaims it to be "very good." Even after human sin, God covenants with creation as a whole, and with every living thing (Gen. 8.21–22; Gen. 9.12–17). Throughout scripture, it is clear that God delights in, values, and continues to care for the whole of creation, quite apart from whether it is useful to human beings or not, or a threat to us or not, or even known to us or not. God's speeches in Job 38–41 are a fierce reminder of this. These speeches do many things in the context of the narrative, and one of them is to put Job, and by extension, all human beings, firmly in our place. God expresses exuberant delight in the rest of creation for its own sake, seeming to take particular care to single out creatures that are useless or dangerous to human beings, or that most human beings would never even encounter.[3] For a gentler, but still pointed example, we can turn to

---

[2] For detailed exploration of the centrality of God's aseity, and creation as the fitting but non-necessary expression *ad extra* of the triune God's being-as-love *ad intra*, see, e.g., Gunton, *Triune Creator*, 9–10, where he briefly sets out the foundational concepts which he will continue to explore in the remainder of the volume, particularly in ch. 4 (65–96). See also McDonough's exploration of these issues in *Creation and New Creation*, particularly chs 2 and 3 (19–66); and Begbie, *Resounding Truth*, 190–92.

[3] For a detailed exploration of Job 38–41 as a reminder of God's delight in and care for all of his creation, and the implications of this for a non-utilitarian view of the rest of creation, see Bauckham, *Bible and Ecology*, ch. 2 (37–63). More briefly, see also

Psalm 104, which sets forth God's sovereignty over every aspect of creation, and the intimate, providential care of God towards a range of creatures. It is important to note that the focus in this Psalm is primarily upon the non-human creation, with human beings mentioned only in passing as one creature among many. The Psalm also reminds us that we are the wreckers in God's good creation, as the creatures who willfully sin: the final verse expresses a longing for the time when sinners will be consumed from the earth and the wicked will be no more.

As this very brief glance at some key texts suggests, from Genesis 1 onwards there are abundant scriptural indications that God's attitude towards and engagement with the whole of his creation precludes an exclusively instrumental and human-oriented utilitarian approach towards the rest of creation. The idea that the rest of creation only exists and only matters to God because of what human beings can do with it or get out of it is both scripturally inaccurate and theologically inadequate.[4]

Continuing our overview of God's engagement with and purposes for the whole of creation, if we are going to declare the fullness of the gospel, this has to include how the incarnation, life, death, and resurrection of Jesus Christ are not simply for us human beings and our salvation, but also for the whole of creation. As Colossians 1.15–20 reminds us, just as τα παντα (*ta panta*)— absolutely everything—was created by, though, and for Christ, and in him all things hold together, so also τα παντα is reconciled to God through the blood of the cross. This is not a text about soteriological universalism. It is a text about the creation-wide scope of the redeeming work of Christ.[5] The close binding of human flourishing with the flourishing of the rest of creation before the fall has its sad counterpart in the equally close binding of the rest of creation to human beings in the aftermath of the fall. Part of Christ's triumph over sin and death is the undoing of the damage our sin has done to the rest of God's good creation. As Romans 8.19–23 indicates, the fact that we human beings are out of right relationship with God has distorted the whole of creation, and the whole of creation is waiting with eager longing for the eschatological consummation. When the relationship between God and God's

---

Bouma-Prediger, *For the Beauty of the Earth*, 93–98; Moo and Moo, *Creation Care*, 61–64.

[4] See e.g. Bouma-Prediger, *For the Beauty of the Earth*, 165–67; Moo and Moo, *Creation Care*, 51–52; Moo and White, *Let Creation Rejoice*, 83.

[5] For an example of the exegesis of Col. 1.15–20 with implications for the creation-wide scope of Christ's redeeming work in mind, see Bauckham, *Bible and Ecology*, 151–61.

people is fully and finally set right, then creation itself will be set free fully to flourish, to the glory and praise of God.[6]

Turning to this eschatological hope, the resurrection of Jesus Christ gives us a glimpse not simply of the eschatological future for human beings, when we will have a glorious body like his glorious body, but also of God's intentions for the whole material creation.[7] The continuity and discontinuity that we see in the pre- and post-resurrection body of Christ points us not towards the annihilation of the present, good creation, but towards its eschatological transformation and glorification. While there may be differing views on exactly how and when this will happen, the consistent witness of the whole of scripture—including even 2 Peter 3.10–13[8]—is that this world has a glorious eschatological future with us, and we have a glorious eschatological future with it. Our flourishing and that of the whole of creation will be bound together through all eternity.

With that broad-brush theological and scriptural sketch in place, we will now narrow the focus to some scriptural themes and principles we can glean with regard to the relationship between human beings and the rest of creation pre- and post- fall, and the implications of these for the flourishing of human beings and creation as a whole in the "in between" time.

First and foundationally, while human beings are creatures just like all the other creatures, we are also set apart from everything else in creation by virtue of the unique relationship God has chosen to establish with us, made clear in the creation accounts of Genesis 1 and 2. We are the only creature made in God's image and able to have a self-conscious relationship with him.

From this unique relationship with God flows a unique relationship with everything else in creation. God gives us dominion over the rest of creation. "Dominion" is a powerful word, both in Hebrew and in our English

---

[6] For a brief but careful account of Rom. 8.19–23 and its implications for the redemption of the whole of creation, see Moo, "Environmental sustainability," 259–61. For this passage and its implications for the future of creation in the wider context of Romans, see Moo and Moo, *Creation Care*, 147–52. Bauckham situates the implications of this text in a broader scriptural context in *Bible and Ecology*, 95–101.

[7] As N.T. Wright summarized in a recent popular article, ("New Testament Doesn't Say," ". . . God is going to do for the whole of creation what he did for Jesus in his resurrection . . ." The transformed and glorified resurrection body of Jesus is our proleptic glimpse into the future God has in store for the whole created order. For a brief but luminous summary of the implications of both the incarnation and resurrection of Jesus Christ for the whole of creation, see Begbie, *Resounding Truth*, 197–98.

[8] For some of the textual and interpretive issues at stake here, and why this text does not refer to the eschatological destruction of the present creation, see Middleton, *New Heaven*, 160–63 and 189–200; Moo and Moo, *Creation Care*, 153–64; and Moo and White, *Let Creation Rejoice*, 118–24.

translation. This needs to be acknowledged before we move too quickly to parse it with the more popular and gentle term, "stewardship."[9] Dominion is a kingly word, reflecting our role as God's representatives—his vice regents—in and to the rest of creation. We are creaturely kings representing the divine King, and as such we are not permitted to define for ourselves what the word "dominion" signifies. Instead, we must ask, "Who is this King whose vice regents we are, and what does his rule look like?" Or if you prefer, we can go back to the Latin root of our word "dominion" and say that we are called to exercise our dominion in a way that reflects our *Dominus*, our Lord. Since our *Dominus* is the one who loved creation into being, continues to care for it, has included it in the redemption won on the cross, and has a glorious eschatological future for it, that should tell us everything we need to know about the nature of the dominion human beings are called to exercise.[10]

In case we are in any doubt, however, God indicates as much in Genesis 2.15. Most translations express the key terms here as Adam's call to till and keep the earth, or to work it and care for it. The Hebrew verbs are עָבַד (*avad*) and שָׁמַר (*shamar*), and they could, and perhaps should, be translated more accurately as "to serve" and "to protect." It is especially noteworthy that the second of these two verbs is at the heart of the Aaronic blessing (Num. 6.24–26), which opens with the words, "The LORD bless you and *keep* you." The second verb here is *shamar*. We are called to engage with the creation God loves in a way that is analogous to God's promises to bless and *keep* (or "protect") his people.

Once we have acknowledged the power, privilege, and responsibility that goes with the kingly word "dominion," and once we have allowed God's self-revelation to define what that signifies, then we are able to turn to the softer language and implications of stewardship.[11] The world belongs to God, not to us. We are only vice-regents, and we are accountable to God for how we treat his good creation.

We are indeed called to cultivate, domesticate, and develop. The cultural mandate of Genesis 1 and 2 is clearly intended to be part of what it means to

---

[9] While the term "stewardship" has become almost universal as a gloss on "dominion," it raises a number of issues. See Bauckham, *Bible and Ecology*, 2–12, for five key reasons why the term is problematic, and also the introduction to Warners and Heun, *Beyond Stewardship*, 5–19.

[10] For accounts of the key terms in Gen. 1 regarding human beings as created in the image of God, being called to fill the earth and to subdue it, and to have dominion over it, and also the following discussion of Gen. 2.15, see Davis, *Scripture, Culture, and Agriculture*, 53–65; Moo and Moo, *Creation Care*, 72–80; Bauckham, *Bible and Ecology*, 16–22.

[11] While the term "stewardship" remains useful in the sense noted here, see n.9 above for contemporary critiques of the concept.

be human. Nevertheless, from the outset we are called to do that with an attitude of care and restraint, rather than wanton exploitation or unnecessary harm. God has placed us in a world in which we need the rest of creation to flourish, and the rest of creation needs us to come to its fullest flourishing too. We are, therefore, called to act in ways that seek the flourishing of the rest of creation as well as ourselves, and with an eye to long-term well-being not merely short-term gain. These principles are at the heart of the many commands God gives to his people about how they are to relate to the rest of creation, to which we will shortly turn.

For the moment, however, this protological framework for the intertwined flourishing of human beings and all of creation sets out the creational ideal. Under the conditions of sin, the relationship between our flourishing and that of creation as a whole is no longer straightforward. We are now in the midst of the curse of thorns and thistles, sweat and toil. What theological help does scripture give for the relationship between—and also the tension between—human flourishing and the flourishing of the rest of creation in our fallen world, when even with the best of intentions, our dominion over the rest of creation will inevitably be deeply distorted?

While we will not find detailed answers to the very particular questions that confront us today, scripture offers highly specific commands concerning how God's people are called to treat the rest of creation, and in doing so it gives us very clear guidance for our discerning here and now. God gives any number of commands to Israel about how to relate well to the land and other creatures, and the principles behind these commands are as challenging to us as they must have been to the people of Israel. It is all too easy for us to skim over these commands, filtering them out as merely a word to the people of God in the agrarian ancient Near East. This becomes a highly convenient way to avoid the challenge of the word of God for the people of God in our relationship with the rest of creation today. As we will see, these commands continue to confront us with truths that are hard both to hear and to act upon.

We begin with the very familiar: the sabbath command in the ten commandments (Exod. 20.8–11; Deut. 5.12–15). I suspect we rarely note that it is not simply all people who are to have a day of rest. The animals are included too. Of course, if human beings are to refrain from work, this automatically entails that animals will not be put to work either. Even so, built into the ten commandments is the intertwined provision for animal as well as human rest, which is for animal as well as human flourishing. Added to this are commandments such as the provision for oxen to eat grain while they are treading it out (Deut. 25.4). Paul picks this up as a metaphor for making sure that those who labor in the gospel are properly supported (1 Cor. 9.9), but, *pace* Paul, in the Deuteronomy text, God is clearly concerned about oxen too. Before this is a metaphor, it is a command about the just treatment of animals.

We can add to these examples various other commands for looking to the well-being of livestock (even the livestock of one's enemies).[12]

It is worth noting that all of these kinds of commands are costly to human beings and require significant trust that God will provide sufficiently. Time when animals and people are not working is lost productivity and lost profit. Grain that the ox is eating is grain that will not get baked into bread. Short-term human self-interest (and straight-up human greed) would say "No" to these practices. Nevertheless, God imposes limits on the fulfillment of our immediate perceived needs and desires for the expression of a rightly ordered relationship between people, between us and the creatures in our care on whom we depend, and between us and God himself.

Most of us will not be directly responsible for animal husbandry, and most of us are so distanced from the sources of our food that we are completely unaware of how the meat we eat is raised, slaughtered, and packed into those neat, plastic covered polystyrene trays, or what has to happen for those eggs to appear in their cartons and so on. But the many commandments of God about the proper treatment of animals should at least make Christians ask some serious theological questions about aspects of CAFOs, for example. Likewise, the more we learn about the slaughter and meat-packing industry, the more we will see that the commodification and exploitation of creatures and human beings often go together. There are layers upon intertwined layers of practices that lead to the very opposite of flourishing for humans or animals, at both the production end and the consumption end of our industrialized food system.[13]

---

[12] For a brief account of the commands of God mentioned here and below (and many more), see Moo and Moo, *Creation Care*, 88–97. For a more detailed treatment of God's commands to Israel with regard to how they are to treat the rest of creation, and the ongoing implications of those commands, see Davis' seminal *Scripture, Culture, and Agriculture*. Central to her concerns in this volume is not only exegesis with an eye to an ecological hermeneutic, but also making clear and strong connections to contemporary issues such as those mentioned briefly below (e.g., Concentrated Animal Feeding Operations—industrialized livestock farming in other words [CAFOs]) and the disproportionate burden on the poor and marginalized as a result of harmful environmental practices). For a similar approach aimed at a more popular audience, see Tull, *Inhabiting Eden*.

[13] Both Davis, *Scripture, Culture, and Agriculture*, 97–99, and Tull, *Inhabiting Eden*, 97–104, set out some of the issues with regard to CAFOs. While the reforms championed most famously by Temple Grandin have led to some improvements at the slaughter end of the process with regard to cattle, significant ethical issues remain for Christians, both with regard to the treatment of all animals in the industrialized farming complex, from birth to slaughter, and also of (often undocumented) migrant workers employed by slaughterhouses. For an ethical examination of broader issues with regard to the treatment of animals from within the structures of the market economy by a Christian economist, see McMullen, *Animals and the Economy*.

Returning to the sabbath theme, it is also worth reminding ourselves that God commands Israel to give the cultivated land sabbaths. It is certainly open to dispute as to whether Israelite farmers ever did any such thing, just as it is extremely unlikely that they ever kept the year of Jubilee. Even so, the command is there. Every seventh year, the land is to rest and lie fallow: "For six years you shall sow your land and gather in its yield; but the seventh year you shall let it rest and lie fallow, so that the poor of your people may eat; and what they leave the wild animals may eat. You shall do the same with your vineyard, and with your olive orchard." (Exod. 23.10–11).[14]

Any good farmer even today would tell us that this is wise practice for the good of the soil, and that over-cultivation and over-fertilizing will lead to a barren waste where nothing will grow without the addition of more and more chemicals, none of which is particularly conducive to the full flourishing of the farmer, the land, or food consumers. Note, however, that the good of the soil is not actually God's primary concern in this commandment. The specific reasons given for the land sabbath are so that the poor may eat, and so that the wild animals can take what is left. Treating the land well is about the flourishing not just of the land, but also of the poor, and of the wild creatures.

The connection between treating the rest of creation well and the well-being of the poor speaks directly to us in a number of ways. It is almost always the poorest and the most vulnerable who are hit first and hardest by environmental degradation and destruction. Superfund sites in the United States offer one example. These dumping grounds for toxic byproducts are considered to be the most dangerously industrially polluted areas. Research has shown that industries deliberately target low income and minority communities for these sites, because they are least likely to have the time, resources, and political influence to put up a fight.[15] Further afield, we should all be at least vaguely aware of the extent to which our individual and societal choices, made to support the kind of lifestyle we treasure, extort a high cost from poorer nations. That often includes a very high environmental cost, which they have to bear, and we mostly do not.[16]

---

[14] See also the parallel command in Lev. 25.1–7. All scripture citations are from the NRSV.

[15] For a recent analysis of the location of superfund sites, see Mohai and Saha, "Which came first, people or pollution?" See also, e.g., Tull, *Inhabiting Eden*, 111–28, and Brunner, *et al.*, *Introducing Evangelical Ecotheology*, 164–76, for reflections on ecojustice, particularly with regard to economically disadvantaged communities and those with a high concentration of people of color.

[16] For a powerful account of milestone examples of environmental injustices affecting the poorest around the world in the twentieth century and the opening decade of the twenty-first century, see Nixon, *Slow Violence*. For a recent popular account of the impact of climate change on some of the most vulnerable communities around the world, see Robinson, *Climate Justice*.

Not doing what is right by the rest of creation therefore very often also means not doing what is right by the poorest. This is a painful reminder and warning that while we have the luxury of reflecting on the concept of "human flourishing," we often implicitly mean the flourishing of certain kinds of people in certain kinds ways. The rest of creation, and other kinds of people, then become unfortunate but necessary collateral damage to sustain that particular vision of "flourishing."

I will offer just two more examples of God's many commandments for the flourishing of the rest of creation, and how these are ultimately for human flourishing too. Like the others I have mentioned, they offer God-given principles for what our attitude should still be now when it comes to our engagement with the rest of creation, even if the presenting issues are very different.

In the first, God explicitly forbids wantonly chopping down trees. Deuteronomy 20.19–20 states, "If you besiege a town for a long time, making war against it in order to take it, you must not destroy its trees by wielding an ax against them. Although you may take food from them, you must not cut them down. Are trees in the field human beings that they should come under siege from you? You may destroy only the trees that you know do not produce food; you may cut them down for use in building siegeworks against the town that makes war with you, until it falls."

First, note God's rather fierce aside: are the trees humans that you should besiege them? The trees are God's good creation. God is demanding that his people pause and exercise restraint, even if it would be more convenient to destroy them all. Note also that there is pragmatism here. God allows his people to use some of the trees to make siege engines, but they are not permitted simply to chop down whatever trees are in their way, for example. The pragmatism cuts both ways. God also reminds his people not to destroy the fruit trees, warning them that if they chop those trees down now, just because it would be more convenient for fighting their battle, they will live to regret it later.

Very obviously, this command is not simply about trees and sieges. Commands such as these are giving God's people then, and God's people now, some clear principles for how we are to interact with the rest of creation, for its flourishing and ours. Those principles are very similar to what we have already seen in the previously noted commands. Above all, we are being reminded that not everything is all about human beings and our immediate needs, or our convenience. For the long-term flourishing of everyone and everything, God is making clear that we sometimes need to call a halt to the easiest thing we might want to do in the moment in order to find other ways of doing things that are less destructive to the rest of creation, and that will be better for us in the long run too. It is hardly difficult to make a very wide array of uncomfortable connections for us here and now from commands and principles such as these.

One of my passions outside of theology is birding, so the final command to which I will draw our attention is irresistible to me. It is Deuteronomy 22.6–7, "If you come on a bird's nest, in any tree or on the ground, with fledglings or eggs, with the mother sitting on the fledglings or on the eggs, you shall not take the mother with the young. Let the mother go, taking only the young for yourself, in order that it may go well with you and you may live long."

Once again, very evidently this command is not simply about how to treat birds. It is about what we would call today "sustainability," and the message is simple. If God's people keep on killing mother birds as well as baby birds, eventually there will no longer be any mother birds, and then there will not be any more baby birds either. So, leave the mother birds alone!

We might well consider this to be completely obvious, and so it is, but it should not escape our notice that we are doing the equivalent of what God forbids in this command all the time. We are overexploiting natural resources of every kind. We are destroying habitats and driving species to extinction at an alarming rate.[17] In addition to extinctions, the sheer number of other living creatures has dropped precipitously in recent decades. The World Wildlife Fund's *Living Planet Report* in 2018 indicated a sixty percent drop in the overall numbers of animals, birds, aquatic creatures, and reptiles *since 1970*. This means there are sixty percent fewer creatures in the chorus of creation's praise to God within many of our lifetimes.[18]

In other words, to return to Deuteronomy 22.6–7, we are taking the mother birds as well as the baby birds, so to speak, and God knows that if we continue to do that, it will *not* go well with us, and we will *not* live long in the land.

Just like the people of Israel, however, we do not want to be forced to reassess our priorities for the sake of the flourishing of the rest of creation, even though that is also for the sake of our own flourishing too. Likewise, we do not want to have to reconsider our preferences based on doing what is right by the poorest and most vulnerable. Neither do we want to be asked to take into account the impact of our wishes now on the rest of creation and other people far into the future (although that thoroughly unpleasant future might be rushing towards us sooner than we think).

This is why God had to *command* his people in scripture—and through his living Word, still commands us now—to think bigger and longer than we

---

[17] For a recent account of ecosystem degradation, extinctions, and related issues, see the 2019 IPBES *Global Assessment Report on Biodiversity and Ecosystem Services*. For helpful overviews of related issues in the context of biblical and theological reflection, although with statistics that are already significantly out of date, see Bouma-Prediger, *For the Beauty of the Earth*, ch. 2 (23–55); and Moo and White, *Let Creation Rejoice*, 21–79.

[18] The World Wildlife Fund's *Living Planet Report, 2018*, sets out the evidence for the 60% overall decline in animals/birds/aquatic species/reptiles in the past fifty years.

otherwise would. The implications for us are the same as they were for ancient Israel: requiring us to put limits on our perceived needs, and to stop our willful exploitation of the rest of creation for short-term gain, and to look instead to the flourishing of the whole of creation, and of the poor, and own longer-term flourishing too. And the flip side of this is clear in scripture as well. Sinful disobedience to God's commands leads to devastating consequences for the rest of creation as well as for us.[19]

All of this means that as the people of God, Christians are summoned to keep on seeking ways of relating to the rest of creation that are closer to what God expects of his image bearers, to whom he has given dominion over his good and beautiful creation. Intentionally seeking the flourishing of the rest of creation, even when that is costly for us and pushes against what seems to be our immediate self-interest, should not be a matter of indifference to Christians, still less of the kind fierce resistance which is a lamentable feature of the current political polarization in the United States and elsewhere. Wise earthkeeping should be an intrinsic element of Christian discipleship, as part of what it means to love the triune Creator God with all of our being, and to love our neighbor as ourselves. As Moo and White point out,

> When we take seriously the cosmic scope of Christian hope and our call to live as God's children now, we find the scope of our love and of our ethics extends even beyond our fellow human creatures to embrace all of God's creation . . . Our casual selfishness in how we use earth's resources, in how we treat our global neighbors and in how we treat creation itself is revealed for what it is: an affront to God, an abrogation of the responsibility he has given us and a rejection of our identity as his children in Christ.[20]

For this aspect of our discipleship we need a strong eschatology, and in particular a proper eschatological reserve, to sustain us and to ensure that our hope is rightly oriented.[21] First, a reminder of the point made very briefly earlier: there *is* eschatological hope for this creation. Its future is not to be utterly annihilated, but to be renewed, transformed, and glorified. Second,

---

[19] 2 Chr. 36.20–21 connects Jeremiah's prophesy of seventy years in exile (Jer. 25.11) to the refusal of Israel to give the land its sabbaths. See also Lev. 26.34–35 and 43. For more general examples of the impact of Israel's disobedience upon the rest of creation, see, e.g., Isaiah 24 and Hos. 4.1–3. For discussion of these and related texts, see, e.g., Davis, *Scripture, Culture, and Agriculture*, ch. 7 (120–38); and Marlow's exegesis of texts from Amos, Hosea, and Isaiah in chs 4–6 of *Biblical Prophets*, and her "Law and the Ruining of the Land."

[20] Moo and White, *Let Creation Rejoice*, 113.

[21] Moo and White, *Let Creation Rejoice*, chs 4–9 offer extended reflections on the implications of a properly scriptural eschatology for Christian attitudes towards and actions in relation to ecological issues.

however, we need to be clear that there is no purely immanent hope for creation. The eschatological consummation will not emerge organically from the way things are, and notwithstanding a plethora of well-meaning book titles, neither are Christians called to "save the planet." The eschatological transformation that will result in the new heavens and the new earth will be an inbreaking, transformative act of God, and not the outcome of any human program or any capacity inherent within the created order.

This is the best news that Christians who are earnest about the relationship between human flourishing and the flourishing of the whole of creation could possibly hear. It means that we are summoned to walk in the trajectory of the fullness of the coming kingdom, but we are set free from the unbearable burden—and the desperate and ultimately hopeless driven-ness—of seeing all of this as dependent upon our actions. Not being called to accomplish the "eschatological everything" liberates us to do the faithful something. This also means there is no excuse for apathy. The attitude of "It's all too hard and we can't make enough of a difference, so let's not bother doing anything and God will sort it all out in the end" is as unscriptural and sub-Christian as the hubris that says that if *we* don't "save the planet" ourselves, there is no hope for it.

Finally, a properly focused eschatology means that even in the face of the bleakest news, and the seemingly intractable complexities of so many of the issues, we do not despair. Our hope is *not* in ourselves and what we can do. Our hope is in the name of the Lord who made the heavens and the earth, and who will redeem them and us. In the meanwhile, it is as much as we can cope with and more to seek to discern and act upon what makes for the flourishing of our neighbor and all of creation now, in the in between time, in our personal choices and our efforts to impact systems and structures, until Jesus Christ comes again in glory to set all things right and make all things new.

## Bibliography

Begbie, Jeremy S. *Resounding Truth: Christian Wisdom in the World of Music.* Grand Rapids: Baker Academic, 2007.

Bauckham, Richard. *The Bible and Ecology: Rediscovering the Community of Creation.* Waco, TX: Baylor University Press, 2010.

Bouma-Prediger, Steven. *Earthkeeping and Character: Exploring a Christian Ecological Virtue Ethic.* Grand Rapids: Baker Academic, 2019.

———. *For the Beauty of the Earth: A Christian Vision For Creation Care.* Grand Rapids: Baker Academic, 2$^{nd}$ edn, 2010.

Brunner, Daniel L., et al. *Introducing Evangelical Ecotheology: Foundations in Scripture, Theology, and Praxis.* Grand Rapids: Baker Academic, 2014.

Davis, Ellen F. *Scripture, Culture, and Agriculture: An Agrarian Reading of the Bible.* Cambridge: Cambridge University Press, 2009.

Gunton, Colin E. *The Triune Creator: A Historical and Systematic Study.* Grand Rapids: Eerdmans, 1998.
Intergovernmental Science-Policy Platform on Biodiversity and Ecosystem Services (IPBES). *Global Assessment Report on Biodiversity and Ecosystem Services.* https://ipbes.net/global-assessment-report-biodiversity-ecosystem-services
Marlow, Hilary. *Biblical Prophets and Contemporary Environmental Ethics.* Oxford: Oxford University Press, 2009.
———. "Law and the Ruining of the Land: Deuteronomy and Jeremiah in Dialogue." *Political Theology* 14 (2013) 650–60.
McDonough, Sean M. *Creation and New Creation: Understanding God's Creation Project.* Peabody, MA: Hendrickson, 2017.
McMullen, Steven. *Animals and the Economy.* The Palgrave MacMillan Animal Ethics Series. London: Palgrave MacMillan, 2016.
Middleton, J. Richard. *A New Heaven and a New Earth: Reclaiming Biblical Eschatology.* Grand Rapids: Baker Academic, 2014.
Mohai, Paul, and Robin Saha. "Which came first, people or pollution? Assessing the disparate siting and post-siting demographic change hypotheses of environmental injustice." *Environmental Research Letters* 10 (November and December 2015), http://iopscience.iop.org/1748-9326/10/11/115008
Moo, Douglas J., and Jonathan A. Moo. *Creation Care: A Biblical Theology of the Natural World.* Grand Rapids: Zondervan, 2018.
Moo, Jonathan. "Environmental Sustainability and a Biblical Vision of the Earth's Future." In *Creation in Crisis: Christian Perspectives on Sustainability*, edited by Robert S. White, 255–70. London: SPCK, 2009.
Moo, Jonathan A., and Robert S. White. *Let Creation Rejoice: Biblical Hope and Ecological Crisis.* Downers Grove, IL: IVP Academic, 2014.
Nixon, Rob. *Slow Violence and the Environmentalism of the Poor.* Cambridge, MA: Harvard University Press, 2011.
Robinson, Mary. *Climate Justice: Hope, Resilience, and the Fight for a Sustainable Future.* New York: Bloomsbury, 2018.
Tull, Patricia. *Inhabiting Eden: Christians, the Bible, and the Ecological Crisis.* Louisville, KY: Westminster John Knox Press, 2013.
Warners, David Paul, and Matthew Kuperus Heun, eds. *Beyond Stewardship: New Approaches to Creation Care.* Grand Rapids: Calvin College Press, 2019.
World Wildlife Fund. *Living Planet Report, 2018.* https://www.wwf.org.uk/sites/default/files/2018-10/wwfintl_livingplanet_full.pdf
Wright, N. T. "The New Testament Doesn't Say What Most People Think it Does About Heaven." https://time.com/5743505/new-testament-heaven/

# Hope

CHAPTER 5

# Lamentable Obligation in Augustine's Political Theology

## Greg Forster

Augustine's political theology is often located as a moderate position on a spectrum between political theologies that celebrate political activity and those that reject it. This chapter evaluates a key concept upon which Augustine builds his political theology in the *City of God*, dubbing that concept "lamentable obligation." It argues that this concept is an important element in Augustine's political theology, and contributes to the attractiveness of Augustine's complex and ambiguous approach to politics, as against theologies that unambiguously celebrate politics or unambiguously reject it. Augustine's concept of lamentable obligation has been an essential element in the emerging story of how Christians live and work in daily life as they participate in public social structures. The chapter then points to theological difficulties in the concept of lamentable obligation, which can be expected to produce ongoing tensions and challenges within the Augustinian approach to politics. Christians in the Augustinian tradition of political thought must take care not to neglect the present-day inbreaking of the kingdom of God in social life, or allow the public square to become a compartmentalized space in which doing evil things is okay so long as we remember to lament.

### The Concept of Lamentable Obligation

Book XIX of the *City of God* turns, in Chapter 6, from general anthropology and ethics (covered in Chapters 1–5) to the specifically political. Here is how that chapter begins: "What of those judgments passed by men on their fellow men, which cannot be dispensed with in cities, however much peace they enjoy? What is our feeling about them? How pitiable, how lamentable do we find them!" (XIX.6, 859.)[1] These sentences summarize the concept we will call "lamentable obligation."

---

[1] Augustine, *City of God*, 859. Subsequent citations to *City of God* appear only in the main text, with book and chapter number followed by page number in the Penguin edition.

By focusing on the act of imposing judgments, Augustine frames politics from the outset in terms of conflict. He mentions many kinds of political conflict, ranging from debates over policy to civil wars. However, conflicts resolved by law—criminal and civil court cases—seem to be the paradigmatic type for him. This harmonizes with the end of Chapter 5, in which Augustine transitions from a discussion of conflict in households to a discussion of conflict in cities by pointing to the courts. Even when the city is not torn apart by legal conflicts, it is always in danger of being so, and this is a permanent hindrance to its peace (XIX.5, 859). It is not surprising that court cases are Augustine's paradigmatic type of political conflict if he sees imposing judgments as the key political act. On the other hand, it is worth noting that this conceptual framework has valid application far beyond the courtroom; it is possible to view all political action as being aimed at the imposition of judgments upon conflicts (e.g., when the legislature enacts a law upholding Policy A rather than Policy B, it is imposing its judgment upon the conflict between those who favor Policy A and those who favor Policy B).

Judgments are lamentable, he goes on to explain in Chapter 6, because they cannot be carried out without using violence against the innocent. This is partly because the judge will sometimes punish the innocent in error, but the more important issue for Augustine is that the process of judgment itself involves violence even before verdict and sentence are imposed. Lack of perfect information about who is guilty, which is especially due to a lack of trust that suspects and witnesses will cooperate, is unavoidable in the present age. This permanent ignorance makes violence against the innocent permanently necessary ("it is through unavoidable ignorance and the unavoidable duty of judging that he [the judge] tortures the innocent," XIX.6, 860).

As the Chapter develops, Augustine rejects the possibility that we might celebrate political action for the good it can achieve in spite of its harsh necessities. Violence against the innocent is intrinsically lamentable, regardless of consequences. Against the view that the wise and virtuous judge should experience "happiness" as the reward of his good labors, Augustine writes, "How much more mature reflection it shows, how much more worthy of a human being it is, when a man acknowledges this necessity as a mark of human wretchedness, when he hates that necessity in his own actions and when, if he has the wisdom of devotion, he cries out to God, 'Deliver me from my necessities!'" (XIX.6, 860–61)

Here we must observe that Augustine's account focuses on an issue that was specific to his culture, but his general point is applicable in all cultures. Augustine's specific focus is the practice of torturing witnesses in criminal trials as a way of obtaining confessions or testing the truth of their testimony. However, we should not conclude that Augustine's argument is applicable only to cultures with such practices. Because we cannot fully trust one another, at least in the present age, some mode of violence against the innocent is necessary for legal judgment. Forcible arrest and imprisonment of suspects is unavoidable—even if a suspect surrenders voluntarily, they must be imprisoned lest they change their mind and flee. Inevitably, the corrupt will abuse this power, and (more germane to Augustine's point) even the innocent will make mistakes in the course of these coercive processes. We may reform our practices to reduce the number of innocent people who are injured or killed as a byproduct of the processes of justice, but in the present age we do not have the power to eliminate such injuries and deaths. And, of course, as we look beyond what is involved in criminal law, all major policy decisions (in areas ranging from medical care to economic development) involve hard choices that will leave at least some citizens worse off for the sake of the common good no matter which option we choose—and all those policies are enforced coercively.

Interestingly, Chapter 6 does not explain in detail why judgments are "unavoidable." Several passages later in the Chapter make it clear that he is asserting the necessity of judgment as a moral imperative and not merely an observable natural inevitability—he is saying not only that judgment always does occur in fact, but that it always ought to occur in principle. For example, we have already quoted his line about "the unavoidable *duty* of judging" (emphasis added). But he does not say at length why it is a duty. He only points out that imposing judgments is necessary to keep the peace because the city experiences conflict. This is true, but Augustine does not establish in Chapter 6 why keeping the peace is morally obligatory even if it involves violence against the innocent. A pacifist position would deny this. The full argument for the moral necessity of judgment emerges gradually in subsequent chapters, because Augustine must establish a more complex conceptual framework to support it, which we will look at below.

In sum, Chapter 6 frames the subsequent discussion of politics in Book XIX in four ways:

1. Politics centers on imposing judgments upon conflicts.
2. Imposing judgments is a moral duty because it is necessary for peace.
3. Imposing judgments always involves inflicting some amount of violence upon the innocent.
4. Imposing judgments should not produce an unambiguous happiness for those who do it, even though it promotes peace, because violence against the innocent is intrinsically lamentable.

This is what we mean by the concept of "lamentable obligation."

## Sources of Lamentable Obligation

A comprehensive review could connect the concept of lamentable obligation to a wide variety of theological and philosophical constructs. We will focus on three theological sources of the concept that seem highly germane to the use Augustine makes of it in his political theology.

The most proximate theological source of the concept can be found in its immediate literary context. This is Augustine's anthropology, his evaluation of human needs and desires, affirming the intrinsic sociability of humanity. Chapters 1–5 of Book XIX critique pagan philosophical accounts of what is the supreme good, and happiest life, for human beings ("supreme good" and "happiest life" were treated as synonymous, or at least inextricably interdependent, in the eudemonistic ethics of the era). Augustine contrasts the Christian view that our supreme good is outside ourselves (in God) with the pagan view that our supreme good is within ourselves (in virtue and knowledge). The crowning argument, in Chapter 5, is that the philosophers agree with Christian theology that human beings are social in nature, but this is inconsistent with the philosophers' view that we can achieve the highest happiness purely from internal sources. So long as our life is a social life, and social life is riven with conflict, we cannot achieve our highest happiness.

Augustine's critique of pagan eudemonism on this point is an essential corrective to widespread misreadings of Book XIX, which attribute this same world-negating pagan view to Augustine himself, as something he allegedly learned from Plato. As Eric Gregory emphasizes, just because Augustine did not think we could have full happiness in the present life because of social conflict, that does not imply he shared Plato's view that the social world was merely worthless; in fact, the point of Chapter 5 is to attack that view.[2]

Augustine focuses on conflict in households for most of Chapter 5, then transitions to conflict in cities near the end. This leads directly into the concept of lamentable obligation in Chapter 6. Imposing judgments is obligatory because we are social, and it is also lamentable because we are social—the view that the good judge should be happy in spite of the violence he inflicts is, for Augustine, associated with the pagan philosophies that locate our highest good and supreme happiness in our own virtue and knowledge.

A second key source of the concept of lamentable obligation is Augustine's soteriology, particularly his view of sin and regeneration, affirming the permanence of conflict between sanctified and depraved communities within the polity. If Augustine's anthropology is the immediate literary context, his soteriology is the general literary context; the very title of the *City of God* illustrates how the contrast between the regenerate community (the city of God) and the unregenerate community (the city of man) is a defining framework of the entire book. Because human beings have no power of their

---

[2] See Gregory, *Politics and the Order of Love*, 35–47.

own to overcome sin, the grace imparted in regeneration is decisive. This implies that the contrast between the regenerate and unregenerate will be sharp, and highly consequential. This is why imposing judgments is obligatory, because conflict is inevitable (both among the unregenerate, who quarrel with one another, and between the regenerate and unregenerate, whose lives are defined by conflicting loves) and this conflict must be resolved for the sake of peace. This is also why imposing judgments is lamentable, because inflicting violence upon the innocent is an action whose intrinsic quality is characteristic of the city of man, not the city of God.

A third key source of the concept of lamentable obligation is Augustine's eschatology, affirming that in the present age, even the sanctified do not have full communion with God. Our separation from God in the present age is the underlying cause of the problems inherent in imposing judgments. This eschatological concern is deeply embedded in the analysis of Chapter 6 (as it is in so many other chapters of the *City of God*). It is implicit in the analysis of why imposing judgment is obligatory; conflict occurs in the city because Jesus has not yet returned. It is especially implicit in the analysis of why imposing judgment is lamentable; it is our ignorance—especially our inability to trust one another—that makes violence against the innocent necessary to judgment. And this implicit connection becomes painfully explicit in the anguished cry in which the Chapter culminates, "Deliver me from my necessities!" This is, of course, an eschatological plea, equivalent to "Come, Lord Jesus!"

### Consequences of Lamentable Obligation for Augustine's Political Theology

The concept of lamentable obligation is not left behind after Chapter 6. It plays an important role in the overall architecture of Book XIX. Augustine spends most of the rest of the book solving the problem he sets for himself in Chapter 6; that problem is not whether political activity is good or bad, but how political activity can be obligatory in spite of the fact that it is lamentable. To trace the consequences of lamentable obligation for Augustine's political theology, a brief outline of subsequent chapters will be helpful.

After applying the concept of lamentable obligation at the international level, both affirming and lamenting just war (Chapter 7), Augustine develops an argument that earthly peace is our highest temporal good, just as peace with God is our highest eternal good (Chapters 8–11). A key conceptual move in this section is his argument that we can distinguish between temporal and eternal goods; this is an important point of contrast with other political theologies.[3] Augustine goes on to argue that there is a law or order of nature that preserves earthly peace—though imperfectly—even among the unregenerate, through a process of compromise among people's different wills

---

[3] O'Donovan, *Desire*, 24, points out that Augustine also draws this distinction in *On the Letter and the Spirit*.

(Chapters 12–13), and that this earthly peace, imperfect as it is, is an important temporal good (Chapter 14). Then he argues that all people are spiritually free and equal by nature (Chapter 15), but this spiritual freedom and equality can coexist with legitimate law and political hierarchy (Chapter 16).

At this point we return to the obligation to impose judgment, which (as we have noted) is not fully supported by justifications in Chapter 6. Augustine's political theology reaches its culmination in Chapter 17, where he argues that "the heavenly city in her pilgrimage here on earth makes use of the earthly peace, and defends and seeks the compromise between human wills in respect of the provisions relevant to the mortal nature of man, so far as may be permitted without detriment to true religion and piety" (XIX.17, 878). While the eternal peace of heaven is the only peace that fully deserves the name, nonetheless the church "relates the earthly peace to the heavenly peace," participating in and defending the earthly peace of the city as an analogue or shadow of the eternal peace of heaven (XIX.17, 878). The church does this because "the life of a city is inevitably a social life," and living out our faith involves loving our neighbors as well as loving God (XIX.17, 879). The remaining chapters of Book XIX return to the contrast between these views and various pagan views, including those of Varro, Cicero and Porphyry, and unpack miscellaneous reflections arising from these contrasts. Eschatology returns to the forefront at the end of the book, where the final culmination of the city of God's quest for peace through Christ (Chapter 27) is contrasted with the final culmination of the city of man's quest for peace through its own powers (Chapter 28).

Lamentable obligation helps define both the structure and character of this argument. Structurally, it defines the problem Augustine's political theology is constructed to solve. If imposing judgments is so lamentable, why is it morally obligatory? The whole point of Augustine's political theology is to demonstrate that political activity is legitimate *without* arguing that the content of political action is intrinsically praiseworthy.

Appropriately, the character of Augustine's argument reflects the paradoxical nature of this enterprise. He avoids using positive constructions to describe political activity, describing the church's life in the city as "a life of captivity in this earthly city as in a foreign land" (XIX.17, 877)—this comment of Augustine's being the most important origin for Christian appropriation of Israel's captivity in Babylon as a political model.[4] He carefully stresses the contrast between the full peace of heaven—which alone really deserves the name—with the merely analogous or shadowy peace of the present.

Augustine even introduces a dual language to accommodate the paradoxical nature of his undertaking, which must both affirm and lament political

---

[4] See O'Donovan, *Desire*, 83.

activity. In Chapter 21 he endorses Cicero's view that there is no true commonwealth without public justice, and then argues that because there is no true justice without true religion, there were no true commonwealths before the rise of Christianity! This emphasizes the contrast between the purity of heaven and the imperfection of earth. Then, in Chapter 24, he introduces an alternative set of definitions under which "justice" and "commonwealths" can be said to occur without true religion, making earthly politics possible. But in Chapter 25 he returns to making the case that there is no true virtue without true religion.[5] This moving back and forth between different linguistic constructions—justice and commonweal are both possible and not possible without true religion—illustrates the depth of paradox in Augustine's political theology.

### What Is Attractive in Lamentable Obligation

Lamentable obligation is a key factor in making Augustine's political theology an attractive alternative for many, in contrast with political theologies that unambiguously celebrate politics as an opportunity to glorify God and love God and neighbor, or that reject all politics outside the church as intrinsically worldly. Here it is important not to draw simplistic divisions between "Augustinian" political theology and such familiar schools of thought as Kuyperianism, liberation theology or the neo-Anabaptist movement. So great is Augustine's influence in the history of theology that almost all schools of thought contain at least some figures who can be described as "Augustianian"—thus there are Augustinian Kuyperians, Augustinian neo-Anabaptists, etc. The relevant contrast is between those whose theology embodies the Augustinian ambiguity toward political action, engaging in at least some civil activity to seek peace while lamenting the necessity of violence in that activity, and those who more wholeheartedly embrace or reject politics.

One advantage of approaches grounded in lamentable obligation is that it deliberately maintains tensions between competing theological imperatives (e.g., the duty to love and serve our neighbors in the public square and the duty to strive for the kingdom of God rather than worldly power). It thus provides resources for processing both the positive and negative sides of politics honestly, removing artificial pressure to minimize the reality or the importance of factors on one side or the other for the sake of synthesis. Where more pro-political theologies are tempted to downplay the ugly side of politics and the more anti-political theologies are tempted to exaggerate it, Augustinian approaches have freedom to take both seriously. Herbert Deane

---

[5] O'Donovan, *Desire*, 7, observes that in making this point, Augustine is building on the earlier views of the Roman Cynics, who held that all political orders were corrupt. However, Augustine relates the corruption of political orders to the fall of humanity and the coming of Christ, as the Cynics obviously did not.

emphasizes this aspect of Augustine's political theology as a source of his continuing influence, observing that Augustine created a bridge between the classical and medieval eras by his ability to affirm—with suitable reforms—some aspects of classical culture (such as its emphasis on the connection between moral virtue and political action) while rejecting others (such as its view that politics is the highest form of human activity).[6]

Another advantage of lamentable obligation is that it emphasizes depending upon God for true justice, rather than any human institution. More unambiguously pro-political theologies put enormous weight on seeking justice from political institutions, while more anti-political theologies invest the same level of importance in seeking justice from ecclesial institutions. Both these views emphasize (with significant theological and philosophical warrant, of course) that God has authorized human institutions in the present age to carry out justice. But Augustinian political theologies emphasize instead that the "justice" done in the present age by any human institutions, civil or church, is truly just only to the extent that God's supernatural intervention (building the kingdom of God by regeneration and sanctification) makes it so. Augustine's striking statement in Chapter 21 that there were no true commonwealths until the coming of the gospel illustrates this. In fact, as Oliver O'Donovan notes, in his political theology Augustine was responding in part to Christians in his own day who thought that with the conversion of ruling Roman authorities to Christianity, the "age of martyrdom had passed forever" and "the sequence of suffering and glory could be read out of church history"; Augustine saw that such thinking "had failed to understand the struggle of the times and had ceased to long ardently for the church's perfection."[7] In another work, Augustine commented that alliance with political rulers actually created greater temptations for the church.[8] However, Augustine did not reject such alliances, and in this he was responding to others in his own day (including his mentor Ambrose, and above all the Donatists) who were more anti-political. For Augustine, the coexistence of the city of God and the city of man in the present age made it necessary to rely on God—and therefore not to have any hard and fast rules about institutional relationships.[9]

This brings us to a third advantage of lamentable obligation: its eschatological approach. Given the continuing presence of the city of man and the need for a public peace based on compromise, even after the arrival of the gospel it is not clear the extent to which Augustine recognizes Rome as a "true

---

[6] Deane, *Political and Social Ideas*, 2–3 and 10–11.

[7] O'Donovan, *Desire*, 191.

[8] See Augustine, *De Perfectione Iustitiae* 15.35, cited in O'Donovan, *Desire*, 197.

[9] See O'Donovan, *Desire*, 201–2.

commonwealth" until Christ returns. Lamentable obligation makes eschatological anticipation active rather than passive. The more pro-political theologies emphasize that justice can be done in the present age; while they do not always neglect eschatology, they tend to give it a less prominent place. The more anti-political theologies tend to be somewhat more eschatological in the sense that they look forward to the overthrow of worldly political systems with Christ's return. But this disruption is conceived as creating such a strong discontinuity that anticipation of it in the present age consists almost entirely of withdrawal—the decision to disengage from politics outside the church is such a radical act that it leaves little room for further active eschatological anticipation. The focus becomes building pure and just ecclesial structures and communities—a project that tends to have a decidedly present-day emphasis. Thus anti-political theologies can be almost as non-eschatological as pro-political ones. Both types of theology attempt to build a just life in the present; the difference being where they expect to find that continuity. A telltale mark of the difference between Augustine and the pro- and anti-political poles is that, unlike them, Augustine does not work with the expectation that things will get much better until Christ returns *either* in the state *or* in the church. As Deane observes, "If we confine our attention only to the history of this world and do not look beyond it to the future kingdom of God's saints, we cannot call Augustine a believer in historical progress."[10] Augustinian political theologies build politics based on the expectation of discontinuity with the future in all structures, civil and ecclesial. They draw a sharp distinction between the limited and imperfect justice that is possible in the present life and the true justice that is known only to the city of God, and will come in full only with Christ's return. (This is why the distinction between temporal and eternal goods is such a key conceptual move, as noted above.)

These factors help explain why Augustine's political theology has been an essential element in the emerging story of how Christians live and work in daily life as they participate in public social structures. The Augustinian tension between the obligation to participate in civil life and the lamentable nature of what that involves helped facilitate the emergence of a clear and consistent distinction between political/civil social structures and religious/ecclesial social structures, which had not been present in antiquity. This distinction in turn set the stage both for the drama of medieval political theology, with its "two swords," and the emergence of religious freedom in the modern world—as well as the secularization and pluralization that have accompanied religious freedom. Obviously we cannot trace the roots of all this back to one chapter of *City of God*, but, at the same time, we should recognize how important this concept was to Augustine's political theology, and how

---

[10] Deane, *Political and Social Ideas*, 71.

important Augustine's political theology has been to our various modes of reconciling faith with public life.

## Theological Difficulties in Lamentable Obligation

We can identify three theological difficulties in the concept of political obligation that help explain why non-Augustinian schools of thought continue to exercise important influence in spite of the advantages to Augustinianism. These three difficulties arise out of the three theological sources identified above—anthropology, soteriology, and eschatology.

Anthropologically, does lamentable obligation suggest a functional dualism that undermines human integrity? For obvious reasons, all political theologies must give some account of the tension between living as members of civil communities and as members of ecclesial communities. The more pro-political theologies emphasize methods of managing this tension. They do not deny it exists, but they think it can be coped with well enough to pave the way for a high degree of Christian involvement in civil affairs, and they typically devote much attention to describing how it is to be coped with. (In some ways, the differences between the different theories in this category—Christendom v. modern natural law v. Kuyperianism v. liberation theology—lies in the differences between their proposed coping mechanisms.) The more anti-political theologies deny that this tension can be managed, arguing instead for radical surgery: amputate the diseased limb in order to enter the kingdom of God without it, rather than be cast whole into Gehenna. Both these approaches seek synthesis—an overcoming of tension. We have observed above that the danger of seeking synthesis is the temptation to minimize or dismiss that which cannot be reconciled to the synthesis. But the advantage is that it creates an impetus to integrity. A person's whole life is to become part of the Christ-centered synthesis; there are to be no compartmentalized areas of life where the claims of Christ are hindered. Deliberately maintaining tension may remove temptations to downplay real problems, but it creates temptations to be complacent about whether our behavior in some areas of life is truly Christ-centered. At the extreme, it can lead to a monstrous kind of spiritual double life, in which Christians practice their faith in the private "church" sphere of life and do not seek to apply their faith in the public "civil" sphere of life. This flatly contradicts the imperative to be whole in Christ and to surrender all of ourselves to him. The question is whether we can distinguish the church from the world (Augustine's focus) without distinguishing "religion" as a distinct area of life, implying that in all other areas of activity we are free to order our lives without reference to God.

Soteriologically, does lamentable obligation collapse the distinction between good and bad works? When reading Chapter 6, and especially the passage asserting that the wise and virtuous judge should not be happy in his work, but should lament it due to its ugly nature, one can easily imagine objections from both the more pro- and anti-political theologies. Their question could be: is imposing judgments good, or not? If it is not good, Augustine is saying we have a duty to do what is not good, which would seem to undermine sanctification. But if it is good, Augustine is saying we should lament what is good, which would equally seem to undermine sanctification. The pro-political side says imposing judgments is good, even if it requires us to do things that we will not have to do in the perfected world when Jesus returns; the good judge can therefore be happy in his work because it is good work. As C.S. Lewis puts it in the context of just war,

> War is a dreadful thing, and I can respect an honest pacifist, though I think he is entirely mistaken. What I cannot understand is this sort of semi-pacifism you get nowadays which gives people the idea that though you have to fight, you ought to do it with a long face and as if you were ashamed of it. It is that feeling that robs lots of magnificent young Christians in the services of something they have a right to, something which is the natural accompaniment of courage—a kind of gaiety and wholeheartedness.[11]

Meanwhile, the anti-political theologians—the "honest pacifists" referred to by Lewis—say imposing judgments is not good, therefore we do not have a duty to do it; in fact, we have a duty *not* to do it. Both sides, in their different ways, seek ethical synthesis as well as anthropological synthesis. By contrast, just as Augustine's anthropological tension allows him to process both sides honestly but creates a temptation to a dangerous functional dualism, his ethical tension allows him to maintain a complex psychology of both duty and lament, but creates a temptation to blur the lines between good and evil.

Eschatologically, does lamentable obligation encourage a *de facto* denial of the proleptic inbreaking/inauguration of the kingdom of God today? As we have noted, both the more pro- and anti-political theologies build on areas where they expect the present to be continuous with the future. Pro-political theologies, emphasizing that God has ordained political structures to do justice, expect these structures to do justice today, imperfectly, as God will do it perfectly in the future. Anti-political theologies, emphasizing that the kingdom of God breaks into the present through the church, expect the church to do justice today, imperfectly, as God will do it perfectly in the future. Augustine's emphasis on the discontinuity between the present age and the age to come leads him constantly to emphasize how distant any justice today must be from the justice that is to come. He resists the idea that the justice done by civil authorities today is like the justice that will be done by God in the future. It is an analogy or shadow of heavenly justice (the church "relates the earthly peace to the heavenly peace," XIX.17, 878) and the church can use it, as a tool, to advance good ends ("the heavenly city in her pilgrimage

---

[11] Lewis, *Mere Christianity*, 67.

here on earth makes use of the earthly peace," XIX.17, 878). But to say that X is a shadow of Y is another way of saying that X is not Y, and to say that the church can use X as a tool to promote Z is another way of saying that X is not Z. Earthly justice does not, by itself, even deserve the name of justice (see Chapter 21) although it is possible to call it that in a highly qualified and provisional way (see Chapter 24). The question here is where the future kingdom of God breaks into the present in matters of justice. The more pro- and anti-political theologies each have a clear answer; Augustine's answers are all, at best, extremely hedged and uncertain. But the gospel call with which Jesus (echoing John the Baptist) began his public ministry was that the kingdom of God is at hand—is present, is available now. If the kingdom of God does not break into the present in the matter of justice, or does so only in indirect or analogous or heavily hedged ways, the call to holiness and sanctification among God's people in this critical area of life is imperiled.

## Conclusion

Augustine's political theology as a whole is structured by his concept of lamentable obligation. The problem he sets up in Chapter 6, and spends most of the rest of Book XIX solving, is not whether political activity is good or bad; it is how political activity can be obligatory in spite of the fact that it is lamentable. This approach allows Augustine to avoid some of the dangerous oversimplifications that more unambiguously pro-and anti-political theologies typically struggle with. But it creates its own dangers, and Christians in the Augustinian tradition of political thought must take care not to allow public life to become for them a compartmentalized space in which the kingdom of God is not active, and doing bad things is permissible so long as we remember to lament them. Augustine would not, of course, endorse such a view *de jure*; but when people taking his approach go wrong *de facto*, that is the direction in which they tend to go wrong. Augustinian politics can remain theologically oriented only by constantly remembering this danger and taking concrete steps to counteract it. As Gregory argues, an Augustinian emphasis on eschatological hope must be leavened by an Augustinian emphasis on the ethic of love.[12]

## Bibliography

Augustine, *Concerning the City of God against the Pagans*. Translated by Henry Bettenson. London: Penguin Books, 1984.

Deane, Herbert. *The Political and Social Ideas of St. Augustine*. New York: Columbia University Press, 1963.

---

[12] See Gregory, *Politics and the Order of Love*, 81.

Gregory, Eric. *Politics and the Order of Love: An Augustinian Ethic of Democratic Citizenship*. Chicago: University of Chicago Press, 2008.
Lewis, C.S. *Mere Christianity*, in *The Complete C.S. Lewis Signature Classics*. New York: HarperCollins, 2002.
O'Donovan, Oliver. *The Desire of the Nations: Rediscovering the Roots of Political Theology*. Cambridge: Cambridge University Press, 1996.

CHAPTER 6

# Paying It Forward: Medieval Monastic Economies of Salvation

## Greg Peters

### Introduction

Outside of specialists, it may not be too much of an exaggeration to state that the Middle Ages remain a largely misunderstood era of Christian history. One only needs to think about the ongoing use of the phrase "the Dark Ages" to describe these roughly 1,000 years of rich and varied history. Or, to run across headlines like this one from the magazine *Current Affairs*, published in February 2018, "The Middle Ages were Pretty Interesting, Actually." It is the "Actually" which reveals the underlying assumption that the Middle Ages were a boring, uninspired epoch of history. The article's author was surprised to learn that this is, in fact, not the case and hopes that she can convince her readers of the same. This mentality is not a recent development but one that goes back nearly to the medieval era itself.

It should come as no surprise that the Protestant reformers were, to say the least, a bit down on the millennium of Christian history that preceded their efforts at reformation. That there are problems in the church of God at any given time is, I think, to state the obvious. Thus, it is not so much that they recognized the problems of the medieval church and sought to correct them, some authors (such as John Bale, bishop of Ossory in England, and the writers of the *Magdeburg Centuries*) went so far as to say that there were two churches: one true and the other false. The medieval church, they contend, was, for all practical purposes, the false church whereas the Protestants are continuators of the remnant of the true church found in such proto-Protestants as John Wycliffe and Jan Hus. The oft-read and immensely popular *Actes and Monuments* of John Foxe (frequently known as *Foxe's Book of Martyrs*) illustrates well the judgment of many Protestants when talking about the Christian Middle Ages:

> Although it be manifest that there were divers before Wickliff's time, who have wrestled and laboured in the same cause and quarrel that our countryman Wickliff hath done, whom the Holy Ghost hath from time to time raised and stirred up in the Church of God, something to work against the bishop of Rome, to weaken the pernicious superstition of the friars, and to vanquish and

overthrow the great errors which daily did grow and prevail in the world . . . Through God's providence stepped forth into the arena the valiant champion of the truth . . . to detect more fully and amply the poison of the Pope's doctrine and false religion.[1]

Moreover, "In these days [i.e., the late medieval church] the whole state of religion was depraved and corrupted . . . whereas the poverty and simplicity of Christ were changed into cruelty and abomination of life . . . there seemed to be no spark of pure doctrine remaining."[2] Simply put, many sixteenth-century Protestant historians and controversialists simplified the first 1,500 years of Christian history, at least in Western Europe, to three movements:

1. The purity of the New Testament and early Fathers (up to 313);
2. The Constantinian era of peace and degeneration—the false church (313 to c.1517); and
3. The recovery and repristination of the true church (c.1517 and on).

But this is mostly political and ecclesiastical polemics and does not accurately reflect the reality of much of medieval Christianity.

Perhaps no one has done as much as Cambridge historian Eamon Duffy to correct the many falsehoods laid against the Christian church of the Middle Ages. Though he frames his work binarily (i.e., "that there was a wise gulf between 'popular' and 'élite' religion")[3] his thesis still holds when framed as a medieval church = false church/Protestant church = true church distinction. He writes, "It is my conviction . . . that no substantial gulf existed between the religion of the clergy and the educated élite on the one hand and that of the people at large on the other. I do not believe that it is helpful or accurate to talk of the religion of the average fifteenth-century parishioner as magical, superstitious, or semi-pagan."[4] Rather, Duffy concludes, "late medieval Catholicism exerted an enormously strong, diverse, and vigorous hold over the imagination and the loyalty of the people up to the very moment of the Reformation."[5] Duffy's evidence for reaching this conclusion is based on texts from a host of differing genres and material artifacts. *The Stripping of the Altars* is a *tour de force* of scholarly evidence, so convincing that John Foxe himself may have withdrawn further editions of his *Actes and Monuments*. And what

---

[1] Berry, ed., *Foxe's Book of Martyrs*, 49.

[2] Berry, ed., *Foxe's Book of Martyrs*, 50–51. For more examples see Parish, *Monks, Miracles and Magic*; and Williams, *Retrieving the Tradition and Renewing Evangelicalism*.

[3] Duffy, *Stripping of the Altars*, 2.

[4] Duffy, *Stripping of the Altars*, 2.

[5] Duffy, *Stripping of the Altars*, 4.

Duffy did for late medieval England, other scholars have done (albeit more modestly) for Germany[6] and France,[7] for example, and for Western Europe in general.[8]

Today, then, the general consensus is that the Middle Ages were not the so-called "Dark Ages" but were *actually* a time of technological innovation,[9] intellectual advance[10] and deep piety.[11] Therefore, medieval religious observances that strike us as odd today (not so much because of the practice itself but due to parallel accretions) must not be seen as strange simply because they are medieval; that is, examples of those extraneous peculiarities of the "Dark Ages." Rather, by understanding the full riches and complexities of the era we stand in a proper position to evaluate these observances with a keen eye through a proper historical grid. For example, it was common throughout the Middle Ages for devout Christians to go on pilgrimage, often to the Holy Land, but also to many other local and/or international locations (e.g., Walsingham in England, or Compostela in Spain).[12] The motivation for these journeys was ideally, and I would say predominantly, for the spiritual benefits one accrued. In other words, these pilgrims were not mere tourists eager to visit the next "cool" place and therefore used pilgrimage as an excuse to travel. No, they went on pilgrimage as an act of devotion.[13]

Nonetheless, in time a financial economy grew up around the practice of pilgrimage, so much so that Adrian Bell and Richard Dale can speak of the "medieval pilgrimage business." They "identify and elaborate on three economic aspects of pilgrimage." First, because pilgrims made a donation at the shrine of pilgrimage there is an "implied contract involving reciprocal rights and obligations on the part of the pilgrim and the church." Second, high and late medieval shrines became "a form of franchise business, operating under the umbrella brand of the universal church" marketing "their patron saint" and taking "in large-scale offerings that were recycled . . . to the clergy,

---

[6] E.g., Bynum, *Wonderful Blood*.

[7] E.g., Adam, *La vie paroissiale en France au XIVe siècle*.

[8] See Gurevich, *Medieval Popular Culture*.

[9] For water technologies alone, see Squatriti, ed., *Working with Water in Medieval Europe*.

[10] Colish, *Medieval Foundations of the Western Intellectual Tradition 400–1400*.

[11] See, e.g., Bernard McGinn's multi-volume *Presence of God: A History of Western Christian Mysticism*; and Swanson, *Religion and Devotion in Europe, c.1215–c.1515*.

[12] On medieval pilgrimage generally see Webb, *Medieval European Pilgrimage*; and Whalen, ed., *Pilgrimage in the Middle Ages*.

[13] In spite of her many eccentricities, Margery Kempe is a good illustration of the medieval religious pilgrim. See Bale, trans., *Book of Margery Kempe*.

church building programmes, and the poor." Third, "ancillary pilgrimage services, such as the provision of accommodation, food and wine, transport, banking and pilgrimage badges constituted an important economic activity."[14] Simply put, by the end of the Middle Ages pilgrimage was not only a devotional practice, but a significant source of income for the church and other auxiliary institutions. That does not mean of course that pilgrimage itself, as a spiritual discipline, should be thrown out simply because it gained a business-like stature and, thereby, was abused by some whose only goal was to profit financially and personally from another's piety. Rather, pilgrimage's genesis, as a means of striving for salvation and as an act of devotion,[15] must be kept in view as *the* good of the practice, whereas its financial effects must be seen for what they are too—the economic and financial dimensions and outworkings of a religious practice.[16]

## Medieval Monks and Economics

Students of medieval history understand that monks were well known for their business savvy. For example, "sheep farming . . . became the mainstay of the economy of many Yorkshire religious houses," especially the Cistercians.[17] After an extensive examination of the extant documents, Janet Burton concludes that the usual size of a gift of pastureland was for 200–300 sheep, though the Cistercian monastery of Rievaulx received several large grants that could support 1,000 sheep each. Though this land was often not arable, it was ideal for sheep and thereby for the production of wool so much so that the "very scale of monastic, and particularly Cistercian, pasture lands and flocks suggests that some houses would from an early date have had considerable surplus wool for disposal."[18] So that by "the fourteenth century Yorkshire [monastic] houses were among the leading wool producers" though they did not "overwhelm" wool production since there are non-monastics listed in the sources who also traded wool in large amounts.[19] In addition to sheep farming, it should be noted that medieval monasteries practiced other forms of husbandry. As R.A. Donkin notes, "it is quite clear from surveys of stock, references to tanneries and vaccaries [i.e., dairy farms or cattle-breeding

---

[14] Bell and Dale, "Medieval Pilgrimage Business," 602.

[15] See Hayes-Healy, "Patterns of *Peregrinatio* in the Early Middle Ages."

[16] Bell and Dale, "Medieval Pilgrimage Business," 624.

[17] Burton, *Monastic Order in Yorkshire 1069–1215*, 228. It should be noted, however, that sheep farming was also common with the Benedictines, see Clark, *Benedictines in the Middle Ages*, 142.

[18] Clark, *Benedictines in the Middle Ages*, 269.

[19] Clark, *Benedictines in the Middle Ages*, 271.

stations], and grants of pasture and rights of way that cattle commonly occupied an important place in the Cistercian economy, notwithstanding the well-known interest of the order as a whole and of certain houses in particular in the great wool trade."[20]

Another well-known activity of medieval monks was land reclamation in order to make it both productive and profitable. When first founded, most monasteries received gifts in kind from its patrons (e.g., foodstuffs). "The aim of each monastery," however, "would have been to acquire a certain amount of arable land which could yield produce for home consumption and surplus for sale."[21] For many monasteries this meant a gift of land that they could subsequently assart if they chose. The Cistercians are particularly well known for their work in this area due to their desire to reside in out-of-the-way locations.[22] Nonetheless, monasteries that belonged to other monastic orders were active in this as well. Peterborough Abbey in England reclaimed, for example, nearly 1,000 acres near its manor at Oundle and Glastonbury, also a Benedictine community, assorted waste around the house, drained lakes and built embankments around marshes.[23] The Benedictine abbey of St Bertin in France even changed the course of a river.[24] Suffice it to say, the monks were business savvy inasmuch as it was a necessary offshoot of being, first and foremost, monks. That is, it is not as if a group of proto-monks got into the wool business and only after some time of making money did they decide to organize themselves into a Cistercian monastery. No, they were monks first and business men and women secondarily. Their main occupation each day was to pray the daily office, give themselves over to sacred reading and, in short, seek union with God in the monastery, that "school for the Lord's service."[25] Economic activity existed for the good of the community and was not, or at least in most cases, an end in itself. This remains true to this day, hence the existence of monastic beers, wines and fruitcakes. What is less well known outside of monastic scholarship is the way in which monasteries engaged in another form of economic activity: an economy of salvation, if you will.

---

[20] Donkin, *Cistercians*, 68.

[21] Burton, *Monastic Order in Yorkshire 1069–1215*, 223.

[22] Burton, *Monastic and Religious Orders in Britain 1000–1300*, 238–39, "All over England Cistercian houses were associated to a greater or lesser degree with the clearance of forest, the drainage of marsh and the conversion of waste and scrub land."

[23] Burton, *Monastic and Religious Orders in Britain 1000–1300*, 237.

[24] Clark, *Benedictines in the Middle Ages*, 142.

[25] Benedict of Nursia, *Regula*, Prol. 45.

## Being Saved in the Middle Ages

Like all eras of Christian history, there is no one universal soteriology in the Western Middle Ages, though Anselm of Canterbury's contribution was highly influential, if not the most influential.[26] Briefly, and utilizing only his *Cur Deus Homo*, Anselm argues that humankind owes God something that we cannot repay; thus, only a God–Man can repay the debt. In Anselm's words, "man owes to God for his sin something which he is incapable of paying back, and cannot be saved unless he repays it."[27] Thus, human salvation is dependent on paying back the debt we owe to God, a debt that can only be paid by God made flesh. Hence, the incarnation of the Son of God in the person of Jesus Christ. But how do humans obtain this payment for themselves? That is, how does a medieval farmer in Cologne or a Cistercian monk in York reap the benefits of this payment made to God by God? They co-operate with God in their redemption, says Anselm.

Joan Nuth says that "Anselm is . . . convinced that humanity must play a part in this re-creation [i.e., redemption of humankind] . . . Anselm's stress upon the humanity of Christ is a deliberate way of saying how important it is that human beings be enabled by God to cooperate in their own salvation."[28] This is the case, thinks Anselm, because otherwise humankind would be unhappy: "A human being, therefore, who does not repay to God what he owes, will be incapable of being blessedly happy."[29] Anselm, at least in the *Cur Deus Homo*, lays out only two ways that humans cooperate in their own salvation: the doctrine of merits and the eucharist.

"On whom," asks Anselm, "is it more appropriate for him [the Son] to bestow the reward and recompense for his death than on those for whose salvation . . . he made himself a man, and for whom . . . he set an example, by his death . . . For they will be imitators of him in vain, if they are not sharers in his reward."[30] Humankind, then, shares in the benefits of Christ's suffering and death, an idea that came to be called the "treasury of merit" and "humans can draw [on this treasury] for spiritual growth."[31] Anselm is, however, silent

---

[26] Nuth, "Two Medieval Soteriologies," 612, "Anselm needs little introduction, for his *Cur Deus Homo* has had immense influence upon the development of soteriology."

[27] Anselm of Canterbury, *Cur Deus Homo* 1.25, in Davies and Evans, eds, *Anselm of Canterbury*, 314.

[28] Nuth, "Two Medieval Soteriologies," 623.

[29] Anselm of Canterbury, *Cur Deus Homo* 1.24, in Davies and Evans, eds, *Anselm of Canterbury*, 310.

[30] Anselm of Canterbury, *Cur Deus Homo* 2.19, in Davies and Evans, eds, *Anselm of Canterbury*, 353.

[31] Nuth, "Two Medieval Soteriologies," 626. Later medieval theologians believed that both Jesus Christ *and* the saints contribute to the treasury of merit, a view still

on how Christians can draw on this treasury. Concerning cooperation through the eucharist, "For Anselm, participation in the Eucharist is the way Christians most fully reenact and enter into the sacrificial death of Christ, becoming one body with him, gaining strength for a life of *imitatio Christi*."[32] This is beautifully captured in Anselm's "Prayer Before Receiving the Body and Blood of Christ," especially the last two stanzas:

> Lord, I acknowledge that I am far from worthy
>     to approach and touch this sacrament;
>         but I trust in that mercy
>     which caused you to lay down your life for sinners
>         that they might be justified [justi fierent],
>         and because you gave yourself
>     willingly as a holy sacrifice to the Father.
> A sinner, I presume to receive these gifts
>     so that I may be justified [justificer] by them.
> I beg and pray you, therefore, merciful love of men,
> let not that which you have given for the cleansing of sins
>     be unto me the increase of sin,
>     but rather for forgiveness and protection.
>
> Make me, O Lord, so to perceive with lips and heart
>     and know by faith and by love,
> that by virtue of this sacrament I may deserve to be
> planted in the likeness of your death and resurrection,
>     by mortifying the old man,
>     and by renewal of the life of righteousness.
> May I be worthy to be incorporated into your body
>     'which is the church',
> so that I may be your member and you may be my head,
>     and that I may remain in you and you in me.
> Then at the Resurrection you will refashion

---

taught in the *Catechism of the Catholic Church*, 1477: "In the treasury, too, are the prayers and good works of all the saints, all those who have followed in the footsteps of Christ the Lord and by his grace have made their lives holy and carried out the mission in the unity of the Mystical Body." The idea of a treasury of merits was formally suggested by Pope Clement VI in 1343: "Upon the altar of the Cross Christ shed of His blood not merely a drop, though this would have sufficed, by reason of the union with the Word, to redeem the whole human race, but a copious torrent . . . thereby laying up an infinite treasure for mankind. This treasure He neither wrapped up in a napkin nor hid in a field, but entrusted to Blessed Peter, the key-bearer, and his successors, that they might, for just and reasonable causes, distribute it to the faithful in full or in partial remission of the temporal punishment due to sin" (Papal Bull, *Unigenitus*).

[32] Nuth, "Two Medieval Soteriologies," 626.

> the body of my humiliation
> according to the body of your glory,
> as you promised by your apostle,
> and I shall rejoice in you for ever
>    to your glory,
> who with the Father and the Holy Spirit
> lives and reigns for ever. Amen.[33]

Notice that it is through reception of the eucharistic elements that makes it possible for the believer to "be justified" and to be forgiven. Moreover, the partaker is made "worthy to be incorporated into [Christ's] body," the church. Humankind's cooperation, by way of partaking in the eucharist, leads to their salvation. As R.N. Swanson writes, the Mass "was integral to the process whereby individuals sought and obtained salvation."[34] Therefore, in both ways, through the doctrine of merits and the eucharist, humankind works with God to bring about their salvation.

## Working with God to Be Saved

As the Middle Ages rolled on in the shadow of Anselm, it was left to others to think about the ways in which Christians could draw from the treasury of merit and the ways in which Christians could make use of the eucharist to cooperate in their salvation. Monasteries offered a number of options. By the high Middle Ages "Celebration of the mass was undeniably the central point in catholic devotion."[35] However, it was common for most Western believers only to partake of the eucharist once a year—at the High Mass on Easter Sunday. In its place had developed the practice of gazing on the eucharistic host: "But for most people, most of the time the Host was something to be seen, not to be consumed . . . seeing the Host became the high point of lay experience of the Mass."[36] Because of this, it became common for priests, after saying the words of institution ("This is my body . . ."), to elevate the Host for all to see. Also, a bell was rung just before the moment of consecration so that those present would abandon their private prayers to look up. This was necessary given the fact that much of what the priest said, including the words of institution, were inaudible or unintelligible (because they were spoken in Latin) to those present. And in some parishes there was often more than one

---

[33] Ward, trans., *Prayers and Meditations of St. Anselm*, 100–101.

[34] Swanson, *Religion and Devotion in Europe*, 138.

[35] Swanson, *Religion and Devotion in Europe*, 137. See also Duffy, *Stripping of the Altars*, 91, "The liturgy lay at the heart of medieval religion, and the Mass lay at the heart of the liturgy."

[36] Duffy, *Stripping of the Altars*, 95–96.

Mass being said at the same time. These Masses were staggered so that those present could see more than one moment of elevation during their time in the church. In the sixteenth century, Thomas Cranmer recalls that worshippers would "run from their seats to the altar, and from altar to altar, and from sacring [i.e., consecration] (as they call it) to sacring, peeping, tooting and gazing at that thing which the priest held up in his hands."[37] For Cranmer this is all bad medieval superstition, but for the medieval Christian herself this was necessary for her salvation.

The centrality of seeing the eucharistic elevation for one's salvific benefit is made evident further by the presence of extant "elevation squints" (also called "hagioscopes") in medieval churches. These squints, often placed at eye-level for kneeling adults, made it possible for those attending Mass to see the elevation while kneeling, particularly for those near the rood screen, which blocked their sight of the high altar. Though these squints are located within the church, there were also squints in some churches through the exterior walls so that believers who were not even in the worship space could see the elevated host from outside.[38] The presence of squints are clear architectural indicators of the importance of the eucharist (or, at least, the elevation of the host) in the medieval economy of salvation.

Monasteries, too, took advantage of this salvific economy by not only offering "regular" Masses that were open to the laity but also by meeting a felt need of many medieval Christians. Though Masses for the Dead had existed for centuries, the mature development of the doctrine of Purgatory in the twelfth century[39] introduced an important question—could a Mass be said for the soul of one particular person? As Miri Rubin notes, "The mass itself offered moments for commemoration of the dead. Thirteenth-century rubrics directed the priest to say, while holding the host over the chalice, 'gracias agimus tibi', offering thanks for the beatified, for those in purgatory, as for the living … But these were not controversial aspects; more difficult were the masses directed at particular souls."[40] In the end, however, *contra* Peter Lombard, for example, and despite Lollard criticism, it was decided that Masses could and should be said to benefit the dead. And no one more than monasteries took the lead in providing these Masses, often through the establishment of chantries (also known as *chapellenie, cappellaria* or, in Germany, Altarpfründe). For "it was the spiritual welfare of the dead to whose salvation a substantial part of the economy was committed, and the monastery and the chantry were the institutions in which a numerous priesthood was

---

[37] Quoted in Duffy, *Stripping of the Altars*, 98.

[38] Raguin and Stanbury, eds, *Women's Space*, 7.

[39] See Le Goff, *Birth of Purgatory*.

[40] Rubin, *Corpus Christi*, 51.

employed in systematic intercession for Christian souls in general and for those of their founders in particular."[41]

Simply put, a "chantry ... was essentially an endowment for the performance of masses and other works of charity for the benefit of the souls of specified persons."[42] They might be established in perpetuity or for some shorter amount of time and though they are not unique to monasteries (chantries were also set up in parish churches or independently, for example) they thrived in the monastic context often because it was already fashionable, if you will, and salvifically beneficial to patronize monasteries[43] and monasteries were already in the business of commemoration and intercession. For instance, "In every abbey the names of all deceased abbots, monks and *confratres*, both lay and ecclesiastical, were inscribed in a *Liber Vitae*, or 'Book of Life', which lay on the high altar as a symbol of their participation in the *opus dei*."[44] At its core, setting up a monastic chantry in order for a monk-priest to say Masses for the Dead was an economic transaction. The deceased benefitted from the Mass being offered by the monk-priest and the monastery benefitted from the endowment provided for the chantry. There was a cost to the saying of Masses (e.g., for consumables like bread, wine and candles) so the gift needed to cover these expenses, but the monk-priest assigned to the task was already a member of the monastery and could, thereby, work "on the cheap." Moreover, one monk-priest could say more than one Mass a day (though the saying of multiple Masses per day was looked down upon in the late Middle Ages), thereby making it possible for the monastery to accept even more bequests for Masses for the Dead.

## Conclusion

As mentioned above monasteries were in the commemoration business—for their own deceased abbots and community members, but also for non-monastic laypersons, especially royalty and those with the means to endow

---

[41] Colvin, "Origin of Chantries," 163–64.

[42] Colvin, "Origin of Chantries," 164.

[43] See, e.g., Stöber, *Late Medieval Monasteries*, 9, "From the start the lay community looked up to these groups of pious men and women [i.e., the monks and nuns]" recognizing "the potential that these holy communities afforded for the salvation of their own souls." And Colvin, "Origin of Chantries," 166, "But in the past what had inspired so many men and women to help to endow monasteries was not so much disinterested piety as the need to ensure the salvation of their souls. Every monastic cartulary contains the texts of hundreds of charters giving this or that estate or church or rent *pro salute anime mee*—'for the salvation of my soul'."

[44] Colvin, "Origin of Chantries," 167. See also Choy, *Intercessory Prayer and the Monastic Ideal*.

some form of commemoration. With the ascendency of a theology of Purgatory, however, it became impossible, it is argued, for monasteries to keep up. As Colvin writes,

> In origin the chantry can therefore be seen as the answer to what was essentially a monastic problem: how to continue effectively to intercede for an army of the dead whose ranks were already growing uncontrollably even before the official recognition of Purgatory had drawn fresh attention to their predicament. It was a privatised means of salvation devised to cope with an increasing demand for intercession with which the established monastic corporations could not cope.[45]

At their core, then, chantries with their Masses for the Dead were not just "get rich schemes" for monasteries; these monastic communities were meeting a real need, a need with life or death, salvation or damnation consequences. Again, the nature of this form of commemoration (as with most forms of commemoration) was transactional with economic benefits. Yet, like pilgrimage, this should not detract from the greater reality that these transactions were conducted with a much more costly currency—the souls of Christian men and women. The medieval soteriological system gave each baptized Christian the opportunity to access the treasury of merit and to benefit from the performance of the holy eucharist. Concerning the latter, by the late Middle Ages those who could chose to benefit not only during their lives by attending Mass and gazing on the host but to benefit also in death through the endowed recitation of the holy eucharist. Monasteries in particular were well suited to this economy of salvation.

## Bibliography

Adam, Paul. *La vie paroissiale en France au XIVe siècle*. Paris: Sirey, 1964.
Anon. *Catechism of the Catholic Church*. Liguori, MO: Liguori Publications, 1994.
Bale, Anthony, trans. *The Book of Margery Kempe*. Oxford: Oxford University Press, 2015.
Bell, Adrian R., and Richard S. Dale. "The Medieval Pilgrimage Business." *Enterprise & Society* 12 (2011) 601–27.
Berry, W. Grinton, ed. *Foxe's Book of Martyrs*. Grand Rapids: Baker, n.d.
Burton, Janet. *Monastic and Religious Orders in Britain 1000–1300*. Cambridge: Cambridge University Press, 1994.
———. *The Monastic Order in Yorkshire 1069–1215*. Cambridge: Cambridge University Press, 1999.

---

[45] Colvin, "Origin of Chantries," 172.

Bynum, Caroline Walker. *Wonderful Blood: Theology and Practice in Late Medieval Northern Germany and Beyond.* Philadelphia: University of Pennsylvania Press, 2007.
Choy, Renie S. *Intercessory Prayer and the Monastic Ideal in the Time of the Carolingian Reforms.* Oxford: Oxford University Press, 2016.
Clark, James G. *The Benedictines in the Middle Ages.* Woodbridge: Boydell, 2011.
Clement VI. *Unigenitus.* New Advent, ww.newadvent.org/cathen/07783a.htm
Colish, Marcia L. *Medieval Foundations of the Western Intellectual Tradition 400–1400.* New Haven, CT: Yale University Press, 1997.
Colvin, Howard. "The Origin of Chantries." *Journal of Medieval History* 26 (2000) 163–73.
Davies, Brian and G.R. Evans, eds. *Anselm of Canterbury: The Major Works.* Oxford: Oxford University Press, 1998.
Donkin, R.A. *The Cistercians: Studies in the Geography of Medieval England and Wales.* Toronto: PIMS, 1978.
Duffy, Eamon. *The Stripping of the Altars: Traditional Religion in England 1400–1580.* New Haven, CT: Yale University Press, 1992.
Fry, Timothy, ed. *RB 1980: The Rule of Saint Benedict in Latin and English with Notes.* Collegeville, MN: Liturgical, 1981.
Gurevich, Aron. *Medieval Popular Culture: Problems of Belief and Perception.* Translated by János M. Bak and Paul A. Hollingsworth. Cambridge: Cambridge University Press/Paris: Editions de la maison des sciences de l'homme, 1988.
Hayes-Healy, Stephanie. "Patterns of Peregrinatio in the Early Middle Ages." In *Medieval Paradigms, Volume II: Essays in Honor of Jeremy duQuesnay Adams*, edited by Stephanie Hayes-Healy, 3–24. New York: Palgrave Macmillan, 2005.
Le Goff, Jacques. *The Birth of Purgatory.* Chicago: University of Chicago Press, 1984.
McGinn, Bernard. *The Presence of God: A History of Western Christian Mysticism.* 6 vols. Provenance: Crossroad, 1991–2017.
Nuth, Joan M. "Two Medieval Soteriologies: Anselm of Canterbury and Julian of Norwich." *Theological Studies* 53 (1992) 611–45.
Parish, Helen L. *Monks, Miracles and Magic: Reformation Representations of the Medieval Church.* London: Routledge, 2005.
Raguin, Virginia Chieffo and Sarah Stanbury, eds. *Women's Space: Patronage, Place, and Gender in the Medieval Church.* New York: State University of New York Press, 2005.
Rubin, Miri. *Corpus Christi: The Eucharist in Late Medieval Culture.* Cambridge: Cambridge University Press, 1991.
Squatriti, Paolo, ed. *Working with Water in Medieval Europe: Technology and Resource-Use.* Leiden: Brepols, 2000.

Stöber, Karen. *Late Medieval Monasteries and Their Patrons: England and Wales, c. 1300–1540*. Woodbridge: Boydell, 2007.
Swanson, R.N. *Religion and Devotion in Europe, c.1215–c.1515*. Cambridge: Cambridge University Press, 1995.
Ward, Benedicta, trans. *The Prayers and Meditations of St. Anselm with the Proslogion*. London: Penguin, 1973.
Webb, Dian. *Medieval European Pilgrimage*. London: Palgrave, 2002.
Whalen, Brett Edward, ed. *Pilgrimage in the Middle Ages: A Reader*. Toronto: University of Toronto Press, 2011.
Williams, D.H. *Retrieving the Tradition and Renewing Evangelicalism: A Primer for Suspicious Protestants*. Grand Rapids: Eerdmans, 1999.

CHAPTER 7

# Bankrupting Heaven: The Printing Press and the Collapse of the Indulgence Market

## Nathan Hitchcock

Students of the Protestant Reformation are uniformly disappointed to discover that many of the details about Martin Luther's posting of the *95 Theses* are apocryphal at best. If Luther posted the theses at all, he did so in conventional fashion, using the All Saints church door as a bulletin board. Moreover, while it is true that his disputations spread throughout the Holy Roman Empire in a matter of weeks, his *95 Theses* (1517) was in fact followed by two better-selling publications, *Sermon on Indulgences and Grace* (1518) and *The Freedom of the "Sermon"* (1518).[1] The truly sensational fact about Luther in those heady days, it turns out, is that—if one will forgive a gross anachronism—he was able to dominate the media cycle. According to Jacques Le Goff, Luther *alone* printed five times as many publications as all the Catholic controversialists put together.[2] He stands out as the shining star of early adopters of pamphleteering. Yet even here the Wittenberg professor was hardly alone. Ronald Deibert acknowledges the media advantage belonged to Protestants in general: "While the printing environment may have favored the strategic interests of Protestantism, it worked against those of the Roman Catholic Church."[3]

That "the printing environment" proved so punishing to the Catholic cause requires some explanation. Is it not ironic that the western magisterium, so experienced and invested in the printing press, was outstripped by the reformers? More specifically, why would the printing presses, devoted to the manufacture of indulgences, so quickly become the dominion of the critics of indulgences? Various arguments have been adduced to explain Protestants' print power.[4] But a sufficient answer, I think, must explain the changing

---

[1] Wengert, "Introduction," 59.

[2] Goff, *Medieval Civilization*, 92.

[3] Deibert, *Parchment, Printing, and Hypermedia*, 73.

[4] Was it the flowering of humanism with its anti-clerical bias and advent of populist "self-understanding," Matheson, *Rhetoric of the Reformation*, 21–24? Was it

dynamic around indulgences. Particularly illuminating in this vein is Bernd Hamm's comment that "the media event" of the reformer's diatribes against indulgences was really "a consequence arising from the media event of late-medieval indulgence propaganda."[5] Similarly, Falk Eisermann focuses attention on Protestants' ability to take the "ready availability, variability of form, [and] the simultaneous omnipresence of standardized contents" of indulgence printing—and weaponizing the culture against traditionalists.[6]

Going further down the line marked by Hamm and Eisermann, I suggest an interdisciplinary explanation to account for the shift in printing power. By the time of Luther, the late medieval indulgence market was ready to collapse, having exhausted itself through an overabundance of indulgences. The introduction of the printing press, so crucial to the expansion of indulgence campaigns, had become a liability. Analogous to the crisis of a central banking system, the Western Church found itself in a situation of runaway inflation in which a surplus of debt notes (indulgences) precipitated a crisis of salvation-currency for the Catholics. Decades before the Reformation, printed indulgences were too numerous and too much in circulation, devaluing them to the point, it seemed, of bankrupting heaven. Christians were losing confidence in papal-run soteriological banking and its printed media. While Catholics struggled to disentangle themselves from the economics of penance, the Reformers successfully used the printing press to proliferate religion guided by "free" salvation. By poking around at the intersection of theology, media history and monetary theory, I hope to offer an account of the rapid collapse of the indulgence industry.

## The Indulgence as Currency

By necessity I start with a brief history of the rise of the indulgence, which itself was grounded in the practice of penance. Christians in the patristic era faced the thorny problem of restoring those who had forsaken Christ under threat of discrimination, torture or death. Instead of permanent excommunication, the lapsed were put into a restoration program of penance involving acts of contrition. Restoration could last months or even years. From an early stage, however, Christians showed openness to the commutation of disciplinary periods. Dramatic expressions of almsgiving, fasting or self-imposed humiliation could result in the shortening of separation from the life of the Church.

---

that the defenders of the old faith did not wish to rely on lay authors, the very voices most eager to contend with the reformers, Edwards, *Printing, Propaganda, and Martin Luther*, 11?

[5] Hamm, "Die Reformation als Medienereignis," 162.

[6] Eisermann, "Indulgence as a Media Event," 330.

In the early Middle Ages one discovers attempts at the systemization of sins and discipline. Certain early medieval monasteries created lists of sins and ecclesiastical disciplinary measures. In Cummean's *Penitential* (mid-seventh century), for example, the Celtic Church entered into a graded system of tariff penance, with specific lengths of punishment assigned to specific sins, then modified for various factors.[7] Naturally, systematized penance welcomed the notion of systematized commutation. If sin could be appraised numerically, so could forgiveness.

To understand how punishments might be quantified, applied and reduced, consider a contemporary analogy. A woman is on a softball team and shows up late for practice three days in a row. Then, in a moment of recklessness, she accidentally hits the coach with a pitch during batting practice. The coach is irate. Even after the player apologizes and grovels, he tells her she is on probation and will miss the next ten games. She feels bad, so bad that, in an expression of sincere humility, she decides to clean the whole team bus after a trip. She makes it sparkle. The coach is a little surprised, but pleased. He takes her aside and says, "I can see you're sorry for what you did. How about this? Buy the whole team a steak dinner tonight and I'll reduce your sentence to three games." That kind of logic, pastorally well-meaning and ethically fraught, characterized the emerging sacrament of penance.

Explicit, direct, standardized exchanges of goods for soteriological relief did not figure into religious practice over the first 1,000 years of Christianity. That changed in the eleventh century. In 1029 one finds something like indulgences proper, in the form of certain European Christians receiving remission of Lenten days for monetary offerings.[8] High-priced items were soon to follow: Cardinal Peter Damian imposed a lengthy penance on the Archbishop of Milan for simony, a penance accompanied by a price tag for the commutation of the sentence.[9] Indulgences had entered the Church as an identifiable practice. Bishops or popes increasingly turned to offers of the remission of sin on the basis of some penitent gift or action.

Two qualifications were in place from the fore, emphasizing the secondary nature of indulgences. One, indulgences were never to take the place of repentance. Sinners were to confess their sins to a cleric. The indulgence was an accessory to penance, an extra-sacramental initiative that could only augment, not replace, confession. Two, an indulgence, rather than forgiving all dimensions of sin, simply reduced disciplinary punishments for sins. Though popular use of indulgences could blur the categories, baptism dealt with guilt (*culpa*) where penance, potentially in tandem with an indulgence, eliminated temporal penalties (*poena*). The many miscellaneous sins warranted

---

[7] Pfeil, "Penitentials as Literature," 129.

[8] Paulus, *Geschichte des Ablasses im Mittelalter*, 96.

[9] Lindberg, *European Reformations*, 74.

periods of discipline. Indulgences therefore adjusted periods of punishment in this life, shortening or eliminating the disciplinary periods conducted by the Church.

Indulgences were widely recognized by the time of the First Crusade. Under threat of Muslim invasion, Pope Urban II in 1095 rallied European forces by offering an indulgence for all those taking up the sword to liberate "the Church of God at Jerusalem." It was the first *plenary* indulgence, no less: an absolution of *all* temporal punishments. Urban II conditioned the indulgence by requiring confession of sins as well as an undertaking of the crusade "from devotion alone, and not for the purpose of gaining honors and wealth."[10] Militant Christians across Europe responded to the call, though one with good reason doubts the purity of their motives. Prospects of land or riches or military glory aside, soldiers were eager to acquire ready-made righteousness in the eyes of God and Church. Rainer Christoph Schwinges argues that the crusaders took "the imprecise terminology" of indulgences to mean that, beyond mere elimination of temporal punishments, service in the crusade would mean total satisfaction for guilt and all related penalties. He concludes that "God's militia" perceived that warfare would merit them "remuneration from God."[11]

Astonishingly, the Western Church went a full 150 years without any concerted effort to justify indulgences theologically. This historical quandary is explained in part by understanding that the salvation matrix had been centralized but not commercialized. It was indeed centralized: with the crusades it became incontestable that satisfaction of sins flowed from the pope himself. Indeed, the twelfth and thirteenth centuries represented the high water of papal power. For instance, in 1215 mandatory confession to a priest once a year was imposed, thus extending "branch offices" of the pope to all quarters. Still, one gets the impression that salvific transactions of this period moved slowly. Salvation was, to wit, resistant to the flow of commerce.

Only in the 1200s does one encounter a true commercialization of indulgences. That peculiar development was achieved through the treasury of merits, a doctrine first articulated by the Dominican scholar Hugh of Saint-Cher.[12] Hugh's writings have been lost, but his teaching is relayed through his contemporary, Henry of Susa:

> The Son of God shed not only a drop, but all his blood for the sinners; and besides, the martyrs shed their blood for the faith and the Church, and they were punished beyond that for which they had sinned. It so occurs that in the said effusion of blood, all sin is punished, and this effusion of blood is the stored

---

[10] Mansi, ed., *Sacrorum Conciliorum Nova et Amplissima Collectio* 20:816.

[11] Schwinges, "Die Kreuzzugsbewegung," 188.

[12] Palmer and Tavard, "Indulgences," 437.

treasury in the cask of the Church, of which the Church possesses the keys. Hence, when the Church wishes, she is able to open the cask, and will be able to grant to anyone her treasury, through granting indulgences and remissions to the faithful. And thus sin goes not unpunished, because it was punished in the son of God, and by his holy martyrs, according to the lord cardinal Hugh.[13]

One might conclude that Henry is merely leveraging the biblical concept of blood atonement, were it not for his addition that blood can be stored and turned into a monetary unit, stowed in the "treasury" (*thesaurus*) or the "cask" (*scrinium*) of the Church. Only a few years after Hugh and Henry, Bonaventure and Thomas Aquinas enshrined the idea of the treasury of merit. The banking of salvation-points, as it were, is possible through the mystical body of Christ, in which the satisfaction of God's justice may be accomplished through a "union of charity." Friends loan friends money; there is a joint account. Therefore, only in the thirteenth century did the Western Church have the basis of a salvific banking *system*. The account was fully capitalized.

The treasury of merit doctrine became increasingly important through the late medieval period (1300s and 1400s) on account of the severe testing of catholicity. In the age of the Avignon Papacy and the Western Schism, the idea of a collective heavenly bank account conferred some sense of unity. Kingdoms and regions had different currencies and high transaction costs, but the Western Church maintained a universal form of spiritual capital.

Later medieval moves toward centralization included the tightening of the heavenly bank account by assigning but one signatory, the Pope. The Pontiff was increasingly in control of, and active in, releasing merit. Indulgences were issued for an expanded array of crusades: against Muslim armies in Spain, Italy, North Africa, and the Levant; also against pagans in the Baltic, heretics in European cities, and even Christian groups in Scandinavia, Russia, and Greece. Because the treasury of merit was communal property in some sense, many clamored for access. Ane Bysted explains that the treasury "provided a theological justification for the extension of the plenary indulgences to classes of people who did not go on crusade personally, but sent a substitute or money instead."[14] The treasury ensured proper compensation for all. Accordingly, non-military indulgences were commissioned, offered to the masses with proceeds going toward churches and hospitals. Indulgences could be and were authorized for fundraising for civic projects such as bridges, dams, canals, and guilds. From 1300 on popes declared jubilee years in which the pious could obtain satisfaction of sins in exchange for pilgrimages, almsgiving or other godly acts.

Still, quantifying righteousness was a tricky proposition. As mentioned before, remission of temporal punishments was derivative of the early penance

---

[13] Cited in Bysted, *Crusade Indulgence*, 135.

[14] Bysted, *Crusade Indulgence*, 147.

system in which disciplinary periods could be shortened by months or years. Plenary indulgences were desirable in that they took care of all possible durations of punishment. But what about lesser indulgences? Exactly how much reduction of penalty-time were they good for?

The question of quantification took on special importance when medieval Christians contemplated the state of the dead. In the twelfth century a related development, the doctrine of purgatory, had formalized. Those who were not ready for the pure bliss of heaven were sentenced to a period of purification in an intermediate state (or space), one characterized by purification by fire. Purgatory finished the sanctifying work partially accomplished in one's earthly life. It falls outside the scope of this study to document the rise of the doctrine, but purgatory is important here insofar as it pressed the accounting of righteousness and punishment. How long would a soul need to spend in the unfortunate purgatorial place? Various clerics, building on the work of Alexander of Hales, came to rather precise measurements. Just as temporal punishments on earth could be numerated and adjusted, so could temporal punishments in the afterlife. Thus, in the thirteenth century, "There came to be established in the hereafter a variable, measurable, and, even more important, manipulable time-scale."[15]

It was precisely the manipulable time-scale that permitted the boldest move of the centralized spiritual banking system yet: the jurisdiction of the earthly Church over the dead. Well into the high Middle Ages the institutional Church had claimed authority only to forgive sins in this life. On the other side of death, remission was entirely in God's hands. When applying the treasury of merit to the doctrine of purgatory, however, one could see the possibility of remitting "otherworldly penalty," a move first made by Albertus Magnus.[16] In reality, rank and file Christians had long assumed an equivalence of accounting on either side of death. So it was perhaps only a matter of time before indulgences were authorized for application to the dead, a practice popularized in the fourteenth century through the influence of the monastery at Cluny.

So far I have traced the rise of a soteriological bank for salvation in the Western Church. Early forms of penance included the commutation of temporal punishments. Early medieval standardization and consolidation and creative theologizing about sin's penalties resulted in the identifiable practice of indulgences. In the high Middle Ages indulgences were part and parcel of a fully commercialized soteriology.

It is appropriate to think of the high medieval Western Church as a bank. The institution as such was the account manager of moral debts and credits. In this light, indulgences operated as a technology. They regulated spiritual

---

[15] Goff, *Birth of Purgatory*, 292.

[16] Schirrmacher, *Indulgences*, 54.

debt. They communicated salvific credit and "moved around" righteousness. They kept the ledgers operative.

Truly, it is even appropriate to think of the high medieval Western Church as a spiritual version of a central banking system. Economist Thammarak Moenjak lists five essential marks of a central bank: 1) issuance of money; 2) conduct of monetary policy; 3) payment systems facilitation; 4) lender of last resort; and 5) banking supervision.[17] Going into the late Middle Ages, the institutional Church had developed all five: 1) issuance of spiritual currency with various notes of indulgence; 2) a penance policy infrastructure covered by bulls, canon law and sacerdotal manuals; 3) distribution and collection through deputized commissaries; 4) a treasury of merit in which Jesus and the saints were responsible for covering deficiencies of credit; and 5) campaign supervision through episcopal, imperial and regional offices, with the Pope as final signatory. Indulgences were part and parcel of the Church's central banking operations.

It should be noted that not everyone was happy about indulgences. They were criticized by the likes of Peter Abelard, the Waldenses and John Wycliffe. Restrictions could be imposed on the exact terms of indulgences, as at the Fourth Lateran Council (1215). But so long as the Western Church kept a rein on its credit system there were no wide-scale objections. After all, few think about a central bank until its policies begin to fail.

## The Printing Press and the Devaluation of Indulgences

Before returning to the history of indulgences, an economic excursus is required. When it comes to the late medieval indulgence industry, money supply theory helps explain its rise and fall. Without ignoring the consequences of political and theological moves, one does well to pay attention to an economic disturbance created by the movable type printing press.

According to one line of thinking, inflation is the great enemy of economic stability. Common to nearly all central banking systems, inflation is the sustained increase in price of goods, or, alternatively, the persistent loss of purchasing power of a currency. Thus, a pack of gum that costs $1.00 this year will likely cost a few cents more the next year even if business goes on like usual. Governments sometimes cope with inflation by generating additional currency and increasing the money supply. Poorly conceived policies with money supply can be catastrophic, however, leading to runaway inflation. To call upon two famous examples, Germans in the Weimar Republic in 1923 began using devalued Deutschmark notes as wallpaper, and not long ago in Zimbabwe runaway inflation led to the issue of a 100 *trillion* dollar bill. Unless

---

[17] Moenjak, *Central Banking*, 37–38.

checked, overzealous printing of bank notes creates a chain reaction of devaluation.

A time-honored way of thinking about inflation is the quantity theory of money (QTM). It holds that there is a direct relationship between the supply of money and price levels. Elevated money supply causes elevated prices as the money's marginal level decreases. In the Fisher Equation version of QTM, money supply multiplied by the velocity of money circulation is equal to the average price level multiplied by the volume of transacted goods. While reformers and detractors of QTM abound, the basic theory has persisted in economic thought.[18] Money supply plays an important, even determinative, role in a banking system.

QTM helps to frame the fragile place of indulgences in the late Middle Ages. Theoretically at least, the value of indulgences was under threat from the thirteenth century. As Bysted puts it, "With an infinite treasury of merits, there was less reason to be cautious in the administration of indulgences, if not for the concern that the indulgence might be devalued."[19] Yet the Church kept close tabs on the number of active indulgences. In most cases a new indulgence would be proclaimed only with the termination of an old one.

It helped that there were few physical units for which the Church, the grand bank of salvation, was responsible. Before the printing press, there were few notes or artifacts. The indulgence was, principally speaking, a decree, a message promulgated by voice. It was transmitted by scribes, written on vellum (calf skin), and read to various crowds. The only material evidence of a crusader being under the indulgence was a small cloth cross sewn to his clothes. Individual Christians did not necessarily carry around evidence of the remission they were owed. If one did possess a physical note, there was a strict statute of limitations: the indulgence had to be redeemed during a certain time period, "cashed in" when confessing to a priest. Fundamentally immaterial, regulated and non-transferable, the indulgence eluded the dynamics governing other currencies.

The introduction of Johannes Gutenberg's printing press changed the dynamic completely. His print shop in Mainz, up and running by 1450, had intentions of manufacturing copies of the Vulgate. The first dated text from Gutenberg, however, is an indulgence. In 1454–55 Gutenberg spun out perhaps 2,000 of them.[20] One can see why: the Catholic Church paid for indulgences up front, which yielded a lucrative return for the cash-strapped

---

[18] For a list of modifications of the Fisher Equation and an empirical defense, see Crowder and Hoffman, "Long-run Relationship," 102–18.

[19] Bysted, *Crusade Indulgence*, 163.

[20] Stallybrass, "'Little Jobs,'" 316.

publisher.²¹ Printed as broadsides (one-sided printings) in thirty-one lines, each indulgence had at the bottom a blank space for the commissary to ink in certification of the indulgence. It was a highly successful project, with copies showing up from Copenhagen to Constance, from Saint Gallen to Westphalia.²²

Not least among the reasons for printing indulgences, fundraising was made considerably easier. With such ready-made currency, official pardoners (*quaestores*) could hawk indulgences to common Christians with great success. Local lords and the emperor had much to gain, as generous portions of indulgences began going to civic projects. Rome might extract its gold, but indulgences were helping to build churches, bridges, roads, hospitals and funding armies for the latest crusade.

Other print shops were quick to join in the bounty. Soon, runs of indulgences were eclipsing what Gutenberg ever produced: from one Augsburg press, 20,000 units, from a fecund printer named Johann Luschner, 142,950 indulgences over a two year period.²³ Just how far the expansion of the indulgence currency could go was tested by the actions of Raymund Peraudi in the latter half of the fifteenth century. At the height of Peraudi's campaigns, from 1488 to 1490, over thirty editions of an indulgence were in circulation each year, with a run of 5,000 to 20,000 copies each edition.²⁴ Even with a conservative number, that makes for a million indulgences disseminated over three years by one commissary.

Before Gutenberg, others had been able to copy indulgences in smaller number by means of wood presses or by hand. But the movable press type opened up the possibility of ubiquity. Christians everywhere could possess a physical copy of the indulgence. In a new and profound sense, the personal documentary unit had become the indulgence itself. At the very least, the document was something of a receipt. Just as merchants had done all along, Western Christians were keeping a ledger of what the Church owed them.

Perhaps more consequential, pardoners were changing the terms of the notes. Again, Raymund Peraudi is outstanding in this regard. From 1477 on

---

²¹ One may observe the irony of Gutenberg's situation. He had experienced monetary problems already as a goldsmith. Things got worse when he undertook to construct the first movable type press. Borrowing florins from moneylender Johann Fust resulted in nothing of value. With his Bible project not yet completed, it appears Gutenberg turned to printing indulgences (spiritual debt notes) in 1454 to get himself *out* of debt. Not that it worked. He wound up owing Fust 20,000 florins in the end and, facing insolvency, was forced to turn the print shop over to the angry lender. In a warped, poetic way, everyone involved with indulgences was drowning in debt.

²² Eisermann, "'Hinter Decken versteckt'," 59–60 and 64.

²³ Flood, "'Volentes Sibi Comparare Infrascriptos Libros Impressos.'"

²⁴ Eisermann, "Indulgence as a Media Event," 327.

he claimed that the letters of confession (*confessionale*) were a "chief grace." He removed from his indulgences the clause requiring Christians to use the note to confess and be absolved in a certain time frame. Now indulgences were tied to the life of the holder, rather than the duration of the indulgence decree or some other ecclesiastical measurement. Peraudi's policy changes were manifested in the materials used. Where common indulgences were typically made from parchment (which at this time was fabricated from fermented and reconstituted rags), Peraudi hawked premium indulgences made of vellum. Indulgences were made to last. With Peraudi's ministry the Western Church experiences the transformation of indulgences from "a mere receipt for confession to a comprehensive form of spiritual life insurance, with validity in this life and the life to come."[25]

One might wonder why inflation did not take hold at this juncture, undercutting the value of the indulgences. Would not millions of spiritual banknotes in circulation result in rapid devaluation? Not necessarily. Currency collapse does not happen so long as demand for the notes is high and public confidence in the issuing government is sustained.[26] Several historical factors are worth noting in this regard. First, lay piety among Christians, especially in the Holy Roman Empire, was waxing. Historians Johannes Jannsen and Johannes Geffken have showed convincingly how passionate fifteenth-century European Christians were in their sincerity and fear about matters of eternal salvation. Indulgences aside, the laity exhibited a voracious appetite for prayer books, catechisms, moral tracts, songbooks, histories, calendars and, significantly, confessional manuals. A fascination with relics and religious wares abounded. That is, piety kept demand in step with the supply. Second, incursions by Muslim armies kept the populace fearful and eager to donate. For instance, a Turkish invasion of Italy from 1480 to 1482 elicited a spike in the sale of indulgences.[27] Western Christians were well aware of the fact that Constantinople, the great Christian capital of the East, had fallen in 1453. Thus, political anxiety propped up demand.

A change in doctrine provides yet another reason for the torrid consumption of indulgences in the latter half of the fifteenth century. Preachers of indulgences opened up new markets by targeting the dead. Offering alms to spring others from purgatory earlier was slow to receive

---

[25] Eisermann, "Indulgence as a Media Event," 326.

[26] "A vast expansion of currency, with its depreciation of money, in the issue of notes by banks or governments, is perfectly practicable among a credulous people, or where, from the popularity of the issuer, or, in the case of government, from patriotic motives, the public are disposed to grant an easy confidence, and encourage the issue, before this inevitable reflux will demonstrate the fact of the overissue and consequent depreciation of the value of money," Carroll, *Organization of Debt*, 242.

[27] Eisermann, "Indulgence as a Media Event," 314.

formal recognition. In 1476, however, Pope Sixtus IV issued a cautious call for the faithful to donate on behalf of the deceased.[28]

As with so many social phenomena, sacred or profane, the boom years were followed by collapse. The market was flooded with indulgences, many of which had an endless shelf life. Though in theory they were non-transferrable, indulgences were being applied to the accounts of the dead. Making matters worse, from 1479 questions of authenticity, even of papal bulls declaring an indulgence, were being raised.[29] Wilhelm Ernst Winterhager reports "an effect of erosion and a loss of credibility" between 1501 and 1503, leading to dwindling revenues.[30] This undoubtedly had to do with the fact that, in the words of Diarmaid MacCulloch, indulgences were as ubiquitous as today's lottery ticket.[31]

All this to say, the preferred fundraising method was in jeopardy well before the beginning of the Protestant movement. The obnoxious Johann Tetzel—who purportedly used the quip, "As soon as a coin in the coffer rings, a soul from purgatory springs"[32]—was notorious before Martin Luther's theological tirade. For example, in 1509 Tetzel was openly criticized by Johann Geiler von Keyserberg because of an insufficient emphasis on personal penitence.[33] Pope Leo X authorized new and unpopular indulgences for broad civic purposes. In 1515 one was commissioned to raise funds for the repair of dikes in the Netherlands, coupled with another to finance King Francis I's crusade (which turned out to be nothing more than an elaborate graft). By 1517, when Leo authorized a campaign to extract gold for the rebuilding of St Peter's Basilica in Rome, many people were openly criticizing indulgences, including Luther's confessor, Johann Staupitz.[34]

What I have been working up to is an answer for why the indulgence industry failed so thoroughly and immediately in the face of the Protestant Reformation. The demise of the industry had much to do with a doctrinal failure, no doubt. The belief structure connecting standardized penalties,

---

[28] It was proclaimed in the bull *Salvator noster* (1476), though even here Sixtus IV implied that an indulgence for the dead was a petition (*per modum suffragi*) rather than an absolution.

[29] Printed bulls would be read first, often bearing seals and ribbons to confirm their own authenticity, for "those who were involved in the indulgence trade were concerned to preserve the documentary character the papal promise of indulgence, thereby proving its legal validity," Eisermann, "Indulgence as a Media Event," 317.

[30] Winterhager, "Ablasskritik als Indikator historischen Wandels vor 1517," 22.

[31] MacCulloch, *Christianity*, 556.

[32] The phrase appears in Thesis 27 of Luther's *95 Theses*.

[33] Rapp, "Les campagnes d'indulgences dans le diocèse de Strasbourg," 80.

[34] Schirrmacher, *Indulgences*, 75.

monetized remission of sin, communal merit, purgatorial rules and vicarious satisfaction for the dead was, to say the least, speculative to the point of incoherence. But my chief argument has been that the downfall of indulgence culture had to do with something better described as an ecclesio-economic collapse. The printing press had multiplied remission notes to an unsustainable level, placing them in too many hands, functionally removing the Church's monetary controls and thereby crashing the value of the indulgence. The argument once more: the central bank that was the institutional Church failed to control the money supply and, to some extent, its velocity, leading to wholesale devaluation of the indulgence as a trustworthy vehicle of spiritual credit. In the end, Western Christians lost confidence in the currency, which is a small step from losing confidence in the governing organization behind the currency.[35] A market correction loomed.

### The Currency of the Gospel

When Martin Luther was first called to account for his dangerous teachings, in Heidelberg in 1518, the perceived threat was to the sacrament of penance. Luther at that time had not rejected the penance complex or papal authority. All the same, he had uncovered the ecclesio-economic instability. Poetic is Thesis 52 of the *95 Theses*, "It is vain to trust in salvation by indulgence letters, even though the indulgence commissary, or even the pope, were to offer his soul as security."[36] Luther's monetary inflection should not be missed. Indulgence letters—the myriads and myriads of them—were not properly securitized. They were untrustworthy because they were not tapping into anything. The papacy was writing bad checks.

It is not my intention to speculate about how the traditionalists could have reined in the presses or revised canon law to prevent a collapse. Rather, I conclude by observing that Protestantism evaded the ecclesio-economic conditions of the medieval salvation-bank entirely. The Protestant reformers appealed to the gratuitous currency of the gospel of grace. Merit could be preached and disseminated freely because the Protestant notion of righteousness did not function like a currency. Here no bank was needed: no

---

[35] In the fifteenth century a range of new financial instruments had been introduced, such as bills of exchange, drafts, letters of credit, insurance and foreign exchange, cf. Grimm, *Reformation Era*, 10–11. By the end of that century Europeans were wary of financial fraud, having faced persistent discrepancies with minting and having witnessed the ruination of the Venetian banking system, cf. Sider, *Handbook*, 208–11. Emblematic is the woodcut of Jörg Breu the Elder, "Question to the Mintmaker" (c.1530), depicting a juxtaposition of three drains on the common good: the merchants' unjust weights; deception in the mintmaker's coins; and the chicanery of the indulgence commissary.

[36] Pelikan *et al.*, *Luther's* Works, 31:30.

reserve, no disbursements, no signatory. Salvation was grounded in the preaching of the word of God and securitized solely by the absolute merit of Christ. The reformers could offer salvation without any of the limitations of the medieval Church's debilitated central banking system. Heralding this new economy, the printing presses erupted with activity for the Reformers.

As for the traditionalists, a difficult season of collapse and contraction ensued. While Catholic clergy and laity continued to defend their use, indulgences were being issued in smaller and smaller quantities. Only a handful of campaigns were successful, and from 1530 to 1570 the practice of indulgences, while not eradicated, was in steep decline.[37] The medieval economy of salvation had come perilously close to bankruptcy. The Catholics would restructure and regroup, finding ways to rehabilitate the doctrines undergirding sin management and, indeed, even the indulgence itself. Never again, however, would they use the printing press to manufacture so prodigal a currency.

## Bibliography

Bysted, Ane L. *The Crusade Indulgence: Spiritual Rewards and the Theology of the Crusades, c. 1095–1216*. Boston, MA: Brill, 2015.

Carroll, Charles Holt. *Organization of Debt into Currency and Other Papers*. Auburn, AL: Moses von Mises Institute, 2002.

Crowder, William J., and Dennis L. Hoffman. "The Long-run Relationship between Nominal Interest Rates and Inflation: The Fisher Equation Revisited." *Journal of Money, Credit, and Banking* 28.1 (1996) 102–18.

Edwards, Mark U. *Printing, Propaganda, and Martin Luther*. Minneapolis, MN: Fortress, 2004.

Eisermann, Falk. "'Hinter Decken versteckt': Ein weiteres Exemplar des 31 zeiligen Ablaßbriefs (GW 6556) und andere Neufunde von Einblattdrucken des 15. Jahrhunderts." *Gutenberg-Jahrbuch* 74 (1999) 58–74.

———. "The Indulgence as a Media Event." In *Promissory Notes on the Treasury of Merit: Indulgences in Late Medieval Europe*, edited by R.N. Swanson, 309–30. Leiden: Brill, 2005.

Flood, John L. "'Volentes Sibi Comparare Infrascriptos Libros Impressos': Printed Books as a Commercial Commodity in the Fifteenth Century." In *Incunabula and Their Readers: Selling and Using Books in the Fifteenth Century*, edited by Kristian Jensen, 139–51. London: The British Library, 2003.

Goff, Jacques Le *The Birth of Purgatory*. Translated by Arthur Goldhammer. Chicago: University of Chicago, 1986.

———. *Medieval Civilization*. Oxford: Blackwell, 1990.

---

[37] Tingle, "Indulgences in the Catholic Reformation," and *Indulgences after Luther*.

Grimm, Harold J. *The Reformation Era*, 1500–1650. New York: MacMillan, 2nd edn, 1973.
Hamm, Bernt. "Die Reformation als Medienereignis." *Jahrbuch für biblische Theologie* 11 (1996) 137–66.
Lindberg, Carter. *The European Reformations*. Oxford: Blackwell, 1996.
MacCulloch, Diarmaid. *Christianity: The First 3,000 Years*. New York: Viking, 2009.
Mansi, Johannes Domenico, ed. *Sacrorum Conciliorum Nova et Amplissima Collectio*. 31 vols. Florence and Venice, 1758–98.
Matheson, Peter. *The Rhetoric of the Reformation*. London: T. & T. Clark, 2004.
Moenjak, Thammarak. *Central Banking: Theory and Practice in Sustaining Monetary and Financial Stability*. Singapore: John Wiley and Sons, 2014.
Palmer, P.F., and G.A. Tavard. "Indulgences." In *New Catholic Encyclopedia:* Volume 7, 2nd ed., edited by Charles George Herbermann *et al.*, 436–41. Detroit, MI: Thomson-Gale, 2003.
Paulus, Nikolaus. *Geschichte des Ablasses im Mittelalter*. Darmstadt: Wissenschaftliche Buchgesellschaft, 2000.
Pelikan, Jaroslav, et al. *Luther's Works:* Volume 31. *Career of the Reformer I*. Trans. by Lowell J. Satre. Philadelphia: Fortress, 1957.
Pfeil, Margaret. "The Penitentials as Literature." In *The Encyclopedia of Christian Literature:* Volume 1. *Genres and Types/Biographies, A–G*, edited by George Thomas Kurian and James D. Smith III, 128–31. Lanham, MD: Scarecrow, 2010.
Rapp, Francis. "Les campagnes d'indulgences dans le diocèse de Strasbourg à la fin du moyen age." *Revue d'Histoire Moderne et Contemporaine* 83 (2003) 71–88.
Ronald Deibert, *Parchment, Printing, and Hypermedia*. New York: Columbia University Press, 1997.
Schirrmacher, Thomas. *Indulgences: A History of the Theology and Reality of Indulgences and Purgatory: A Protestant Evaluation*. Eugene, OR: Wipf & Stock, 2012.
Schwinges, Rainer Christoph. "Die Kreuzzugsbewegung." In *Handbuch der europaischen Geschichte II*, edited by Theodor Schieder, 174–98. Stuttgart: Klett-Cotta, 1987.
Sider, Sandra *Handbook to Life in Renaissance Europe*. Oxford: Oxford University Press, 2005.
Stallybrass, Peter. "'Little Jobs': Broadsides and the Printing Revolution." In *Agent of Change: Print Culture Studies after Elizabeth L. Eisenstein*, edited by Sabrina Alcorn Baron *et al.*, 315–41. Amherst, MA: University of Massachusetts, 2007.
Tingle, Elizabeth C. *Indulgences after Luther: Pardons in Counter-Reformation France, 1520–1720*. London: Routledge, 2016.

———. "Indulgences in the Catholic Reformation: Polemic and Pastoral Uses in France c. 1520–1715." *Reformation & Renaissance Review* 16.2 (2014) 181–204.

Wengert, Timothy J. "Introduction." In *The Annotated Luther:* Volume 1. *The Roots of Reform*, 1–11. Minneapolis, MN: Fortress, 2015.

Winterhager, Wilhelm Ernst. "Ablasskritik als Indikator historischen Wandels vor 1517: Ein Beitrag zu Voraussetzungen und Einordnung der Reformation." *Archiv für Reformationsgeschichte* 90 (1999) 6–71.

CHAPTER 8

# Godly Non-Profits: Extending the Porterfield Thesis

## Robert E. Wright

In *Corporate Spirit: Religion and the Rise of the Modern Corporation*, Amanda Porterfield lays bare the Pauline Christian theological roots of the modern corporate form. Those who understand that corporations took non-profit, municipal, and mutual forms and were not just vehicles for joint-stock companies to gain monopoly or limited liability privileges should easily "buy" the connections she makes between the corporate body, a.k.a. the body politick, and the corpus of the church.[1]

Even for-profit business corporations were not, at first, primarily interested in limitations on liability but rather sought perpetual succession and entity shielding. The latter is the converse of limited liability in that it protects the corpus from the sins of the flock, the corporate entity from the bankruptcy of any or all of its owners in other words. Perpetual succession did not mean perpetual life, as too often claimed, but simply the ability to change ownership without having to dissolve and settle accounts as common law partnerships had to do. It came to early America via "corporations sole," a vehicle through which Anglican church officials, among others, could separate their flawed flesh from the rights and responsibilities of their respective religious offices. Perpetual succession, limitations on liability, and entity shielding also applied to "corporations aggregate," or agglomerations of numerous individuals into a single body or entity.[2]

This paper seeks to extend Porterfield's thesis by arguing that the church's influence went beyond the modern corporate form to the creation of actual corporations, specifically early American secular non-profit charities and beneficial voluntary associations. By longstanding definition, a non-profit may take in more money than it pays out in any given period (i.e., it can earn a "profit"), but it cannot distribute any of those net earnings to the people who control the institution without giving up its non-profit status, a condition that

---

[1] Porterfield, *Corporate Spirit*, 14.

[2] Wright, "For- and Non-Profit Special Corporations," 480–509; Silber, *Corporate Form*, 16.

Yale law professor and economist Henry Hansmann calls the "nondistribution constraint."[3]

Alas, a database of non-profits analogous to the one for business corporations that my research assistants at NYU compiled a decade ago, with help from several grants and financial historian Richard Sylla, remains incomplete. The for-profit data can be downloaded[4] and is contextualized in my *Corporation Nation*.[5] When the non-profit data is complete, look for my book *Liberty Lost* for additional details. The general outlines of the story, however, are already clear. Before the Civil War, organizations that sought the undoubted privileges of perpetual succession, entity shielding, and some limitations on liability, if not full-blown limited liability, could incorporate under special statute or, when available, general incorporation laws. Under a general incorporation law, individuals could charter a church, charity, or other pre-specified type of organization, profit or non-profit, merely by filing paperwork and paying a fee. Under special incorporation, a new law, often called a charter, granted corporate privileges to specific individuals to undertake specific tasks.[6]

Special incorporation was slower and more expensive but could be tailored precisely to each organization's specific needs. General incorporation was generally faster and cheaper and worked best for standard, well-understood types of non-profits like hospitals and, tellingly, churches. In fact, the first general incorporation laws applied not to manufacturers, as sometimes claimed, but to churches. When Catholics encountered difficulty obtaining charters for their churches in early New York, advocates of religious freedom in 1784 passed a general incorporation law for churches of all denominations to encourage the voluntary financing of religious bodies. Pennsylvania followed in 1791, but Virginia, Arkansas, Kentucky, and Missouri long prohibited even the special incorporation of churches. Most states, though, readily incorporated churches by special charter.[7]

By 1830, over a dozen general incorporation statutes for secular non-profits had been passed in more than half a dozen states, including large ones like Massachusetts, New York, Pennsylvania, and Virginia, covering specific types of non-profits such as agricultural societies, colleges and other educational associations, fire companies, and libraries. New York in 1848 passed a general

---

[3] Hansmann, *Ownership of Enterprise*, 227–54, and "Economic Theories," 28; O'Neill, *Third America*, 2.

[4] https://repository.upenn.edu/mead/7/.

[5] Wright, *Corporation Nation*.

[6] Silber, *Corporate Form*, 18–20.

[7] Porterfield, *Corporate Spirit*, 101–2; Butterfield, *Making of Tocqueville's America*, 70; Bloch and Lamoreaux, "Voluntary Associations," 242.

non-profit general incorporation statute that became widely emulated by other states over time, though in most jurisdictions, including New York itself, special incorporation also remained possible.[8]

## How Important Is This Story?

It is a truism that religion played an important role in early American history. The specifics, at least in matters business and economic, remain hazy, but quantification can aid clarification. In 1800, about one in every fifteen Americans were official members of a church and about forty percent were at least loosely connected to a church. By 1835, for reasons explained below, official membership had improved to one in eight and some seventy-five percent of Americans had some church connection. Although early Americans were not uniformly religious, churches were clearly an important part of their institutional and physical landscapes. In 1776, the number of church buildings in America was already north of 3,200. Americans built about 10,000 new churches between 1780 and 1820, and by 1850 boasted 38,000, and by the Civil War 54,000. Almost all were built and maintained primarily by private donations, many protected by charters.[9]

Religious charities were also numerous. Several major colonial religious leaders inspired charitable giving through their sermons and writings. In 1710, for example, Cotton Mather, in a pamphlet called *Bonifacius: Essays to do Good*, beseeched colonists to "be as Wise to Do Good, as Many People are Wise to do Evil" and to set aside time each Sunday to ask themselves, "What Good may I do?"[10] In addition, colonial church leaders and acolytes generally agreed that a strong economy strengthened religious life, and *vice versa*. Moreover, John Locke's notion that rational individuals enjoyed a natural right to freely associate had taken a strong hold, creating a consensus that transcended traditional class/caste, religious, geographical, or social boundaries and that included both for- and non-profit corporations. Little wonder then, that, in addition to their ubiquitous churches, colonists established non-profit colleges, hospitals, orphanages, and learned societies as well as debate societies, bell ringing associations, and supper clubs. However, other than the Quakers, who helped the poor and Indians, few denominations took much interest in poor relief until after the Revolution.[11]

---

[8] Silber, *Corporate Form*, 22; Bloch and Lamoreaux, "Voluntary Associations," 241, 259.

[9] Butterfield, *Making of Tocqueville's America*, 33; Burke, "Religious Organizations," Table Bg 320–33.

[10] Mather, *Bonifacius*, 30, 41.

[11] Porterfield, *Corporate Spirit*, 75–76; Brooke, *Heart of the Commonwealth*, 81–83, 187, 270, 278–79; Carp, "Orphanages vs. Adoption," 123; Nielsen, *Endangered Sector*,

Catholics became important contributors to social services provision in the early Southern and Middle Atlantic states, especially in Maryland. Before 1830, eight orders, from Carmelites to Sisters of Our Lady of Mercy, formed and operated elementary, negro, female, and normal schools; orphanages; and hospitals, all of which served non-Catholics as well. Later, as Irish immigrants began to pour into the country, Catholic charities began to form in significant numbers in the North and Old Northwest as well. Not all were formally incorporated but the largest ones tended to be, though some fairly large ones took the form of trusts and smaller ones formed around informal constitutions called articles of association or articles of agreement.[12]

Remarkably, despite the wide variance due to differences in state-level legal environments, nobody has bothered to count the non-profits chartered in each state before, or for a long time after, the Civil War.[13] Exact numbers are difficult to ascertain because no government or other body regularly tracked their formation, leaving, as philanthropist Richard Cornuelle put it, no "easy trace for historians to follow."[14] What we do know, however, suggests that churches and religious charities were an important but not dominant subset of all non-profit formation and that non-profits may have outnumbered for-profit corporations. For example, between 1790 and 1860, Georgians formed 528 academies, 314 churches, eighty-five fraternal lodges, forty charitable societies, fourteen scientific societies, twelve mutual benefit groups, ten libraries, and six temperance societies.[15]

Non-profit corporations were just as prolific, and religiously oriented, in other states. When Alexis De Tocqueville visited America in the early 1830s, he was struck by how easily Americans banded together to form corporations and associations to meet a wide variety of socioeconomic needs:

> Americans of all ages, all conditions, and all dispositions constantly form associations. They have not only commercial and manufacturing companies, in which all take part, but associations of a thousand other kinds, religious, moral, serious, futile, general or restricted, enormous or diminutive. The Americans make associations to give entertainments, to found seminaries, to build inns, to construct churches, to diffuse books, to send missionaries to the antipodes; in this manner they found hospitals, prisons and schools. If it is proposed to

---

26–28; Butterfield, *Making of Tocqueville's America*, 24; Cnaan *et al.*, *Newer Deal*, 114–16.

[12] Weaver, *U.S. Philanthropic Foundations*, 21–22; Misner, *"Highly Respectable,"* 8, 247, 280–83.

[13] Campbell, "Social Federalism," 152.

[14] Cornuelle, *Reclaiming*, 22.

[15] Butterfield, *Making of Tocqueville's America*, 67; Heath, *Constructive Liberalism*, 293–308.

inculcate some truth or foster some feeling by the encouragement of a great example, they form a society.[16]

In 1830, Francis Lieber called the United States "a concatenation of various corporations, political, civil, religious, social and economical,"[17] but as early as 1763 Massachusetts attorney James Otis had made much the same observation.[18] Historians have concurred. "The historical record of America's voluntary accomplishments," noted two scholars in 1995, "is nothing short of phenomenal."[19] Two decades before and two decades later, other scholars claimed much the same.[20]

Although no one knew for certain, as nobody kept close track until very recently, scholars often assumed that the number of for-profit corporations, now known to have been about 22,000 specially incorporated businesses chartered before the Civil War, must have outstripped the number of non-profits. For-profits clearly formed due to the lure of lucre, but the number and size of non-profits were also a function of supply and demand. The supply of new non-profits, some scholars have reasoned, must have been weak.[21]

One reason for that belief, which may prove to be mistaken, was that New York, Virginia, Maryland and several other major states repealed the Statute of Charitable Uses and passed laws that seemed hostile to the development of private eleemosynary corporations. Only in the Girard case in 1844 did SCOTUS (the Supreme Court of the United States) make clear that charitable trusts were valid in those states and at the federal level. Or so the story went, but it turns out that that narrative was overblown. While the attack on charitable endowments certainly reduced giving by some unknowable amount, overall, the Virginia Charity Doctrine, which was rooted in Virginians' long struggle to dis-establish the Anglican church, represented a mere speed bump temporarily put in place in reaction to the efflorescence of non-profit formation and charitable giving sweeping across the new nation. If the attack did anything, it was to spur incorporation, which clearly provided more protection for property rights than unchartered voluntary associations could count upon.[22]

---

[16] As quoted in Silber, *Corporate Form*, 21.

[17] As quoted in Butterfield, *Making of Tocqueville's America*, 66.

[18] Butterfield, *Making of Tocqueville's America*, 195.

[19] Bennett and DiLorenzo, *Unhealthy Charities*, 1.

[20] Butterfield, *Making of Tocqueville's America*, 2; Neem, *Creating a Nation*.

[21] Cuninggim, *Private Money*, 12–13; Silber, *Corporate Form*, 23–25.

[22] Wyllie, "Search for an American Law," 210; Hall, "Historical Overview," 5–6; Wright, "Corporate Social Responsibility," 120–21; Zunz, *Philanthropy in America*,

Another reason why scholars presumed that for-profits outnumbered non-profits lay in assumptions about the incentives of individuals to try to create new organizations, which presumably were heavily weighted towards for-profits, and the incentives of state legislators to charter them, which again were presumably heavily weighted towards for-profits because commercial enterprises could pay higher taxes and/or bribes. Even for-profits sometimes found it difficult to obtain charters and according to recent research by Ruth Bloch and Naomi Lamoreaux, legislators regularly blocked the formation of non-profits thought to be socially or politically disruptive. Unfortunately, however, those scholars did not read through legislative records and so could present only anecdotal evidence of non-profits being denied charters for politicized reasons. *Ergo*, the exact extent of non-profit repression, particularly outside of abolition, labor, and other "radical" associations, remains unclear.[23]

Scholars have missed the fact, however, that the supply of non-profits was augmented by an important group largely excluded from supplying the for-profit corporate sector, women. Early American women often used the non-profit sector to enter public life in lawful and socially acceptable ways, as they had in Christian lands since Roman times. Although women were active in business, especially in the nation's first few decades before Victorian mores strengthened and work increasingly moved out of the home, they were largely excluded from the for-profit corporate sector, except as passive investors. They could lawfully vote in corporate elections but were not encouraged to do so, and only a handful were elected to corporate boards before the Civil War.[24]

By contrast, women maintained a large presence in the antebellum non-profit sector.[25] English traveler James Silk Buckingham noted that "there are perhaps ten times the number of women in good society in New York who interest themselves in the support and direction of moral objects and benevolent institutions than could be found in any city of the same population in Europe."[26] In 1836, the Rev. C. Gayton Pickman reminded his audience that it was "to female influence and exertion that many of our best schemes of charity are due."[27] The following year, the Rev. Jonathan Stearns made the same point, noting that "the cause of benevolence is peculiarly indebted to the

---

14–17; Campbell, "Social Federalism," 152, 174–77; Katz *et al.*, "Legal Changes," 55–57; Bloch and Lamoreaux, "Voluntary Associations," 233–34.

[23] Bloch and Lamoreaux, "Voluntary Associations," 240.

[24] Porterfield, *Corporate Spirit*, 18; Wright, *Hamilton Unbound*, 173–94, and *Financial Exclusion*, 213–74.

[25] Butterfield, *Making of Tocqueville's America*, 93.

[26] As quoted in Sander, *Business of Charity*, 20.

[27] Ginzberg, *Women*, 1.

agency of woman."[28] Many were not loose clubs but rather formal associations, incorporated by state governments, that followed their charters and by-laws as solemnly as if they had been multi-million dollar banks, insurers, or manufacturers.[29]

Well before they could vote in most political elections, women stood in the vanguard of the creation, development, and maintenance of a wide variety of non-profit organizations that sought to abolish slavery, aid the deaf, dumb, blind, and insane, agitate for broad social change, alleviate the pain and suffering of the sick, fight prostitution, reduce alcoholism, spread the word of God, train the unemployed for productive work, and, finally, to bolster their own civil rights. They learned how to form non-profit corporations from each other, from males in their familial and social networks, and, when necessary, attorneys. Incorporation protected the assets devoted to their respective organizations. Many women were named as incorporators of non-profit corporations, including Hannah Stillman, the founder of the Boston Female Asylum in 1800.[30] By 1816, Hannah Kinney, president of the Newark Female Charitable Society, noted that "applications to legislators by females to become incorporate bodies are not novelties."[31] Jonathan Roberts of Pennsylvania also noted that even married women frequently incorporated non-profit institutions in many states.[32]

Through non-profits, women could act as agents of change in ways they could not in the for-profit and government sectors. Although parts of it were considered more feminine than others, and many non-profits remained segregated into male and female contingents, non-profits constituted the first gender-integrated sector of the economy, a social space where male and female spheres overlapped.[33] As historian Lori Ginzburg showed, "women did everything most men did, worked alongside men, and maintained permanent organizations and institutions."[34]

On the other side of the equation, demand for non-profits was strong because the government was, by design, a limited one. It purposely did not involve itself in the thousands of activities that interested its citizens but rather left it to them to solve their own problems, in their own ways, with their own resources. Political scientists make substantially the same point somewhat

---

[28] As quoted in Sander, *Business of Charity*, 20.

[29] Butterfield, *Making of Tocqueville's America*, 93–96.

[30] Ginzberg, *Women*, 1–5, 38–39, 50–51; Anon., *Reminiscences*, 14.

[31] As quoted in Ginzberg, *Women*, 53.

[32] Anon., "Washington."

[33] Ginzberg, *Women*, 15–16, 31–32.

[34] Ginzberg, *Women*, 37.

differently, by implying or even outright asserting that the government was insufficiently "developed" or lacked the "capacity" to solve numerous problems.[35] The limited purview of early American governments was, however, quite purposeful, and arguably a sign of their great strength, not of weakness or underdevelopment.

Another reason many scholars assumed that for-profits outnumbered non-profits is the free rider problem, the ability of people to obtain the benefits of something without paying for it themselves. Free riding certainly imposed costs that reduced the expected effectiveness of non-profit organizations, and hence the demand for them, but its effects were not as severe as commonly believed.

Charity presented a serious but not insurmountable free rider problem because donors and their customers, the recipients of charity, were not the same group, at least not at the same time. Those who did not donate could not be excluded from the benefits created by charities, like reductions in begging, crime, disease, and so forth, suggesting that charities would find it difficult to raise money as everyone shirked, hoping to benefit from their neighbors' donations. But even secular charities found it possible to reduce free riding because the various streams of Protestantism that dominated the American antebellum religious scene stressed the Golden Rule, the notion that good Christians should do unto others rather than follow the dictates of a strict rationality.

Many believed, in addition, that maintaining a good charitable safety net might personally help them in the future. Downward socioeconomic mobility was real enough that many charitable donors could easily envision a future where they, or their loved ones, would feel the wolf of hunger and hence wanted to ensure that a private safety net was in place to catch them should their fortune reverse.[36] Middle class families were even more vulnerable. Everyone knew at least one "man who had a respectable establishment, for many years ... [who] was gradually reduced ... to abject penury ... at last houseless and pennyless."[37] A donation to an orphanage, one who understood this precarity reasoned, could provide "a respectable and comfortable asylum for our own descendants."[38] Even if one's descendants were never burdened with the loss of their parents, another intoned, supporting orphan asylums that paid due attention to their charges' morals and "habits of industry" would create a better society in the future by ensuring that its inhabitants, even the

---

[35] Skowronek, *Building a New American State*, 3–9.

[36] Sander, *Business of Charity*, 17.

[37] Carey, "Public Charities of Philadelphia," 163.

[38] Anon., "Orphans' Asylum."

least fortunate ones, were sober and hard-working.[39] Charitable giving, in other words, hedged against their own possible future difficulties, and those of their descendants, while also performing God's work. Free riding, therefore, was not as big a problem as economists sometimes imagine.[40]

Non-profits also offered intangible club goods, like feelings of community or companionship.[41] Those who tried to free ride by obtaining such intangibles without contributing were excluded from membership in non-profits just as easily as for-profits excluded non-paying customers. Moreover, when faith, reason, and intangible goods proved insufficient, other techniques were employed to reduce free riding. Early on, sermons often served as major charitable fund-raising events for secular non-profits.[42] Fear of the Lord effectively reduced free riding by some, including a nine-year-old girl who after hearing the words of Dr Freeman in 1808 decided that she had to increase her nine pence charitable contribution to the Boston Female Asylum another $1.25, a huge sum then, especially for one so young.[43] Other inhabitants of Boston were also moved, to the point that Samuel Eliot asserted "that a much larger amount has been distributed by the individual inhabitants of Boston than by the City government," an act "done freely, voluntarily, by no compulsion of any sort."[44] No worldly compulsion anyway.

Religion may be the mother of philanthropy and the godmother of the non-profit sector but annual sermons soon lost their novelty, inducing secular non-profits to try other fundraising activities.[45] Fairs (rummage sales), "balls, entertainments, oyster suppers, and other devices for inveigling money from the pockets of those who would not otherwise contribute the same amounts," were found to mitigate free rider problems to some extent.[46] Purists balked but when one fair raised $500 for an antislavery society, abolitionist Mary Robbins called it "a blossom on the tree of liberty."[47]

---

[39] Anon., "Washington Orphan Asylum Society."

[40] Sander, *Business of Charity*, 17; Holcombe, *Writing Off Ideas*, 212–13.

[41] Butterfield, *Making of Tocqueville's America*, 40.

[42] See, e.g., Anon., "A Sermon."

[43] Anon., *Reminiscences*, 36.

[44] As quoted in Wright, "Corporate Social Responsibility," 127.

[45] Weaver, *U.S. Philanthropic Foundations*, 19–20; O'Neill, *Third America*, 20–42; Anon., *Reminiscences*, 37–38; Ginzberg, *Women*, 46–47.

[46] Warner and Coolidge, *American Charities*, 385.

[47] As quoted in Ginzberg, *Women*, 47.

For all those reasons, it is unsurprising to find that non-profit formation exceeded that of for-profit formation in aggregate through at least 1810.[48] Additionally, non-profit special charter formation outpaced for-profits in eight of twelve states sampled through 1860. In aggregate, however, specially chartered non-profits trailed slightly because of the influence of Indiana, where for-profits outnumbered non-profits 602 to 310, apparently due to the state's early penchant for passing popular non-profit general incorporation laws for agricultural societies, churches, educational establishments, fire companies, fraternal lodges, horse anti-theft associations, and libraries.[49]

### Direct Influences of Religion on Secular Non-Profits

Direct religious influences on secular non-profits were both positive and negative. Most importantly, the distinction American secular charities long made between the deserving and undeserving poor was an old one, with deeply religious roots.[50] Religions that used "their charities as engines for church extension," on the other hand, often induced vigorous competition from secular charities.[51] Joseph Tuckerman, a Unitarian clergyman in Boston, at first tried to save the poor by saving their souls but he later realized that the poor were often the victims of bad luck and bad social policies, which he tried to alleviate in various ways, including urging churches to aid the poor regardless of their religious affiliation.[52]

Some, but not all, heeded Tuckerman's call. The Orphaline Charity School in Baltimore, for example, attracted "little public notice" over its first twenty-one years but managed to help over 100 female orphans to mature, physically and intellectually, until they could "be placed in respectable families."[53] The largest number were Catholics, but they were not a majority as the group included numerous Methodists as well as a smattering of girls from other Protestant denominations. In Washington, DC, by contrast, the female orphan asylum was assailed for not being open to girls from all religions.[54]

The United States remains one of the world's most religious nations because of its tradition of limited government, which meant that even colonies

---

[48] Kaufman, "Corporate Law," 413–17.

[49] *Statutes of Indiana*: 1816, 156; 1819, 70; 1820, 56; 1823, 380; 1828, 9; 1831, 526; 1834, 87; 1846, 97; 1850, 133.

[50] Rothman, *Discovery of the Asylum*, 8–9.

[51] Warner and Coolidge, *American Charities*, 382–84.

[52] Cnaan et al., *Newer Deal*, 117.

[53] Anon., "Baltimore Female Orphan Asylum."

[54] A Citizen, "Washington Female Orphan Asylum."

like Massachusetts, Pennsylvania, and Maryland, dominated at first by a single sect, did not establish strong state religions. The dearth of tithes and religious oaths and tests helped to attract new settlers, who aided in defense and economic development. The colonies therefore remained, for the most part, religiously tolerant, especially within Protestantism. The new state governments completely disestablished churches following the Revolution and the new federal government swore off a close connection between church and state in the Bill of Rights.[55]

Separation of church and state kept the government out of America's churches and other religious organizations. Americans thereafter enjoyed the undeniable right to join the church, or churches, of their choice, or none at all. As a result, religions had to compete for acolytes, which made them highly responsive as Adam Smith famously explained.[56] Small religious sects were nimble and customer-oriented, especially compared to religions with large endowments or state-sponsorship, which tended to make them sclerotic and hence sowers of the seeds of atheism, Deism, Rastafarianism, Pastafarianism, and other non-Christian beliefs.[57]

In America, everything from church services to theology evolved to please parishioners enough to keep them coming back and paying their pew rents, dues, Sunday assessments, and so forth. Competition also gave church officials tremendous incentives to win over new acolytes. Consider, for example, the exploits of Francis Asbury, a Methodist bishop who traveled 300,000 miles on horseback and in the process increased the size of the Methodist community in the US from 5,000 in 1776 to over 200,000 in 1816. Love of the Lord drove him forward, but so too did hatred of Baptists! Intense competition meant that American churches tended to be plentiful but small and highly focused on the needs of their members. By the 1850s, the small town of Princeton, Illinois, boasted eleven different Presbyterian churches. Free African-Americans established their own churches, as did members of every other group that felt unwelcomed in other houses of worship.[58]

Open competition meant that secular charities could offer spiritual services as well, and many did so. The Boston Female Asylum, for example, believed it necessary to provide the girls in their charge with religious as well as knitting and sewing instruction and secular schooling "suitable to their age, sex and

---

[55] O'Neill, *Third America*, 26–28; Cnaan *et al.*, *Newer Deal*, 113.

[56] Smith, *Wealth of Nations*, Book V, Chapter 1, Article 3.

[57] O'Neill, *Third America*, 20; Butterfield, *Making of Tocqueville's America*, 29–30; Wright, "Corporate Social Responsibility," 117–36.

[58] Wright, "Business," vii–xix; O'Neill, *Third America*, 32; Burke, "Church and Congregation Membership," Table Bg334–348; Butterfield, *Making of Tocqueville's America*, 32.

station."[59] The New York Mission and Tract Society also ministered to the poor, the imprisoned, and new immigrants.[60] Other non-denominational groups formed for spiritual reasons, including one in Newport dedicated simply to praying for "the universal benefit of mankind."[61]

In 1828, political economist Mathew Carey divided American non-profits into three categories, religious, beneficial (i.e., club), and charitable, the last mentioned of which he further subdivided into three types, educational, reformative (of the individual), and physical, i.e., "to relieve physical wants."[62] Education and religion often went hand in hand. In 1784, for example, several wealthy inhabitants of Worcester County, Massachusetts, chartered the Leicester Academy with "the purpose of promoting true piety and virtue, and the education of youth."[63] The Salem Society for the Moral and Religious Instruction of the Poor operated religious schools for poor men and women in their Massachusetts town.[64]

Even beneficial non-profits borrowed heavily from religion. Although a British import from the colonial period, Masonic Lodges proliferated in the US in the 1790s, growing to eleven grand lodges and 347 lodges by 1800. By the 1820s, about 80,000 American men, roughly one in twenty, were Masons. Critics lambasted the society's secret rituals, its membership levels and initiation rites, and, most importantly, its secularization of traditional religious tropes. Other beneficial societies, like the Redmen, also employed vaguely spiritual rituals to help bind members together.[65]

### Influence of the Christian Religion on the Development of the Non-Profit Sector

Christian churches also influenced the general development of the entire American non-profit sector. Religious and secular non-profit organizations undertook activities that businesses and governments would not touch, the former because they were insufficiently remunerative and the latter because they were insufficiently popular. They allowed Americans to put real resources into causes they believed to be important, without the distorting influence of profits or politics interceding. While businesses were driven by the "profit

---

[59] Anon., *Reminiscences*, 39–43, 57.

[60] Cnaan *et al.*, *Newer Deal*, 117.

[61] As quoted in Butterfield, *Making of Tocqueville's America*, 93.

[62] Carey, "Public Charities of Philadelphia," 170.

[63] As quoted in Brooke, *Heart of the Commonwealth*, 186.

[64] Ginzberg, *Women*, 36.

[65] Butterfield, *Making of Tocqueville's America*, 26–29, 173.

motive," and governments by "the will to power," the "urge to serve" drove non-profits, in large part due to their religious origins. Some people want to help others, often desperately. The Third Sector harnessed those humanitarian impulses and directed them to do good, and at low cost.[66]

Some people today believe that Jesus of Nazareth would have been a New Deal Democrat. Jesus, the argument goes, wanted his disciples to aid other people. Policymakers who want to cut taxes and hence aid to the poor are, according to this logic, in league with Beelzebub himself. Such claimants, students no doubt of Socialist presidential candidate Eugene V. Debs, who believed that Christ was pro-labor union,[67] seem to be under the impression that Jesus was not in favor of economic freedom and that the only way to help others was through bigger government.[68] That anti-business, pro-government interpretation of Jesus is, however, directly contrary to the view held by most American colonists, who came to the New World to celebrate what Porterfield calls "liberty in Christ."[69] From a society that asked what individuals could do to help others, America has become a society that asks what individuals can do to ask government to help others. A Good Samaritan today is somebody who votes for more government spending, blithely ignoring costs and alternatives.[70]

Early Americans, by contrast, believed that the best way to palliate most economic and social problems was by means of voluntary civil society, not formal government or commercial enterprise, the instruments of which are too often crude or cruel. That legacy of voluntarism is largely forgotten today because non-profits tended to be, like good Christians, humble entities that did not seek to bring attention to their activities. But that meant their efforts were too easily forgotten, downplayed, or ignored. When the US government formed the Peace Corps to much ballyhoo in 1961, major media outlets forgot to note that religious groups then had 33,000 Americans stationed overseas doing the same work, and had been at it since 1809, with American missionaries ensconced in Africa, Burma, Ceylon, China, India, and the Sandwich Islands (Hawaii) even before the Civil War.[71]

---

[66] Cornuelle, *Reclaiming*, 65, 98.

[67] Porterfield, *Corporate Spirit*, 126. Equally extreme, of course, was Billy Graham's claim that God is anti-union. Porterfield, *Corporate Spirit*, 156.

[68] According to Bastiat, *The Law*, 32–33, "Socialism . . . confuses the distinction between government and society. As a result of this, every time we object to a thing being done by government, the socialists conclude that we object to its being done at all."

[69] As quoted in Porterfield, *Corporate Spirit*, 70. See also 73–74.

[70] Nielsen, *Endangered Sector*, 185–86; Cornuelle, *Reclaiming*, 69–70, 137.

[71] Cornuelle, *Reclaiming*, 105, 141; O'Neill, *Third America*, 128.

The vast majority of the members of America's founding generations believed in a limited government, particularly at the national level, the main goal of which was to protect Americans' lives, liberties, and property from foes foreign and domestic. The commitment to limited government spurred America's economic growth miracle, its robust average annual increase in inflation-adjusted *per capita* output after 1790. Although its fruits were not equally distributed, the productivity increases at the root of America's economic efflorescence substantially improved the quality of life for all Americans, rich and poor, young and old, white and black, Jew and Gentile.[72]

Wealth, though, was not the sole goal of early Americans, whose non-monetary aspirations waxed along with their material prosperity. They perceived many social ills, from alcoholism to hunger to slavery, that they wanted to reduce, if not outright destroy. Instead of turning to government for aid, which evoked fears of tyranny and inefficiency, they turned to civil society, and they looked to their churches and religious charities for direct aid as well as inspiration for secular associations and corporations designed to address the sundry economic and socials ills that they had identified.[73]

Non-profits offered an alternative to the growth of the state and commercial power.[74] Moreover, in many circumstances characterized by high levels of asymmetric information or market power (monopoly), non-profits outcompeted for-profits by more easily reassuring customers that they provided higher quality services at reasonable prices than for-profit firms did, or could. Activities that many people did not want governments to undertake, usually because they believed governments to be too inflexible and inefficient, were provided by non-profits without controversy. Even the economically-challenged Thomas Jefferson understood that taxpayer funds used to further some specific social goal, like the improvement of agricultural productivity, were likely to be lavished upon a "few idle favorites & in little further."[75] Moreover, unlike most governments, non-profits provided services to just those who wanted them, and paid for just by those who wanted to pay for them.[76]

Voluntary association, however, was no panacea. Non-profits did not, and indeed could not, solve all social problems completely. The early nineteenth-century asylum movement died, for example, because the focus switched from reform to custody, from helping to locking away, from religious goals to purely

---

[72] Wright, *One Nation Under Debt*.

[73] Cornuelle, *Reclaiming*, 22.

[74] Cornuelle, *Reclaiming*, 74–79.

[75] As quoted in Butterfield, *Making of Tocqueville's America*, 101.

[76] O'Neill, *Third America*, 15–16; Hall, "Historical Overview," 3; Hansmann, "Economic Theories of Nonprofit Organization," 28–35.

secular ones. Asylums for the insane lost their status as institutions worthy of charitable donations not because the insane were unworthy but because the asylums themselves became overcrowded pits of iniquity and injustice.[77]

## Conclusion

Due to the failure of some voluntary efforts, an increasingly pervasive statist worldview, and the failure of non-profits and historians to remind the public of the Third Sector's many contributions, Americans started to believe that the government could solve social problems by using its power of taxation to defeat the budget constraints thought to underpin all social ills.[78] The hoary notion that forcibly taking resources from one person and giving them to another may breed animosity and contempt in both parties lost much of its force despite admonitions from political leaders like President Herbert Hoover, who tried to remind Americans that "a voluntary deed by a man impressed with the sense of responsibility and brotherhood of man is infinitely more precious to our national ideals and national spirit than a thousandfold poured from the treasury of the government under the compulsion of law."[79]

The Great Depression and New Deal reduced the importance and changed the mission of the Third Sector, the charitable component of which adroitly adapted to the rise of America's modern welfare state. Crushed by the unprecedented depth and length of the Depression, even churches retreated as deacons once the main intermediary between church charity funds and aid recipients found their roles reduced. After World War II, US governments felt they could intercede in areas of socioeconomic life previously left to non-profits. The US federal government during the Cold War continued to extend its reach ever deeper into Americans' private lives. Many acquiesced because with the ascendance of industrial mammoths like General Motors and General Electric, Americans increasingly believed the only viable alternative to government was large-scale commercial enterprise, an inappropriate tool for addressing many social problems.[80]

Nonprofits did not disappear from postwar America's political or economic landscape, but some conservative observers sensed a change in public sentiment and urged a return to older values. In 1960, for example, Republican politician Barry Goldwater felt the need to beseech Americans to "not blunt the noble impulses of mankind by reducing charity to a mechanical

---

[77] Rothman, *Discovery of the Asylum*, 238, 265–68.

[78] Hall, "Historical Overview," 3.

[79] Hoover, "Address."

[80] Morris, *Limits of Voluntarism;* Hawley, "Herbert Hoover," 161–90; Cornuelle, *Reclaiming*, 10–12, 135.

operation of the federal government." Instead, he argued, we should "encourage those who are fortunate and able to care for the needs of those who are unfortunate and disabled." In other words, "let welfare be a private concern. Let it be promoted by individuals and families, by churches, private hospitals, religious service organizations, community charities and other institutions that have been established for this purpose." Private philanthropy would not "lack sufficient funds" for such projects, he noted, if federal taxes and "the overhead charge for processing the money through the federal bureaucracy" were not so high.[81]

Goldwater's pleas went largely unheeded, but politicians continued to support voluntary service in general, most importantly by allowing non-profits to remain tax-exempt. Some politicians used the exemption, however, to intimate that churches and other non-profits somehow "owed" something to the rest of the country.[82] Due to the nature of their funding base and restrictions, some regulatory and some self-imposed, on their political and publicity activities, foundations and secular, non-educational philanthropic organizations found it especially difficult to rally sufficient popular support to contest such claims. Much of the publicity they garnered focused on their failures rather than on their successes. Moreover, many non-profits remained content with what Cornuelle called "rustic methods" instead of embracing new, more efficient technologies.[83] The Third Sector sometimes accomplished great things, like the eradication of polio, but also often wasted resources because non-profits often did not "know when to start spending money or when to stop."[84] It therefore lost donors' trust over time and then its financial independence from government, leaving only large endowments, due to their stash of cash, and religions, due to the doctrine of separation of church and state, independent from government control.[85]

It therefore may be time, once again, for secular non-profits to learn from their religious brethren about how to tap the "urge to serve." At the same time, however, religious non-profits might learn from secular ones the limits on non-profit activities that donors, politicians, regulators, and taxpayers will tolerate.[86]

---

[81] Goldwater, *Conscience*, 69.

[82] Hall, "Historical Overview," 19; Cornuelle, *Reclaiming*, 151.

[83] Cornuelle, *Reclaiming*, 45; Cuninggim, *Private Money*, 3, 19–22.

[84] Cornuelle, *Reclaiming*, 51.

[85] Cornuelle, *Reclaiming*, 161; Nielsen, *Endangered Sector*, 187.

[86] See, for example, the issues raised in Moss and Baden, *Bible Nation*.

## Bibliography

Anon., "Baltimore Female Orphan Asylum." *Daily National Intelligencer*, 22 September 1823.
Anon., "Orphans' Asylum." *Daily National Intelligencer* 3 October 1815.
Anon. *Reminiscences of the Boston Female Asylum*. Boston: Eastburn's, 1844.
Anon., "A Sermon." *Daily National Intelligencer*, 25 January 1817.
Anon. "Washington." *Daily National Intelligencer* 14 March 1816.
A Citizen, "Washington Female Orphan Asylum." *Daily National Intelligencer*, 11 October 1825.
Anon., "The Washington Orphan Asylum Society." *Daily National Intelligencer* 27 November 1815.
Bastiat, Frederic. *The Law*. Translated by Dean Russell. Irvington-on-Hudson, NY: Foundation for Economic Education, 1972.
Bennett, James T., and Thomas J. DiLorenzo. *Unhealthy Charities: Hazardous to Your Health and Wealth*. New York: Basic, 1994.
Bloch, Ruth H., and Naomi R. Lamoreaux. "Voluntary Associations, Corporate Rights, and the State Legal Constraints on the Development of American Civil Society, 1750–1900." In *Organizations, Civil Society, and the Roots of Development*, edited by Naomi R. Lamoreaux and John J. Wallis, 231–90. Chicago: University of Chicago Press, 2017.
Brooke, John L. *The Heart of the Commonwealth: Society and Political Culture in Worcester County, Massachusetts, 1713–1861*. Amherst, MA: University of Massachusetts Press, 1989.
Burke, Colin B. "Religious Organizations—Membership, Churches and Synagogues, Clergy, and Attendance, by Denomination and Region: 1776–1998." *Historical Statistics of the United States*, edited by Susan B. Carter, Scott Sigmund Carter, Michael R. Haines, Alan L. Olmstead, Richard Sutch, Gavin Wright. New York: Cambridge University Press, 2006.
Butterfield, Kevin. *The Making of Tocqueville's America: Law and Association in the Early United States*. Chicago: University of Chicago Press, 2015.
Campbell, Bruce A. "Social Federalism: The Constitutional Position of Nonprofit Corporations in Nineteenth-Century America." *Law and History Review* 8 (1990) 149–88.
Carey, Mathew. "Public Charities of Philadelphia." In *Miscellaneous Essays*, edited by Mathew Carey, 153–203. Philadelphia: Carey & Hart, 1830.
Carp, E. Wayne. "Orphanages vs. Adoption: The Triumph of Biological Kinship, 1800–1933." In *With Us Always: A History of Private Charity and Public Welfare*, edited by Donald Critchlow and Charles H. Parker, 123–44. New York: Rowman & Littlefield, 1998.
Cnaan, Ram, et al. *The Newer Deal*. New York: Columbia University Press, 1999.
Cornuelle, Richard. *Reclaiming the American Dream*. New York: Random House, 1965.
Cuninggim, Merrimon. *Private Money and Public Service: The Role of Foundations in American Society*. New York: McGraw-Hill, 1972.

Ginzberg, Lori. *Women and the Work of Benevolence: Morality, Politics, and Class in the Nineteenth-Century United States.* New Haven, CT: Yale University Press, 1990.
Goldwater, Barry. *The Conscience of a Conservative.* Princeton, NJ: Princeton University Press, 1960.
Hall, Peter Dobkin. "A Historical Overview of the Private Nonprofit Sector." In *The Nonprofit Sector: A Research Handbook*, edited by Walter W. Powell, 3–26. New Haven, CT: Yale University Press, 1987.
Hansmann, Henry. "Economic Theories of Nonprofit Organization." In *The Nonprofit Sector: A Research Handbook*, edited by Walter W. Powell, 27–42. New Haven, CT: Yale University Press, 1987.
———. *The Ownership of Enterprise.* Cambridge, MA: Harvard University Press, 1996.
Hawley, Ellis W. "Herbert Hoover, Associationalism, and the Great Depression Relief Crisis of 1930–1933." In *With Us Always: A History of Private Charity and Public Welfare*, edited by Donald Critchlow and Charles H. Parker, 161–90. New York: Rowman & Littlefield, 1998.
Heath, Milton. *Constructive Liberalism: The Role of the State in Economic Development in Georgia to 1860.* Cambridge, MA: Harvard University Press, 1954.
Holcombe, Randall G. *Writing Off Ideas: Taxation, Foundations, and Philanthropy in America.* New Brunswick: Transaction, 2000.
Hoover, Herbert. "Address to the Annual Convention of the American National Red Cross." 13 April 1931. http://www.presidency.ucsb.edu/ws/index.php? pid=22603
Katz, Stanley N., et al. "Legal Changes and Legal Autonomy: Charitable Trusts in New York, 1777–1893." *Law and History Review* 3 (1985) 51–89.
Kaufman, Jason. "Corporate Law and the Sovereignty of States." *American Sociological Review* 73 (2008) 402–25.
Mather, Cotton. *Bonifacius: As Essay Upon the Good . . .* Boston: B. Green, 1710. https://quod.lib.umich.edu/e/evans/N01223.0001.001?view=toc
Misner, Barbara. *"Highly Respectable and Accomplished Ladies": Catholic Women Religious in America, 1790–1850.* New York: Garland, 1988.
Morris, Andrew J.F. *The Limits of Voluntarism: Charity and Welfare from the New Deal through the Great Society.* New York: Cambridge University Press, 2009.
Moss, Candida R., and Joel S. Baden. *Bible Nation: The United States of Hobby Lobby.* Princeton, NJ: Princeton University Press, 2017.
Neem, Johann N. *Creating a Nation of Joiners: Democracy and Civil Society in Early National Massachusetts.* Cambridge, MA: Harvard University Press, 2008.
Nielsen, Waldemar A. *The Endangered Sector.* New York: Columbia University Press, 1979.
O'Neill, Michael. *The Third America: The Emergence of the Nonprofit Sector in the United States.* San Francisco, CA: Jossey-Bass, 1989.
Porterfield, Amanda. *Corporate Spirit: Religion and the Rise of the Modern Corporation.* New York: Oxford University Press, 2018.

Rothman, David J. *The Discovery of the Asylum: Social Order and Disorder in the New Republic*. Rev. ed. New York: Aldine de Gruyter, 2002.
Sander, Kathleen. *The Business of Charity: The Woman's Exchange Movement, 1832–1900*. Urbana, IL: University of Illinois Press, 1998.
Silber, Norman I. *A Corporate Form of Freedom: The Emergence of the Modern Nonprofit Sector*. Boulder, CO: Westview, 2001.
Skowronek, Stephen. *Building a New American State: The Expansion of National Administrative Capacities, 1877–1920*. New York: Cambridge University Press, 1982.
Smith, Adam. *An Inquiry into the Nature and Causes of the Wealth of Nations*. London: W. Strahan and T. Cadell, 1776.
*Statutes of Indiana*. Amherst, NY: Hein Collection. http://home.heinonline.org/content/state-statutes-a-historical-archive
Warner, Amos G., and Mary Coolidge. *American Charities*. 3rd ed. New York: Thomas Y. Crowell, 1919.
Weaver, Warren. *U.S. Philanthropic Foundations: Their History, Structure, Management, and Record*. New York: Harper & Row, 1967.
Wright, Robert E. "Business, Religion, History, and Consilience." In *The Business Turn in American Religious History*, edited by Amanda Porterfield et al., vii–xix. New York: Oxford University Press, 2017.
———. *Corporation Nation*. Philadelphia: University of Pennsylvania Press, 2014.
———. "Corporate Social Responsibility and the Rise of the Non-Profit Sector in America." In *A History of Socially Responsible Business, c.1600–1950*, edited by William A. Pettigrew and David Chan Smith, 117–35. New York: Palgrave Macmillan, 2017.
———. *Financial Exclusion: How Competition Can Fix a Broken System*. Great Barrington, MA: American Institute for Economic Research, 2019.
———. "For- and Non-Profit Special Corporations in America, 1608–1860." In *Research Handbook on the History of Corporate and Company Law*, edited by Harwell Wells, 480–509. Northampton, MA: Edward Elgar, 2018.
———. *Hamilton Unbound: Finance and the Creation of the American Republic*. New York: Praeger, 2002.
———. *One Nation Under Debt: Hamilton, Jefferson, and the History of What We Owe*. New York: McGraw-Hill, 2008.
Wyllie, Irvin G. "The Search for an American Law of Charity, 1776–1844." *The Mississippi Valley Historical Review* 46 (1959) 203–21.
Zunz, Olivier. *Philanthropy in America: A History*. Princeton, NJ: Princeton University Press, 2012.

# Love

CHAPTER 9

# Failure to Thrive in the Lord's Ordered World: Causes for Poverty in the Book of Proverbs

Daniel J. Estes

Human flourishing is a broad subject that includes every area of life. It can refer to political freedom, to educational opportunity, to social wellness, and to psychological wholeness. In this paper, I have limited my topic to poverty, or the absence of economic flourishing, as it is reflected in the book of Proverbs.[1] Given the general correlation in Proverbs between wisdom, righteousness, and life on the one hand, and folly, wickedness, and death on the other hand, what factors cause humans to fail to thrive economically? In other words, what does the book of Proverbs teach about the causes for poverty?

I am firmly committed to exegetical theology, that is, that exegesis of the biblical text must drive and define our theological conclusions. Paul commended the Bereans in Acts 17 because they assessed what he communicated to them by evaluating it in the light of the scriptures. If that was appropriate for Paul's teaching, then it is equally crucial when Christians make claims in fields such as economics. One's economic philosophy must not function as the lens for evaluating scriptural texts, but instead the exegesis of scriptural texts must be the lens through which economic claims are critiqued. It is vital that we never alter our understanding of scripture in order to fit the contours of capitalism or the schema of socialism; rather every human speculation must be scrutinized in the light of what the scriptures teach.

In Proverbs, the general theme of retribution indicates that wisdom leads to life in all of its dimensions, and folly leads to death in all of its manifestations. The retribution principle as formulated by Klaus Koch is a fixed relationship between acts and consequences, in which God does not actively participate in the outworking of the deed/destiny process.[2] Koch's formula of retribution has

---

[1] For a succinct discussion of the vocabulary of wealth and poverty in Proverbs, see Whybray, *Wealth and Poverty*, 11–23. For a detailed exegetical analysis of the relevant texts in Proverbs, see Sandoval, *Discourse of Wealth and Poverty*.

[2] Koch, "Gibt es ein Vergeltungsdogma?" 1–42.

been rightly revised by Patrick Miller, who argues from the biblical data that "while there is always a causal effect in the relationship between someone's or some people's actions and the judgment they receive, that relationship is not necessarily internal but is perceived as resting in the divine decision and not happening apart from that decision or decree."[3] The retribution principle implies that following the path of wisdom will lead necessarily to human flourishing and prosperity, and that it is the path of folly that results in poverty and the failure to thrive in the Lord's ordered world. This formula can be expressed in maxims such as "Acts have consequences," and "You get what you deserve." Or in the memorable words of *The Sound of Music*, "Nothing comes from nothing, and nothing ever could." However, a close reading of Proverbs reveals that in this wisdom collection the causes of poverty are more complex than what the retribution principle alone explains.

## Foolish Behavior Leads to Economic Poverty

It is undeniable that there is much evidence in Proverbs that supports the retribution principle,[4] and therefore that poor people are to blame because of their own foolish and/or wicked acts. Sometimes poverty is attributed to unspecified wickedness and folly. For example, "The righteous eat to their hearts' content, but the stomach of the wicked goes hungry" (Prov. 13.25), and "The wicked are overthrown and are no more, but the house of the righteous stands firm" (Prov. 12.7).[5]

More often in Proverbs the laziness of the sluggard is the specific cause for poverty, a predictable outcome of sloth.[6] In Proverbs 6.10 and 24.33 the sluggard is cited as saying, "A little sleep, a little slumber, a little folding of the hands to rest," as he postpones beginning to work, and then his expected fate is disclosed in 6.11 and 24.34, "and poverty will come on you like a thief and scarcity like an armed man." Alden notes perceptively that these verses do "not say an actual robber victimizes the sleeping man; his sleep itself robs him. In a

---

[3] Miller, *Sin and Judgment*, 134.

[4] For an excellent brief discussion of the theology of retribution in the Old Testament, see Vannoy, "Retribution," 1140–49. He makes the important point that "while there is general agreement that the idea of divine retribution for good and evil is deeply embedded in the OT, the concept does not become solidified into a simplistic dogma in which every misfortune is viewed as evidence of sin and every success is viewed as evidence of obedience and piety" (1141).

[5] Waltke, *Proverbs Chapters 1–15*, 523, notes that the verb *hāpôk* ("overturn") "refers to a sudden upset and reversal of a chain of events or a condition from that hoped for," and that the context in 12.2, 22 turns this verb into a metaphor of divine judgment.

[6] Fox, *Proverbs 10–31*, 571.

sense he robs himself by wasting away his time, talents, and earning power. Precious hours, important opportunities, and years of productivity are squandered because he lacks enthusiasm and initiative."[7] Similarly, "Lazy hands make poverty, but diligent hands bring wealth" (Prov. 10.4), "Those who work their land will have abundant food, but those who chase fantasies[8] will have their fill of poverty" (Prov. 28.19), "All hard work brings a profit, but mere talk leads only to poverty" (Prov. 14.23), and "Do not love sleep or you will grow poor; stay awake and you will have food to spare" (Prov. 20.13). The poverty of the lazy person is not stated explicitly, but it is clearly implied as well in Proverbs 18.9; 19.15; 20.4; and 21.25–26. As Ross remarks trenchantly, "People should be more afraid of idle talk than of hard work. Or, to put it another way, do not just talk about it—Do it!"[9]

A number of sinful attitudes and actions are cited as causes for poverty in Proverbs. These include immorality, because "a companion of prostitutes squanders his wealth" (Prov. 29.3; cf. 5.8–10; 6.26; Luke 15.30). Similarly, presumption can lead to poverty, because "those who trust in their riches will fall" (Prov. 11.28).[10] Loving pleasure, whether that be expressed by drunkenness or gluttony (Prov. 21.17; 23.20–21) impoverishes a person,[11] as also does dishonesty (Prov. 13.11)[12] and a corrupt heart (Prov. 17.20). Greed for acquisition and its converse of miserliness can also result in poverty,

---

[7] Alden, *Proverb*, 57.

[8] Garrett, *Proverbs, Ecclesiastes, Song of Songs*, 226, observes that the Hebrew term *rēqîm* "only describes someone who follows 'empty pursuits.' It could refer to idle fantasies, but it also could be unprofitable occupations or business speculations. The point of the verse is that hard work is the only way to prosperity; anything else is a waste of time."

[9] Ross, "Proverbs," 988.

[10] Clifford, *Proverbs*, 126, comments that the verb *npl* "is used several times of the wicked person's fall into a pit (e.g., 22:14; 26:27; 28:10). In contrast, the righteous are compared to a leaf that not only does not fall but blooms, like the righteous in Ps. 1:3."

[11] McKane, *Proverbs*, 553, reasons, "Feasting and drinking are recipes for poverty, and the man who has a fondness for the extravagances of high living is always short of money and by way of becoming a pauper." Similarly, Kitchen, *Proverbs*, 529, states colorfully, "Industry gives way to indulgence and, soon, indolence and indigence follows."

[12] Instead of the MT *hebel*, rendered by NIV as "dishonest," *BHS* on the basis of the LXX and Vg. readings proposes a metathesis of the first two consonants, thus rendering the word as "haste." Longman, *Proverbs*, 282, argues that this emendation provides a better contrast with the second line of Prov. 13.11. However, the frequent use of *hebel* to speak of what is transitory or non-existent would support the NIV, and it may well be the better reading here.

because "The stingy[13] are eager to get rich and are unaware that poverty awaits them" (Prov. 28.22), and "One person gives freely, yet gains even more; another withholds unduly, but comes to poverty" (Prov. 11.24; cf. 15.27).

In several passages, Proverbs specifically shows how poor financial decisions, and in particular giving surety for the financial obligations of another, can result in poverty. Whether one pledges security for a person who is known (Prov. 17.18) or for a stranger (Prov. 11.15; 20.16;[14] 27.13), he places himself in a precarious situation, because "if you lack the means to pay, your very bed will be snatched from under you" (Prov. 22.26–27). Therefore, the sage urges his son in the strongest terms to free himself from this financial obligation, which he likens to a gazelle in the hand of a hunter and a bird in the snare of the fowler (Prov. 6.1–5). Although generosity is frequently enjoined in the book of Proverbs,[15] that should be in the form of gifts rather than by guaranteeing another's loan.

There is, then, ample evidence in the book of Proverbs that poverty is often attributable to the foolish behavior of the poor, and this accords well with the retribution principle. However, that is not the whole story that Proverbs has to tell.

### Sinful Actions by Other People can Cause Poverty

It is also evident in numerous passages in Proverbs that one's poverty can be attributed to the sinful actions of others that have adversely affected one's financial condition. In other words, though in many cases people are to blame for their own poverty, there are other cases in which their poverty is caused by others, and it is therefore beyond their own direct control.[16] As Washington

---

[13] The Hebrew expression rendered by NIV as "stingy" is literally "evil eye" (cf. 23.6). Hubbard, *Proverbs*, 434, explains that this "is a graphic figure for an attitude of ill-will toward others, motivated by jealousy, hatred, or some kindred disposition. Greed is surely its chief expression in this passage, as 'hastens after riches' (see v. 20) attests."

[14] Fox, *Proverbs 10–31*, 669, observes, "The man who gives surety for others' loans will end up forfeiting his own property. Like 11:15a, this proverb assumes the voice of an unidentified onlooker to dramatize the dangers of giving loan guarantees. Here it sounds like the judge or creditor speaking."

[15] For a brief discussion of the data in Proverbs relating to generosity, see Estes, *Handbook*, 239–43.

[16] Looking at the Old Testament more broadly, Wright, *Old Testament Ethics*, 170–71, argues that a principal cause for poverty is oppression, including exploitation of the socially weak; exploitation of the economically weak; exploitation of the ethnically weak; royal excess, corruption, and abuse of power; and judicial corruption and false accusation." See also Barnard, "Causes of Poverty," 448–65.

assesses the evidence, "of all the passages in Proverbs which take an evaluative stance on wealth and poverty, less than a third imply that the rich and the poor deserve their fates. More frequent is the recognition that much existing wealth and poverty is the result of murder, extortion, and deceit."[17] This data in Proverbs, then, coheres with the Old Testament legal stipulations, as Wong concludes, "Biblical laws were written to protect the poor from exploitation and help them out of the cycle of poverty ... No blame was placed on the poor because many became impoverished through no fault of their own. Even when someone fell into poverty through their own fault, the overriding concern was their restoration. This was based on God's attributes and Israel's covenant with God, and consequently with one another."[18]

In general terms, injustice by wicked people can cause poverty, as is implied in Proverbs 29.7, "The righteous care about justice for the poor, but the wicked have no such concern." As Murphy observes, this saying implies a judicial case in which the just acknowledge what is right, but the wicked fail to have a concern for what is right.[19] Therefore, even though there is the potential of ample food for the poor in an unplowed field, "injustice sweeps it away" (Prov. 13.23; cf. Amos 5.11; Jas. 5.4–5).[20]

Several sayings in Proverbs decry oppression by the rich and powerful against the poor and weak.[21] For example, "a tyrannical ruler practices extortion" (Prov. 28.16). In laconic words of description that imply disapproval, Proverbs 22.7 observes, "The rich rule over the poor, and the borrower is slave to the lender,"[22] and Proverbs 22.16 describes "one who oppresses the poor to increase his wealth." When "the poor plead for mercy," they find that they are powerless when "the rich answer harshly" (Prov. 18.23). This attitude is categorically condemned in Proverbs 14.31, "Whoever

---

[17] Washington, *Wealth and Poverty*, 3.

[18] Wong, "Nature and Theological Basis for Poverty," 194–95.

[19] Murphy, *Proverbs*, 221.

[20] Hubbard, *Proverbs*, 346 concludes, "Whatever else justice may mean in the Old Testament, it calls for the rights of every sector of society and all parties in any transaction to be safeguarded."

[21] For an analysis of some prominent structural factors that cause poverty in the contemporary world, see Sider, *Rich Christians*, 133–79.

[22] McKane, *Proverbs*, 566, compares the frequent prophetic denunciations of the oppressors of the poor. He says, "As the prophets saw it, the power of the mortgage secured the eviction of the peasant and destroyed a style of life which was indispensable to the social well-being of the community." For textual support, he cites Mic. 2.2, 8–9; 3.1–2; Isa. 5.8.

oppresses the poor shows contempt for their Maker, but whoever is kind to the needy honors God."[23]

A particular manifestation of oppression is the exploitation of the needy. This could take specific form in appropriating the land that properly belonged to those who were powerless to stop it, as in Proverbs 23.10 (cf. 22.28), "Do not move an ancient boundary stone or encroach on the fields of the fatherless." As Fox observes, "A field untended or unprotected during the owner's minority would be a tempting target for encroachment."[24] It could occur even in the courts in which justice was supposed to be upheld, because Proverbs 22.22 warns, "Do not exploit the poor because they are poor and do not crush the needy in court," and continues to say in v. 23 that "the LORD will take up their case and will exact life for life."[25] More generally, Prov 30:11–14 describes the despicable behaviors of the wicked, concluding by speaking of "those whose teeth are swords and whose jaws are set with knives to devour the poor from the earth and the needy from among mankind." Pleins observes, "Here the wisdom writer approximates the social criticism of the prophets using traditional phrasing shared with the prophets. If the prophets offer any clue to the interpretation of this material, the agents of the devouring of the *'ānî* and *'ebyôn* are the ruling elite."[26]

To compound their problem, the oppressed poor are left to fend for themselves, because "one who has unreliable friends[27] soon comes to ruin" (Prov. 18.24). Because they have no effective voice sufficient to defend them in legal cases (cf. Ps. 127.5), Lemuel's mother urges him, "Speak up for those who cannot speak for themselves, for the rights of all who are destitute. Speak

---

[23] Ross, "Proverbs," 991, reasons, "How people treat the poor displays their faith in the Creator. Here is the doctrine of the Creation in its practical outworking. Anyone who oppresses the 'poor' (*'ōšēq*) shows contempt for his Maker, for that poor person also is the image of God. Showing favor for the poor (*ḥōnēn*) honors God because God commanded this to be done (see Matt 25:31–46; cf. Prov 14:21; 17:5; 19:17)."

[24] Fox, *Proverbs 10–31*, 730. Waltke, *Proverbs Chapters 15–31*, 244–45, states that throughout the ancient Near East the king bore responsibility to protect the poor who were too weak to defend their own rights.

[25] Garrett, *Proverbs, Ecclesiastes, Song of Songs*, 194, observes, "Yahweh is viewed as protector of the oppressed. Here the text warns the powerful not to use legal devices to exploit the poor, lest they find themselves arraigned before a much higher judge. The warning is punctuated with an image of God doing to the rich exactly what they do to the poor (v. 23)."

[26] Pleins, "Poverty," 64. He cites parallel language in Amos 4.1; 5.11; 6.1–6; Isa. 3.13–14; Jer. 5.4–5, 27–28.

[27] Fox, *Proverbs 10–31*, 646–47, explains that the contrast in Prov. 18.24 is between companions who are good only for socializing and a truly committed friend who is as reliable as a brother.

up and judge fairly; defend the rights of the poor and needy" (Prov. 31.8–9). He must "champion the cause of the one who cannot otherwise get a fair hearing."[28]

This evidence from the book of Proverbs indicates that poverty in some cases is caused by the sinful actions of those who prey upon the needy, and that the wicked oppressors are to blame for the resultant poverty.

**The Good Life is not Necessarily the Prosperous Life**

It is often assumed that the prosperous life, the life that flourishes, is measured by financial affluence. In the book of Proverbs, however, the validity of this assumption is called into question by a number of "better is" sayings. As Waltke notes, Koch's "deed-destiny nexus is modified by counterproverbs that contradict it," specifically several sayings that "link poverty with righteousness and wealth with wickedness and so make it perfectly plain that deeds of piety and morality do not invariably lead in experience to the destiny of social and physical benefits."[29] In these proverbs, it is evident that there are several things that are better than riches, and thus equating wealth with the good life may well misunderstand what makes for true prosperity. These verses suggest that a faulty value system may be to blame for misperceptions of what constitutes wealth and poverty.

Several times in Proverbs it is stated that wisdom is better than riches, and in fact Wisdom is personified as saying, "Choose my instruction instead of silver, knowledge rather than choice gold, for wisdom is more precious than rubies, and nothing you desire can compare with her . . . My fruit is better than fine gold; what I yield surpasses choice silver" (Prov. 8.10–11, 19). The sages also exclaim, "How much better to get wisdom than gold, to get insight rather than silver!" (Prov. 16.16), and "Blessed are those who find wisdom, those who gain understanding, for she is more profitable than silver and yields better returns than gold. She is more precious than rubies; nothing you desire can compare with her" (Prov. 3.13–15).[30] Therefore, the son is challenged, "The beginning is wisdom is this: Get wisdom. Though it cost all you have, get understanding" (Prov. 4.7). Cohen reasons well, "Unless one realizes how essential it is to possess this mental and ethical endowment, he will be

---

[28] Waltke, *Proverbs 15–31*, 509.

[29] Waltke, "Proverbs," 1090. For detailed analysis of the relevant texts in the book of Psalms, see Van Leeuwen, "Wealth and Poverty," 25–36.

[30] Longman, *Proverbs*, 136, observes that the poem in Prov. 3.13–20 "is a description of the qualities and benefits of wisdom, which serves as an explanation for why the person who finds wisdom is blessed. The purpose of such a poem is to encourage those who have not yet begun their quest for wisdom to begin it."

disinclined to make the effort. Having appreciated its essential place in life, he will leave nothing undone to acquire it."[31]

It is also evident in Proverbs that righteousness, or living according to the standard of the Lord, is better than riches. This is stated explicitly in Proverbs 16.8, "Better a little with righteousness than much gain with injustice." More implicit are sayings such as the following: "Wealth is worthless in the day of wrath,[32] but righteousness delivers from death" (Prov. 11.4), and "Better the poor whose walk is blameless than the rich whose ways are perverse" (Prov. 28.6). From these sayings, McKane concludes, "The estate of the poor man whose way of life is morally blameless is better than that of the wealthy man who is sick with a moral turpitude."[33]

Proverbs also indicates that good character is better than riches. This is clearly taught in sayings such as, "A good name is more desirable than great riches; to be esteemed is better than silver or gold" (Prov. 22.1), and "A wife of noble character who can find? She is worth far more than rubies" (Prov. 31.10). Fox notes that a good name refers to how a person is esteemed by others, and concludes, "What makes this kind of regard important is that it is gained through wisdom (Prov 3:4; 13:15a) and is not merely prestige, but true honor."[34] More indirectly, "A kindhearted woman gains honor, but ruthless men gain only wealth" (Prov. 11.16), "Better to be lowly in spirit along with the oppressed than to share plunder with the proud" (Prov. 16.19),[35] and "What a person desires is unfailing love; better to be poor than a liar" (Prov. 19.22). Kitchen comments insightfully that "violent oppression may gain one a measure of tangible, worldly wealth, but that, by gracious living, one may achieve the far more lasting and valuable treasure of 'honor' in the sight of man and God (Prov. 22:1; 31:28, 30)."[36]

---

[31] Cohen, *Proverbs*, 22.

[32] Some commentators have read "the day of wrath" here in the prophetic sense of eschatological judgment, citing as support passages such as Ezek. 7.19 and Zeph. 1.15, 18, but this phrase could also be viewed more generally as a disastrous devastation that threatens life, and that is likely its nuance in Prov. 11.4.

[33] McKane, *Proverbs*, 628.

[34] Fox, *Proverbs 10–31*, 694.

[35] Longman, *Proverbs*, 334, explains, "While riches are not negative, they are not to be gotten at the expense of humility. Humility is valued because it is not the road to pride. Further, read in conjunction with the previous proverb, if wealth comes to the wise, it is likely to be short-lived or a prelude to disaster anyway. The 'needy' are contrasted with those who 'divide plunder,' a warfare term for the victorious dividing the spoils among themselves. Perhaps having won the victory breeds pride, if the victory is thought to come because of human skill or strength."

[36] Kitchen, *Proverbs*, 249.

In addition, riches come in second place to good relationships in Proverbs 15.17, which says, "Better a small serving of vegetables with love than a fattened calf with hatred." Preeminently, the fear of the Lord exceeds riches, because "Better a little with the fear of the LORD than great wealth with turmoil" (Prov. 15.16). Murphy observes, "Fear of the Lord is the beginning of wisdom, but it is no guarantee of prosperity and riches, even if these are the benefits promised to the wise. Wealth is preferable to poverty, but not at any price; it does not guarantee happiness."[37]

## Some Aspects of Yahweh's Moral Order are Inscrutable

Although the book of Proverbs often draws correlations between acts and consequences, it also contains several sayings that teach that there are some things that only the Lord controls and understands fully, and that includes why some people experience poverty. These maxims, which provide a counter-voice to the prominent theme of retribution in Proverbs, are taken up in greater detail in Psalms 49 and 73, and especially in the book of Job. They imply that humans cannot always discern in particular cases why people are experiencing poverty, and therefore they may be unable to prescribe appropriate remedies.

For example, Proverbs 16.9 states, "In their hearts humans plan their course, but the LORD establishes their steps." Similarly, Proverbs 19.21 observes, "Many are the plans in a person's heart, but it is the LORD's purpose that prevails." In life, "a person's steps are directed by the LORD," so "how then can anyone understand their own way?" (Prov. 20.24). Murphy rightly regards these sayings as "warnings that one must be open to the uncertainties along the way. The final result is the Lord's doing, over which humans have no real control, and it may not be the 'success' that is yearned for."[38] In Proverbs, the Lord by his wisdom orders his world in ways that are not always discernable, predictable, or understandable by humans, so as to teach his people to trust in him with all their heart, rather than leaning on their own understanding (Prov. 3.5). Waltke notes perceptively that "the Lord does not uphold a moral order in a tidy calculus wherein righteousness is immediately rewarded and wickedness is punished. If that were so, people would confound pleasure with morality; all would behave righteously for selfish reasons, not out of pure virtue based in faith, hope, and love . . . The

---

[37] Murphy, *Proverbs*, 113.

[38] Murphy, *Proverbs*, 121. Similarly, Garrett, *Proverbs, Ecclesiastes, Song of Songs*, 178, concludes, "In the final analysis we do not understand all that is going on around us or happening to us, and we are guided through life in ways we do not recognize. Trusting in divine providence therefore is best."

wise trust the Lord to uphold his ethical proverbs in his own time and in his own way, even when the wicked prosper and the righteous suffer."[39]

## Conclusion

The information in Proverbs relating to the various causes of poverty is clear, but how is it to be construed and applied? Evangelical Christians affirm that the Bible as the authoritative word of God is the standard for their belief and their behavior, the divine mandate for their faith and life. Nevertheless, evangelical Christians have taken several disparate approaches to the data in Proverbs on poverty. Some evangelicals barely consider the biblical data on poverty when they formulate public policy. They may not be aware of what the book of Proverbs teaches about the various causes of poverty. Although they regard the Bible as the authority for their personal piety and for church teaching, in practice the Bible does not control how they live in or think about their community. This is a stance of fragmentation or disintegration of truth, in which the Christian faith is not linked with life beyond individual piety. This position in effect limits the realm of God's authority, but the Bible insists that the Lord rules as king over all of his creation, not just over the individual lives of his worshipers. This approach is a far cry from Abraham Kuyper's insistence that there is not one square inch in the universe that lies outside the kingly rule of the Lord.[40]

Other evangelical Christians select and accept some portions of the biblical data on poverty, but not all that it teaches. Several years ago, I attended a forum in which a leader in the Christian Left and a leader in the Christian Right debated the Christian approach to poverty. I heard one speaker cite scripture verses that supported his commitment to social justice, as though the Bible said nothing about the factors by which individuals are responsible for their own financial distress. The other speaker cited verses that supported his commitment to free-market capitalism, as though the Bible said nothing about structural factors that produce and perpetuate poverty, factors that are beyond the control of the poor. When the Bible is cited only selectively to support a position that has been adopted on other grounds, then the Bible becomes merely a proof text, and not the final authority. By selecting only part of the biblical data, this approach, whether from the Left or from the Right, has the effect of denying the plenary inspiration of the Bible, because not all of the biblical data is regarded as of equal relevance.[41]

---

[39] Waltke, "Proverbs," 1093. See also the wide-ranging exegetical argument against eudaemonism and its manifestation in the prosperity gospel by Kaiser, "Old Testament Promise of Material Blessings," 151–70.

[40] Kuyper, *Centennial Reader*, 488.

[41] It is also important to consider the fact that most of the published discussions of wealth and poverty in the book of Proverbs have been written by scholars in the

It is my contention that evangelical Christians need to take seriously the verbal, plenary inspiration of the Bible, and as a result hold consistently to its final authority for all of faith and life. Our primary allegiance must not be to our preferred political, economic, and social ideologies, but to all that God has revealed in his authoritative word. If the Bible is used merely to provide scriptural and theological support for one's ideology, then the Bible has in effect bowed to that ideology, and that ideology has in reality become an idol. The Reformation commitment to *sola scriptura* rightly insists that the Bible alone is the ultimate authority by which all truth claims are measured, and that standard must be applied to all areas of inquiry, including how we regard poverty and its causes. When viewed from that perspective, the book of Proverbs has much to contribute to the conversation about human flourishing.

Bibliography

Alden, Robert L. *Proverbs: A Commentary on an Ancient Book of Timeless Advice*. Grand Rapids: Baker, 1983.
Barnard, Philip Alan. "The Causes of Poverty: Is a Biblical Understanding Reflected in the Experiences of Today's Poor?" *Missiology* 44 (2016) 448–65.
Clifford, Richard J. *Proverbs: A Commentary*. Louisville: Westminster John Knox, 1999.
Cohen, A. *Proverbs*. Soncino Books of the Bible. London: Soncino, 1952.
Estes, Daniel J. *Handbook on the Wisdom Books and Psalms*. Grand Rapids: Baker Academic, 2005.
Fox, Michael V. *Proverbs 10–31*. Anchor Yale Bible 18B. New Haven: Yale University Press, 2009.
Garrett, Duane A. *Proverbs, Ecclesiastes, Song of Songs*. New American Commentary 14. Nashville: Broadman, 1993.
Hubbard, David A. *Proverbs*. Communicator's Commentary 15A. Dallas: Word, 1989.
Kaiser, Walter C. "The Old Testament Promise of Material Blessings and the Contemporary Believer." *Trinity Journal* 9 (1988) 151–70.
Kimilike, Lechion Peter. *Poverty in the Book of Proverbs: An African Transformational Hermeneutic of Proverbs on Poverty*. Bible & Theology in Africa 7. New York: Lang, 2008.
Kitchen, John A. *Proverbs*. Mentor. Fearn, UK: Christian Focus, 2006.
Koch, Klaus. "Gibt es ein Vergeltungsdogma im Alten Testament?" *Zeitschrift für Theologie und Kirche* 52 (1955) 1–42.
Kuyper, Abraham. *Abraham Kuyper: A Centennial Reader*. Edited by James D. Bratt. Grand Rapids: Eerdmans, 1998.

Longman, Tremper. *Proverbs*. Baker Commentary on the Old Testament Wisdom and Psalms. Grand Rapids: Baker Academic, 2006.
McKane, William. *Proverbs*. Old Testament Library. Philadelphia: Westminster, 1970.
Miller, Patrick D. *Sin and Judgment in the Prophets: A Stylistic and Theological Analysis*. Chico, CA: Scholars, 1982.
Murphy, Roland E. *Proverbs*. Word Biblical Commentary 22. Nashville: Thomas Nelson, 1998.
Pleins, J. David. "Poverty in the Social World of the Wise." *Journal for the Study of the Old Testament* 37 (1987) 61–78.
Ross, Allen P. "Proverbs." In *The Expositor's Bible Commentary*, edited by Frank E. Gaebelein, 5:881–1134. Grand Rapids: Zondervan, 1991.
Sandoval, Timothy J. *The Discourse of Wealth and Poverty in the Book of Proverbs*. Biblical Interpretation Series 77. Leiden: Brill, 2006.
Sider, Ronald J. *Rich Christians in an Age of Hunger: Moving from Affluence to Generosity*. 5th ed. Nashville: Thomas Nelson, 2005.
Van Leeuwen, Raymond C. "Wealth and Poverty: System and Contradiction in Proverbs." *Hebrew Studies* 33 (1992) 25–36.
Vannoy, J. Robert. "Retribution: Theology of." In *New International Dictionary of Old Testament Theology and Exegesis*, edited by Willem A. VanGemeren, 4:1140–49. Grand Rapids: Zondervan, 1996.
Waltke, Bruce K. *The Book of Proverbs Chapters 1–15*. The New International Commentary on the Old Testament. Grand Rapids: Eerdmans, 2004.
———. *The Book of Proverbs Chapters 15–31*. The New International Commentary on the Old Testament. Grand Rapids: Eerdmans, 2005.
———. "Proverbs: Theology of." In *New International Dictionary of Old Testament Theology and Exegesis*, edited by Willem A. VanGemeren, 4:1079–94. Grand Rapids: Zondervan, 1996.
Washington, Harold C. *Wealth and Poverty in the Instruction of Amenemope and the Hebrew Proverbs*. Society of Biblical Literature Dissertation Series 142. Atlanta: Scholars, 1994.
Whybray, R. N. *Wealth and Poverty in the Book of Proverbs*, 11–23. Journal for the Study of the Old Testament Supplements 99. Sheffield: Sheffield Academic Press, 1990.
Wong, Fook-Kong. "A Reflection on the Nature and Theological Basis of Poverty and Debt Laws in the Pentateuch." *Review and Expositor* 111 (2014) 187–95.
Wright, Christopher J. H. *Old Testament Ethics for the People of God*. Downers Grove, IL: InterVarsity, 2004.

CHAPTER 10

# Paul, Poverty, and Economic Justice

John W. Taylor

Introduction

Our purpose here is to investigate Paul's understanding of economic justice and poverty in its first-century context. Moses Finley claimed that the ancients lacked not simply the vocabulary of economics but they even "lacked the concept of an 'economy'."[1] Nevertheless, given that Paul discusses issues such as wealth, poverty, and giving practices, it is worth asking whether there is some concept of economic justice that can be discerned in his writings. The focus will be limited to economic issues, broadly construed.

There have, of course, been numerous attempts to examine Paul in the light of socio-economic concerns. Particular attention has been paid to establishing the socio-economic location of Paul and his churches through the efforts of scholars such as Edwin Judge, Gerd Thiessen, Ronald Hock, and Wayne Meeks.[2] The so-called "new consensus,"[3] which developed from their work, differed somewhat from the earlier position of Adolf Deissman, who argued on the basis of literary remains that the early church was virtually universally poor, and said, "The social structure of Primitive Christianity points emphatically to the lower, occasionally to the middle class. Primitive Christianity stands in but slight relationship to the upper class at the beginning."[4] The cumulative effect of the "new consensus" was to highlight the importance of socio-economic factors in interpreting Paul's letters, and to demonstrate that the Pauline churches were not homogenous, but contained a mixture of people from various social strata, though weighted strongly towards the poor rather than the rich. The tension created by this socio-economic diversity can help explain some of the issues which Paul addresses, such as the behavior of the Corinthians at the Lord's supper.

---

[1] Finley, *Ancient Economy*, 21.

[2] See Judge, *Social Pattern*, 85; Theissen, *Social Setting*; Hock, *Social Context*; and Meeks, *First Urban Christians*. Also notable is Hengel, *Property and Riches*.

[3] Malherbe, *Social Aspects*, 31.

[4] Deissmann, *New Light on the New Testament*, 66.

More recently there have been a series of attempts to locate the economic level of the early Christians with more specificity, including the work of Justin Meggitt, who, resisting the new consensus, found the evidence for "belief in the presence of affluent groups in the Pauline churches" to be "not convincing."[5] He returned to Deissman's view that the early believers were mired in grim poverty. The work of Steven Friesen and Bruce Longenecker has sought to assess the status of the early church in terms of a precise economic scale.[6] The result has been a reiteration of the severe poverty of most of the early church, while allowing for the presence of a number of people at some higher economic levels. Scheidel and Friesen argue that

> the top 1.5 per cent of households [in the Roman Empire] controlled around one-fifth of total income; that economically "middling" non-elite groups accounted for a modest share of the population (around 10 per cent) but perhaps another fifth of income; and that the vast majority of the population lived close to subsistence but cumulatively generated more than half of overall output.[7]

By way of comparison, according to the World Economic Forum, as of 2016, the richest 1 per cent in India controlled 53 per cent of the nation's wealth (compared to 37 per cent in the USA), the top 10 per cent controlled 76 per cent, while the poorest 50 per cent of the population controlled only 4 per cent of the wealth.[8] Of course, this comparison says nothing about the actual living standards of the rich or poor. To be poor in the twenty-first century is, for most, very different from being poor in the first century.

There is no doubt that Paul is concerned about the economic suffering of the early believers, and to some extent with the suffering of those outside the church. He reminds believers of their obligations to meet the financial needs of the poor, particularly poor believers (2 Cor. 9.12; Titus 3.14), to support the work of travelling Christian missionaries (1 Cor. 9.4–6), to support church leaders (1 Tim. 5.7–8), and to be generous with hospitality (Rom. 12.13). The question, however, is whether Paul has in mind some particular vision of economic justice, and, if so, how does he envisage that justice coming about? Can Paul be brought into modern arguments about equality of outcome versus equality of opportunity? Given the current political and media interest in

---

[5] Meggitt, *Paul, Poverty and Survival*, 153.

[6] Friesen, "Poverty in Pauline Studies," 323–61; Longenecker, *Remember the Poor*.

[7] Scheidel and Friesen, "Distribution of Income," 62–63. The study's comment that the economic control of the elite and middling groups meant "leaving not much more than half of all income for all remaining households," 85, suggests that authors were thinking in terms of a zero-sum game, where the wealth of the upper classes came at the expense of the poor.

[8] Anon., "Inequality in India."

economic and social justice issues, there is a danger of anachronism, whereby modern language and concepts are read into Paul. Edwin Judge warned against anachronistic, ideological interpretations of early Christianity:

> Given a belief in the class struggle, it is easy to take a group of Galilean peasants, add the community of goods, Paul "working with his hands", and the "not many wise . . . , not many mighty, not many noble" at Corinth, and thus discover a movement of protest among the working classes.[9]

Nevertheless, efforts continue to enlist the New Testament on the side of an economic justice agenda taking anti-capitalist form. Richard Horsley, for example, says that "Global capitalism has become the new form of empire, with one percent of the population becoming ever richer and the remaining ninety-nine percent ever poorer."[10] Society, he says, has a biblical obligation to ensure economic livelihood for all, including "food and shelter, health care, education, transportation, and some sort of support network" and economic justice, which requires "an end to or perhaps a roll-back of privatization."[11] Similar ideas are held by Sylvia Keesmat and Brian Walsh, who complain that "in this kind of economy money can grow and a small minority of people can become incredibly rich while the majority of the world's population sink deeper and deeper into poverty."[12] What should be done? They argue that, "for starters, we need to get out of the markets. Christians need to abandon the financial markets and begin to develop more just ways to invest the resources entrusted to us."[13] However, their assumption that the poor are getting poorer is incorrect.[14]

Is the gap between rich and poor, which exercises so many, a concern for Paul? What kind of concern, if any, does he show for economic equality or justice, and how does this compare or contrast with other views of his time? We shall focus particularly on asking whether Paul sees poverty or economic inequality as an issue of justice (or injustice), and, if so, how? To begin with, though we shall address the question in the Roman and Jewish context in which Paul lived.

---

[9] Judge, *Social Distinctives*, 36–37.

[10] Horsley, "Economic Justice in the Bible," 415–16.

[11] Horsley, "Economic Justice in the Bible," 430.

[12] Keesmat and Walsh, "Jesus and the Justice of God," 69.

[13] Keesmat and Walsh, "Jesus and the Justice of God," 86.

[14] According to the World Bank, "Decline of Global Extreme Poverty," "the percentage of people living in extreme poverty globally fell to a new low of 10 percent in 2015," down from 36 percent in 1990. Extreme poverty is defined on living on less than $1.90 per day.

## The Romans, Poverty, and Justice

### Explanations of Poverty

There is little sustained reflection on the causes of poverty in the extant literature of the early Roman Empire, but what we have indicates multiple explanations of poverty. Cicero lamented the failures of the grain harvest which caused great suffering, but also condemned "the avarice of the dealers" who hoarded or diverted grain during crises (*Dom.* 11–12). Tacitus records that food shortages and famine were seen as ill omens (*Annals* 12.43). Plutarch said that "poverty is never dishonorable in itself, but only when it is a mark of sloth, intemperance, extravagance or thoughtlessness" (*Comp. Arist.* 4.1). Poverty can also be inflicted on people, the result of the unscrupulous use of power (*Agis.* 5.3). Plutarch distinguished poverty caused by "laziness, soft living and extravagance," which is "disgraceful and reprehensible" (*Aud. Poet.* 23F–24A), from poverty caused by misfortune, or, literally, by fate (τυχή), or the malevolent daimons.[15] Epictetus shares the Stoic attribution of poverty to the divine will, and with it, therefore, the need to accept poverty: "I have been poor because it was your will, but I was content also" (*Disc.* 3.5.8). Seneca reports how the teaching of the Stoic Attalus made him (temporarily) desire to be poor (*Ep. Luc.* 93). Voluntary poverty, though rare, was a possibility, as was the practice among the Cynics.[16]

### Responses to Poverty

There were also multiple responses to poverty in the empire. These included occasional public benefaction by the wealthy in times of crisis, such as supplying grain during a famine,[17] though the motive was often the honor and recognition the benefaction engendered.[18] A free grain dole was available to Roman citizens in Rome during the early empire,[19] though that, of course, still left out many of the poor.[20] Julius Caesar reduced recipients of grain from 320,000 to 150,000 in 46 BC (Suetonius, *Divus Julius* 41). Augustus claimed, "I furnished from my own purse and my own patrimony tickets for grain and money, sometimes to a hundred thousand persons, sometimes to many more"

---

[15] See Armitage, *Theories of Poverty*, 84–91. He notes that Plutarch's attribution of poverty to impersonal fate was a way of removing the gods from direct responsibility, thus maintaining their virtue.

[16] Malherbe, *Paul and the Popular Philosophers*, 19, and *Moral Exhortation*, 38–39.

[17] See Winter, *Seek the Welfare*, 27.

[18] Longenecker, *Remember the Poor*, 72.

[19] See Rowland, "Grain Dole," 71–72.

[20] Garnsey, *Famine and Food Supply*, 213.

(*Res Gest.* 18). In early second-century AD Italy the state lent money to landowners at a low rate (5 per cent) with the interest payable to local community funds to help poor children.[21] Public works such as the building of aqueducts made life in the cities easier for everyone, including the poor.[22] The growing practice of manumission of slaves formed a class of freedmen, who gradually gained status,[23] and many of whom were able to prosper, such that "the 'wealth of freedmen' became proverbial."[24] But overall there is scarce evidence that structural solutions were sought for poverty, that poverty was considered a justice issue, or that poverty was something that should be addressed in a systematic way. Attention was usually only paid to the poor in times of crisis, such as famine. Perhaps this is to be expected, given that poverty was the lot of the vast majority of people, and that the governing elite were insulated from its effects. There is some evidence of private almsgiving to the poor; the fact that there were complaints about beggars says that there were some people who gave to beggars.[25] There is limited evidence that the Roman custom of patronage sometimes helped the rural poor.[26] And there is also evidence of mutual help among peasant farmers (Dio, *Oration* 7.68–69). Finally, just as some had a broadly religious explanation of poverty, attributing it to fate, evil magic, or to the whims or judgments of the gods and daimons, so also some sought wealth through charms, oracles, offerings, and the like.[27]

*Justice and Poverty*

The Romans prided themselves on their justice. Augustus, writing his own funerary inscription, describes a gold shield which was mounted in his honor in the senate-house in Rome, which acclaimed his justice, along with his virtue, mercy and piety (*Res Gestae* 34). According to the poet Ovid, the emperor Tiberius was honored with a triumph in AD 12, after his return from military victory in Pannonia, and he offered incense on "sacred fires" to

---

[21] Edmondson, "Economic Life in the Roman Empire," 678.

[22] So, e.g., around 100 BC, Lucius Betilienus Varus built a public bath, reservoir, aqueduct and water pipes for the city of Aletrium, and was honored with a statue (*CIL* 10.5807), Lewis and Reinhold, *Roman Civilization*, 1:461.

[23] The *lex papia Poppaea* (AD 9), e.g., allowed freeborn men to marry freedwomen, Vermote, "Roman Freedmen," 151.

[24] Lewis and Reinhold, *Roman Civilization*, 2:167. Horace mocked the wealth and status of Menas, a freedmen, formerly a slave in shackles: "*Fortuna non mutat genus*" ("Fortune does not change nature," *Epod.* IV.6).

[25] Longenecker, *Remember the Poor*, 74.

[26] See Garnsey and Woolf, "Rural Poor," 158–67.

[27] See Knapp, *Invisible Romans*, 13–23.

Augustan Justice, that is to say, the justice of his step-father Augustus (*Ex Ponto* 2.1.32–33). Shortly afterwards, he dedicated a sculpture of Justice, probably on the same site. Ovid wrote, "No god is more lenient than our prince. Justice moderates his powers. Caesar recently established her in a marble shrine, but long ago in the temple of his heart" (*Ex Ponto* 3.6.23–26). A contemporary addition to the Fasti Praenestini calendar inscription (*Inscr It.* 13.2.17) notes that "Tiberius Caesar dedicated the statue of Augustan Justice when Plancus and Silius were consuls."[28] A dedicatory inscription on the "Monument of the Roads" in Patara, from the citizens of Lycia to the Emperor Claudius, honors him for building roads throughout the region, and for "having recovered concord, the equal administration of justice [τὴν ἴσην δικαιοδοσίαν] and the ancestral laws."[29]

This inscription illustrates a key focus for Roman discussion of justice. For the Romans, with their strong legal apparatus, justice meant the fair application of the law. The Emperor Claudius established a number of laws which protected certain classes of people from poverty or oppression. These included laws protecting women's dowries, a law forbidding masters who had abandoned their elderly or sick slaves from reasserting their ownership, and a law making the killing of a sick slave a matter of murder.[30] Some idealized the administration of Roman law, claiming that the poor and rich were equal before the law. Seneca the Elder dramatizes the example of a poor man whose rich neighbor burned down his tree and his house. The poor man claims his legal rights, "There is no difference at law between you and a poor man."[31] Paul's call to avoid public lawsuits between believers (1 Cor. 6.1–8),[32] along with several negative accounts in the New Testament of Roman court proceedings (John 18.28–40; 19.1–22; Acts 16.19–40; 24.1–27), point to a reality that was far below the Roman ideal.

---

[28] Latin text: *signum Iustitiae Augus[tae Ti(berius) Caesar dedicavit Planco] et Silio co(n)s(ulibus)*. For discussion, see Lott, "August Justice," 263–370. Lott suggests that the belief in the recent conflict as a just war may lie behind the sacrifices to justice personified as a goddess.

[29] Jones, "Claudian Monument," 163. See also Onur, "'Monument of the Roads' at Patara," 570–77.

[30] Scramuzza, "Personality of the Emperor," 331. Other laws focused on the protection of wards and children. It should not be supposed, of course, that Claudius was a model of enlightened benevolence. Suetonius, *Claudius* 34.2, comments, "When any person was to be put to the torture, or criminal punished for parricide, he was impatient for the execution, and would have it performed in his own presence."

[31] Seneca, *Controversiae* 5.5. For further examples, see Larsen, "Representation of Poverty," 105–106.

[32] See the discussion in Winter, *After Paul Left Corinth*, 58–71.

There was no assumption that poverty was *prima facie* evidence of injustice or oppression. Quite the contrary, the poor were frequently regarded as "responsible for their own destitution by their own moral failings,"[33] and "The regular attribution of poverty to vice (whether extravagance or laziness) was correlated with contempt for the poor."[34] Of course, the evidence we have for the status of the poor in the early Roman Empire comes from the wealthy and educated.[35] The poor left little record of their passing, nor independent record of their opinions. For some of the wealthy, at least, poverty was evidence of *justice*, not injustice.

The exception may be where poverty was caused by the abuse of power. Not everyone thought of the Romans as just. Even Cicero laments, "All the provinces are mourning, all the autonomous communities are complaining, indeed all foreign kingdoms are protesting over Roman greed and Roman injustice."[36] Evidence from Egypt during the reign of Nero points to significant numbers of people fleeing the district in which they resided, in order to avoid the burden of Roman taxation and compulsory public service.[37] It seemed that Rome treated Egypt as storehouse to be raided, and gave little back. Flight was also a common response to the terrors and trials of slavery.[38] A small but potent ancient literature laments the injustices slaves suffered under Roman masters.[39]

## Poverty and Injustice in Early Judaism

*Explanations of Poverty*

Some of the explanations of poverty in early Judaism are similar to those found in Roman thought. Several of them are found in the one book, Sirach.

---

[33] Osborne, "Roman Poverty in Context," 14.

[34] Armitage, *Theories of Poverty*, 61.

[35] Woolf, "Writing Poverty in Rome," 94, "Latin writing about poverty almost never had anything to do with the actual experience of those whom we would classify as the Roman poor."

[36] Cicero, *Second Speech Against Verres*, 3.89.

[37] Llewelyn, *Review of the Greek Inscriptions and Papyrii*, 103. Rathbone, "Poverty and Population," 108, argues against reading too much significance to the flight statistics, and suggests, 113, that Roman Egypt enjoyed relative prosperity during the early empire.

[38] Knapp, *Invisible Romans*, 137.

[39] See Knapp, *Invisible Romans*, 132–40.

In the manner of Proverbs and other wisdom literature,[40] it critiques behaviors likely to impoverish, such as idleness (22.1–2), drunkenness (19.1) and extravagance (18.33), as causes of poverty and disgrace: "Do not become a beggar by feasting with borrowed money, when you have nothing in your purse" (Sir. 18.33). The same book, however, attributes poverty (and wealth) to God himself: "Good things and bad, life and death, poverty and wealth, come from the Lord" (11.14).[41] And Sirach also predicts the future impoverishment of the unrighteous, implying a divine judgment or settling of accounts: "Panic and insolence will waste away riches; thus the house of the proud will be laid waste" (21.4); "The wealth of the unjust will dry up like a river, and crash like a loud clap of thunder in a storm" (40.13). Thus, the unrighteous wealthy should not be arrogant, because justice is coming, even if it seems to be delayed: "An hour's misery makes one forget past luxury, and at the close of one's life one's deeds are revealed" (11.27).

The judgment of God also features in Philo's reflection on the Deuteronomic curses. Poverty, indigence and destitution are promised "for those who transgress the commandments and the laws" (*Praem.* 127, cf. Deut. 28.33; *Praem.* 136). Yet this curse, is, according to Philo, "the lightest evil" (κουφότατον κακόν). Likewise, the Psalms of Solomon see poverty as one of the ways in which God punishes sinners (*Pss. Sol.* 4.6, 15; 16.13–14). Philo also blames fate, or at least misfortunes (αἱ ἀνθρώπων τύχαι), for the enslavement which happened frequently, even to well-born freemen (*Prob.* 18). And he acknowledges the voluntary poverty of the Essenes (*Prob.* 77).

Philo makes it clear, too, that sometimes poverty is the result of oppression or cruelty. Those who lend to the poor, demanding the payment of interest in addition to the principal, show "inhumanity and terrible hardness, making the poor person even poorer" (*Spec.* 2.75). Josephus recounts the complaint made by a large delegation of Jews against Herod Archelaus before Augustus in Rome, that "when he took the kingdom, it was in an extraordinary flourishing condition," but "he had filled the nation with the utmost degree of poverty" (*Ant.* 17:307), through heavy and unjust taxation. In the *Letter of Aristeas*, King Ptolemy grants freedom to 100,000 Jews who had been captured by his father's troops and brought as slaves to Egypt. He said, "The spoil that fell to the soldiers on the field of battle was all the booty that they should have

---

[40] E.g., "Laziness brings on deep sleep; an idle person will suffer hunger" (Prov. 19.15, NRSV).

[41] M. *Qidd.* 4.14 recounts the opinion of Rabbi Meir, who said, "A man should always teach his son a clean and easy trade. And let him pray to him to whom belong riches and possessions. For there is no trade which does not involve poverty or wealth. For poverty does not come from one's trade, nor does wealth come from one's trade. But all is in accord with a man's merit." This ascription of poverty or wealth to merit implies divine action, rewarding merit as it deserves.

claimed. To reduce the people to slavery in addition was an act of absolute injustice" (*Let. Aris.* 23).

The variety of explanations offered for poverty in early Judaism includes acts of divine judgment, and acts of human injustice. There is no evidence, however, that poverty in and of itself is considered unjust, apart from some unjust cause.

### The Proper Response to Poverty

The attitude to poverty was important. The Qumran text 4Q Instruction calls the poor to endure their hardship, and not to sin through greed, but to live simply, remain generous, avoid debt as far as possible, and trust God, that at least there will be justice for "the sons of his truth" at the final judgment. Poverty is not the most important thing, because, "What is more trivial than a poor man?"[42] Sirach says, "It is better to be poor, healthy, and strong in condition, than rich and afflicted in the body" (Sir. 30.14), and poverty can even be an advantage, because "the prayer of the poor goes from the mouth to his [God's] ears, and his judgment comes speedily" (Sir. 21.5).

There are numerous texts which call for generosity to be shown to the poor.[43] The *Testament of Issachar* says, "Love the Lord and your neighbor, be merciful to the poor and weak" (*T. Iss.* 5.2); "In my generosity I offered the good things of the earth to every poor and every oppressed person" (3.8); and "I shared my bread with the poor person. I never ate alone" (7.5). According to the *Testament of Abraham*, the pious patriarch, a paragon of hospitality, welcomed everyone to his tent, "rich and poor, both kings and rulers, the maimed and the helpless, friends and strangers, neighbors and travelers" (*T. Ab.* 1.2). Tobit describes his almsgiving to his nation (Tob. 1.3), including the first and second tithes, and the third year tithe, which he gave "to the orphans and widows and proselytes" (1.8), and he tells his son to give alms willingly to the poor, or at least to the righteous poor, "Do not turn your face from any poor person" (4.6).[44] The Testament of Job portrays Job and his wife as paragons of virtue through their generosity to the poor.[45] Philo tells the rich not to hoard their wealth but to use it to help the poor (*Spec.* 4.74). The Mishnah says that if a Jew was travelling and found himself in need, he could

---

[42] 4Q416.1; 4Q416.2.II; 4Q17.1.II.10.

[43] For further discussion of charity in Second Temple Judaism, see Longenecker, *Remember the Poor*, 108–15.

[44] Tobit 4.7 is not found in the shorter Tobit manuscripts.

[45] *T. Job* 9.3–6; 10.6–7; 11.3–11; 12.1–2; 13.4; 25.4–5; 30.5; 32.2–7; 40.13; 44.2–4; 45.2; 53.1–5. In the biblical book of Job, Job claims to have been generous to the poor (Job 29.12; 31.16) despite being accused of being callous to the poor (20.19; 34.19, 28).

use the poor man's tithe (*m. Pea.* 5.4). It also gives instructions on gifts of food to the itinerant poor, and distributions from the community fund (*m. Pea.* 8.7). Finally, some Jews, such as the Essenes, lived in intentional community, where the wealth of the rich was shared with the poor (Josephus, *Ant.* 18.20).

### *Justice for the Poor?*

There is discussion in Philo on how the poor are treated in the Mosaic law. One aspect is how the poor are treated in court. He extols the wisdom of Exodus 23.3, which "commands the judge not to show pity to the poor man in judgement" (*Spec.* 4.72). Compassion on the poor, Philo says, "is always proper, except at the time of giving judgement" (*Spec.* 4.76). This concern for legal justice is seen also in Sirach, which says, "The Lord will not show partiality to the poor, but he will hear the prayer of one who is wronged" (35.16), and in Josephus, who has Moses say, while defending himself against the slanders of Dathan, that he has "never condemned a poor man who ought to have been acquitted, on account of the one that was rich" (*Ant.* 4.46).

But Philo also explains how the law itself is filled "with precepts of law and humanity" (*Spec.* 4.72), with protections for the poor, such as the seventh year remission of debts (*Spec.* 2.71, cf. Deut. 15.1); the seventh year sabbatical for the land, from which the poor could eat (*Spec.* 2.86, cf. Lev. 25.4); the command to pay laborers on the day of their work (*Spec.* 4.195, cf. Deut. 24.15); and the requirement to let Israelite slaves go free after seven years, and to make sure they are well-provided for as they go (*Spec.* 2.79, cf. Deut. 15.12). Josephus likewise extols the benefits and the justice which the poor receive under the law, such as the gleanings of the harvest (*Ant.* 4.231).[46]

Finally, there is some evidence in Jewish apocalyptic writings of a promise of future prosperity for the righteous (*Syb. Or.* 3.580, 780, *4 Ezra* 8.51–53, *Test. Levi* 25.4; *Ap. Abr.* 20.15). Justice for the poor, then, in early Judaism, was provided for in two main ways: through the just laws of God, which made provision for the poor, and told the people how to treat the poor, and through

---

[46] Gardner, "Pursuing Justice," 42, insists that leaving the gleanings and the corners of the field for the poor was not an act of charity, but an act of social or distributive justice. He argues that these provisions "never belonged to the householder, they are simply distributed by God directly to the poor." It is true that the gleanings were not literally given to the poor. They had to come and take them. But Gardner's argument ignores a feature of Lev. 19.9–10, which emphasizes the householder's ownership of the property and its fruit: "When you reap the harvest of *your land* [אַרְצְכֶם], you shall not reap *your field* [שָׂדְךָ] right up to its edge, neither shall you gather the gleanings after *your harvest* [קְצִירְךָ]. And you shall not strip *your vineyard* [כַּרְמְךָ] bare, neither shall you gather the fallen grapes of *your vineyard* [כַּרְמְךָ]" (emphasis mine). The same thing is true of Lev. 23.22 and Deut. 24.19–21. Nevertheless, his overall point, distinguishing legal requirements to help the poor from voluntary charity, remains.

direct divine agency: ultimately God will judge those who oppress the poor and give the righteous poor what is due to them.

## Poverty and Injustice in Paul
### Explanations of Poverty

When we look at Paul for explanations for poverty, we have such a small corpus that it is not surprising that we find very little. The poor simply exist. Paul does exhort believers to work for a living, probably because some were becoming unnecessarily dependent on the generosity of believers (2 Thess. 3.12), but also as a righteous alternative to theft,[47] and to enable generosity to the poor (Eph. 4.28). And yet there is explicit reflection on Paul's own poverty, and on the poverty of Christ. To begin with Paul's poverty, he relates his experience in graphic terms: "Until this present hour also we hunger and thirst, and are poorly clothed, and are beaten, and are homeless, and toil, working with our own hands" (1 Cor. 4.11–12). The degree of his deprivation varies. At one level, his times of poverty are a matter of indifference, because he has learned the secret "of being filled and going hungry, both of abounding and lacking" (Phil. 4.12). At times he supports himself through his own prodigious labor, night and day (1 Thess. 2.9; 2 Thess. 3.8). He is occasionally supported by churches (2 Cor. 11.9), though not the ones he is working in at the time, for he refuses to be a burden on the churches (2 Cor. 12.14), wanting to make the gospel free of charge (1 Cor. 9.18), and to set an example of hard work (2 Thess. 3.9). So it appears that Paul could be lumped in with the Cynics and the Essenes, as having chosen a form of voluntary poverty. And perhaps he could be lumped in with the Stoics (and Epicureans) in his willing endurance of hardship. There is no doubt that Paul is willing to endure suffering (Phil. 3.7–11).

Yet Paul's "hardship lists" in 1 and 2 Corinthians (1 Cor. 4.9–13; 2 Cor. 4.8–15; 6.4–10; 11.23–30; 12.10) point to something more. In 1 Corinthians 4.9–13 he is talking about the experiences of the apostles, who have become a spectacle (4.9), the scum and the dregs of the world (4.13).[48] But it is God who has done this. *He* has exhibited the apostles as last (ἔσχατος), as condemned to death (ἐπιθανάτιος). Elsewhere in the letter Paul says that he is compelled to preach the gospel (1 Cor. 9.16). The passage is heavy with irony, of course. The painful experience of the apostles—the emissaries of

---

[47] ἐργαζόμενος ταῖς ἰδίαις χερσὶν τὸ ἀγαθόν. The inclusion of ἰδίαις here is uncertain, and is not supported by 𝔓46, ℵ² or B. However, the same witnesses omit ἰδίαις in the similar expression in 1 Thess. 4.11, ἐργάζεσθαι ταῖς ἰδίαις χερσὶν ὑμῶν.

[48] The two roughly synonymous terms περικαθάρμα and περίψημα are both used metaphorically for ransom in places. Whether they do so here, or there is deliberate ambiguity, is a matter for debate. See Ciampa and Rosner, *First Corinthians*, 185.

Christ himself—is contrasted to the Corinthians' lofty opinion of themselves. But the irony goes deeper. The apostles, Paul says, bless when reviled, endure when persecuted, and encourage when defamed.[49] In other words, Paul is lamenting the injustice he suffers, that when doing good in obedience to God, bringing the best good news to the world, he experiences evil. Thus Paul's apostolic poverty is at once an injustice, and at the same time God-sent. Not that God is causing Paul's hunger or persecution, but God has put him in the position which entails such unjust suffering.

The hardship list in 2 Corinthians 6.4–10 is also ironic. Paul commends himself to the Corinthians, ironically through his suffering and hunger, as well as his love and truth. Once again a contrast is drawn between the horrible treatment the apostles endure, and the truth of who they are: "Treated as deceivers, and yet true; as unknown, and yet well known; as dying and yet behold, we are alive!" The list in 2 Corinthians 11.23–30 is a grim recitation of sufferings, including hunger and cold. And Paul uses this list to boast, ironically, in his weakness, unlike the "super-apostles" (2 Cor. 11.5), who boast in their accomplishments. The list in 2 Corinthians 12.10 explains the suffering that Paul's "thorn in the flesh," the angel of Satan (12.7), is bringing about: the "weaknesses, insults, hardships, persecutions and difficulties" with which Paul is content "for the sake of Christ." The hardship list in 2 Corinthians 4.7–15 points to a key explanation for all of this. The apostles are the earthen pots in which the treasure of the gospel is displayed. They continually experience, at some level, the death of Jesus so that Jesus' life may be displayed through them. Paul's experience of poverty and other suffering is his sharing in the poverty and suffering of Jesus himself, who, according to Paul, "though he was rich, yet for your sake he became poor, that you through his poverty might become rich" (2 Cor. 8.9). Most likely the incarnation is in view here, and "poverty" a summation of Jesus' whole earthly existence including his death.[50] But the context indicates that material deprivation is not out of view. The messengers of the gospel share in the rich blessings of the gospel of Christ, in his glory and resurrection life, but they also participate in the sufferings of Christ (Rom. 8.17). Thus Paul explains his sufferings for Christ, including his poverty, as part of the cross-shaped existence in Christ.

---

[49] Ambrosiaster, "1 Corinthians," 132, comments, "People who were preaching Christ without pretentiousness, and (as it seemed to worldly people) with a degree of foolishness, were regarded as weak and subject to injuries. The Corinthians, on the other hand, were strong because they confessed Christ in such a way as not to offend anybody."

[50] See Martin, *2 Corinthians*, 264–65.

## Responses to Poverty

Paul advocates strongly for giving to the poor in 1 Timothy (1 Tim. 6.17–19), including widows (1 Tim. 5.9–10), but our focus is especially on the collection he organized for the saints at Jerusalem. It provides the most sustained discussions of poverty and related issues in Paul's writings. 1 Corinthians 16.2 instructs each person in the church to put aside weekly contributions, as circumstances allow, or, retaining the passive sense of εὐοδῶται, "as he (or she) is prospered," that is, by God.[51] The NRSV's "put aside and save whatever extra you earn,"[52] as if Paul is demanding any money earned above subsistence, is not accurate. The contributions were to be collected when Paul arrives. 2 Corinthians 8.8 and 9.7 make it clear that this is not compulsory, though Paul expresses himself very strongly: participating will prove the genuineness of their love.

There are two innovations here: first, the voluntary collection for the poor, of money gathered regularly over a long period, in this case a year (2 Cor. 8.10). In the second century, Trajan gave permission for the formation of associations in Amisos in Pontus, "for the relief of hardship among the poor" (Pliny, *Ep*. 10.92–93), but how they were organized is not known. Collections have been recorded for other projects, such as setting up inscriptions to honor benefactors, or for building projects.[53] Jews collected for the poor, the Levites and the temple regularly, but through a system of taxation which was at least nominally compulsory. However, neither the tithes nor the temple tax were necessarily policed. Greco-Roman associations could provide emergency loans to their members who were in financial strife.[54] But the sustained collection of money for the poor was a departure from the norm. The second innovation was international giving by non-elite people for the sake of the poor elsewhere (2 Cor. 8.1). Occasional benefaction took place internationally in the empire, but mostly at an elite level, as might be expected. According to Suetonius, Augustus rebuilt some cities which had treaties with Rome, after they had suffered earthquakes (*Aug*. 47.5). It was generally beyond the resources of the poor to organize internationally. Kloppenborg gives an example of Tyrian *stationarii* in Puteoli asking for funds from the city council of Tyre to pay the rent for the maintenance of their Tyrian civic cult while away from home. The council at Tyre decide to tax its *stationarii* in Rome 250 denarii a year to help.[55] But this is still quite different to Paul's collection. It was a tax imposed by government on its expatriate citizens. Kloppenborg comments, "We have

---

[51] Garland, *1 Corinthians*, 754.

[52] Cf. Barrett, *First Corinthians*, 387, "Save whatever profit he makes."

[53] See Kloppenborg, "Fiscal Aspects," 174, 185.

[54] Harland, "Economics of Group Life," 26–31.

[55] Kloppenborg, "Fiscal Aspects," 180.

no evidence of any ἐπίδοσις [public subscription] organized for the benefit of members of a community other than that of the donors themselves."[56] The early church in any event was likely to have been unattractive to elite benefactors, even those who were sympathetic, because there was little prospect of receiving the kind of honors they normally expected.[57] And the early church, like Judaism (from which it would of course be hardly distinguished in the middle of the first century, at least to outsiders) was distinct from most Greco-Roman associations in not being confined to a local area.[58] Paul also encouraged giving beyond the community of believers (Gal. 6.10; 1 Thess. 5.15).

*Poverty, Justice, and Equality*

Paul uses the language of justice and equality (or fairness) in a key passage which concerns economic issues. In 2 Corinthians 8.13–15 he puts the collection in terms of equality (ἰσότης):[59] "For it is not for the relief of others, and your affliction, but from equality; in the present time your abundance for their lack, so that also [in the future] their abundance might be for your lack, that there may be equality, as it is written, 'The one with much did not have too much, and the one with little had no lack.'"[60] Paul distinguishes equality from a system that afflicts some for the relief of others. Instead, equality is seen as working through voluntary mutual generosity and care *over time*, so that at various times the Greek and Judean churches would be able to help each other. Some have taken Paul's emphasis on equality to mean a radical redistribution of wealth. For Welborn, this means, "The equalization of resources between persons of different social classes through voluntary redistribution."[61] For Ogereau, Paul "aimed at reforming the structural

---

[56] Kloppenborg, "Fiscal Aspects," 191

[57] See Longenecker, "After the First Urban Christians," 54–55.

[58] One exception was the guild of artists (actors and musicians) devoted to Dionysus, which began as local guilds in Greece during the Hellenistic period, but in the imperial period became an international association, with patronage at times from notables such as Mark Antony and Hadrian, see Aneziri, "World Travellers," 222 n.35, 232 n.86.

[59] The LXX uses ἰσότης to translate the Hebrew תְּשֻׁאוֹת in Job 36.29, and Zech. 4.7, likely misreading the root as שׁוא which forms תְּשֻׁאָה (MT), instead of שׁוה which forms the verb שָׁוָה, "to be equal, level."

[60] The quote here from Ex. 16.18 does not include the last part of the verse, which explains the variation as each person gathering what was needed, or, in the LXX, what was fitting for himself, and presumably for his household (εἰς τοὺς καθήκοντας παρ' ἑαυτῷ).

[61] Welborn, "Equality," 11. See also Horrell, "Collection."

inequalities of Greco-Roman society that were also becoming apparent in the early church."[62] For Vassiliadis, "The ultimate purpose of the collection project was to realize the social ideal of the equal distribution and permanent sharing of material wealth."[63]

All this is too political and too grand for Paul's purposes, as Brian Tucker has pointed out.[64] John Kloppenborg also downplays the political significance of the collection: "It is an exaggeration to call Paul's project 'subversive', as some have claimed. Subversion was simply beyond Paul's reach, since he lacked the political power and influence to bring about significant change . . . It is doubtful that Paul's collection would be noticed by those outside the narrow circle of Christ followers."[65]

The term Paul uses for "equality," ἰσότης, has a range of meanings, including fairness, balance, equity and equality, and it is sometimes associated with ideas of justice. The Psalms of Solomon says that the coming messiah "will shepherd the flock of the Lord with faithfulness and justice [δικαιοσύνη]," and "he will lead them all in equality [ἰσότης], and there will be no pride among them to oppress any among them" (*Pss. Sol.* 17.41–42). Philo says, "Equality [ἰσότης] gives birth to justice, which is the mistress and ruler of the virtues" (*Plant.* 122). He discusses the equality of proportion, such as when cities "command every citizen to contribute an equal share of his property, not equal in number, but in proportion to the value of his assessment" (*Her.* 145).

Paul has something like this in mind in 2 Corinthians 8.12, when he says, "For if the eagerness [to give] is there, it is acceptable to the degree that one has, not to the degree that he does not have." As well as proportionality, the voluntary aspect is also emphasized, especially in the case of the Macedonians, who had to beg to be allowed to participate in the collection, in view of their own poverty. Macedonia in the mid-first century was poorer than Achaia. Paul salutes their willingness to give beyond their means, and sees it as a work of the grace of God, but he makes it clear that they were not forced. Perhaps they were not even asked (2 Cor. 8.1–5). This suggests that for Paul, giving can, by God's grace, go beyond the equality of mutual provision for one another's needs out of the excess of what is earned, to that which is truly sacrificial. But for Paul, equality is expressed in the mutual and voluntary willingness of believers to meet the needs of others at times of necessity, and proportionally according to their own resources. In one further passage Paul

---

[62] Ogereau, "Jerusalem Collection," 377.

[63] Vassiliadis, "Equality and Justice," 57.

[64] Tucker, "Jerusalem Collection," 69–70.

[65] Kloppenborg, "Fiscal Aspects," 197. He has an ethnic take on the collection, 193: "Paul's notion of equality in 2 Cor 8:14 is not one of equal civic rights but of Greeks sharing economic resources with Judeans."

uses the language of justice and equality within an economic relationship: "Masters, provide your slaves justice and fairness [or equality], knowing that you also have a master in heaven" (Col. 4.1). It seems odd perhaps to speak of justice and equality right after instructing slaves to obey their masters (Col. 3.22–25), but it does suggest a transformation through Christ in the relationship between master and slave. Masters are warned that they are accountable to God for how they treat their slaves.[66]

Paul also occasionally calls for help for the poor on the basis of the justice of obligation. The explanation for the collection which Paul gives in Romans 15.25–28 also related to ideas of justice. It is at one level a matter of voluntary fellowship or participation: "For Macedonia and Achaia have been pleased to make some contribution [κοινωνία] for the poor among the saints at Jerusalem" (15.26). At another level it is an obligation: "For they were pleased—and they are under obligation to them" (15.27). The debt that the Greek believers owe derives from the spiritual blessings they have received through the Jews, especially the Jerusalem saints. As is now well known, especially due to John Barclay's work in the field,[67] the reception of a gift in both Greek and Jewish cultures frequently implied an obligation to return some blessing or gift, whether of honor, or in some other way. Gentile believers are obligated to help the Jerusalem believers in material ways (15.27). Likewise, children (or grandchildren) who have widowed mothers are obligated "to return recompense" (ἀμοιβὰς ἀποδιδόναι) to their parent (1 Tim. 5.4).[68]

It is clear that Paul was committed to "remember the poor" (Gal. 2.10), as he was exhorted by Peter, James and John. It is unlikely that the apostolic instruction referred specifically to the church in Jerusalem as "the poor,"[69] given that the topic under discussion at the Jerusalem meeting was the gospel which Paul and Barnabas were preaching among the Gentiles (Gal. 2.2). Instead, Paul interpreted it in a much broader sense, and passed this on to the churches, as we see worked out in the churches of Galatia (1 Cor. 16.1), Macedonia (2 Cor. 8.1) and Achaia (2 Cor. 9.1–3).

## Conclusion

Jewish and Greco-Roman reflections on poverty have significant parallels. Both included calls for untroubled acceptance of poverty. Both allow for

---

[66] See O'Brien, *Colossians, Philemon*, 232–33.

[67] Barclay, *Paul and the Gift*, 74.

[68] Cf. also Gal. 6.6, "Let the one who is taught the word share all good things with the one who teaches."

[69] See the discussion in Longenecker, *Remember the Poor*, 183–206.

multiple causes of poverty, including the divine will, fate or misfortune, acts of injustice, and character problems such as laziness and extravagance. Both encouraged charity or benefaction. Both had groups who practiced voluntary poverty. Both made some structural provision for the poor, though for the Romans this was focused in the city of Rome in particular. Both spoke about the necessity for the equality of rich and poor under the law. Neither saw poverty or wealth disparity in themselves as issues of justice or injustice. But there were significant differences. The Jewish emphasis on almsgiving went far beyond what was common in the Roman world. Jewish thought and law was much more engaged with helping the poor. And Jewish eschatology promised a better world to come.

Our brief study of Paul has also shown some overlaps, despite the brevity of the corpus of his letters. Paul is content whether he is poor or affluent. He accepts the poverty that he suffers as a persecuted apostle of Christ, knowing that God has put him in that position, and he chooses to remain in his calling. He exhorts believers to work hard with their own hands, and not become dependent on others, and seeks to set an example of this practice in his own life. He urges and organizes acts of generosity to the poor, especially to fellow believers.

Concerning justice there are several key conclusions. First, as with Romans and Jews, there is no evidence that Paul, who is both Jewish and a Roman citizen, sees poverty in itself as evidence that injustice has been committed. There is no call for mandatory redistribution. Second, Paul upholds the obligation for justice in certain relationships, such as the obligation on families to look after their own elderly widows. Third, Paul sees justice, or equality, being worked out through the mutual care of believers for one another over time, and in response to need, as they give voluntarily, generously and in proportion to their means, shaped by the self-giving of Christ himself. And ultimately, for Paul, hope is in God, not on riches in this age. Life in this age is like shivering in a tent, waiting for the sun to rise—for mortality to be swallowed up by immortality (2 Cor. 5.4).

## Bibliography

Ambrosiaster. "1 Corinthians." In *Commentaries on Romans and 1–2 Corinthians*, edited and translated by Gerald L. Bray, 119–206. Ancient Christian Texts. Downers Grove, IL: InterVarsity, 2009.

Aneziri, Sophia. "World Travellers: The Associations of Artists of Dionysus." In *Wandering Poets in Ancient Greek Culture: Travel, Locality and Pan-Hellenism*, edited by Richard Hunter and Ian Rutherford, 105–36. Cambridge: Cambridge University Press, 2009.

Anon. "Inequality in India: What's the Real Story?" http://weforum.org/agenda/2016/10/inequality-in-india-oxfam-explainer.

Armitage, David J. *Theories of Poverty in the World of the New Testament.* Wissenschaftliche Untersuchungen Zum Neuen Testament 2 Reihe. Tübingen: Mohr Siebeck, 2016.
Barclay, John M.G. *Paul and the Gift.* Grand Rapids: Eerdmans, 2015.
Barrett, C.K. *A Commentary on the First Epistle to the Corinthians.* Black's New Testament Commentaries. London: A. & C. Black, 1971.
Ciampa, Roy E., and Brian S. Rosner. *The First Letter to the Corinthians.* Pillar New Testament Commentary. Grand Rapids: Eerdmans, 2010.
Deissmann, Adolf. *New Light on the New Testament, from Records of the Graeco-Roman Period.* Translated by Lionel R.M. Strachan. Edinburgh: T. & T. Clark, 1908.
Edmondson, Jonathan. "Economic Life in the Roman Empire." In *The Oxford Handbook of Roman Epigraphy*, edited by Christer Bruun and J.C. Edmondson, 671–98. Oxford: Oxford University Press, 2015.
Finley, M.I. *The Ancient Economy.* Sather Classical Lectures. Berkeley, CA: University of California Press, 1973.
Friesen, Steven J. "Poverty in Pauline Studies: Beyond the So-Called New Consensus." *Journal for the Study of the New Testament* 26.3 (2004) 323–61.
Gardner, Gregg E. "Pursuing Justice: Support for the Poor in Early Rabbinic Judaism." *Hebrew Union College Annual* 86 (2015) 37–62.
Garland, David E. *1 Corinthians.* Baker Exegetical Commentary on the New Testament. Grand Rapids: Baker Academic, 2003.
Garnsey, Peter. *Famine and Food Supply in the Graeco-Roman World: Responses to Risk and Crisis.* Cambridge: Cambridge University Press, 1988.
Garnsey, Peter, and Greg Woolf. "Patronage of the Rural Poor in the Roman World." In *Patronage in Ancient Society*, edited by Andrew Wallace-Hadrill, 153–70. London: Routledge, 1989.
Harland, Philip A. "Associations and the Economics of Group Life: A Preliminary Case Study of Asia Minor and the Aegean Islands." *Svensk Exegetisk Årsbok* 80 (2015) 1–37.
Hengel, Martin. *Property and Riches in the Early Church: Aspects of a Social History of Early Christianity.* Translated by John Bowden. Philadelphia: Fortress, 1974.
Hock, Ronald F. *The Social Context of Paul's Ministry: Tentmaking and Apostleship.* Philadelphia: Fortress, 1980.
Horrell, David. "Paul's Collection: Resources for a Materialist Theology." *Epworth Review* 22.2 (1995) 74–83.
Horsley, Richard A. "You Shall Not Bow Down and Serve Them: Economic Justice in the Bible." *Interpretation* 69.4 (2015) 415–31.
Jones, Christopher P. "The Claudian Monument at Patara." *Zeitschrift für Papyrologie und Epigraphik* 137 (2001) 161–68.
Judge, E.A. *Social Distinctives of the Christians in the First Century: Pivotal Essays.* Peabody, MA: Hendrickson, 2008.

———. *The Social Pattern of the Christian Groups in the First Century: Some Prolegomena to the Study of New Testament Ideas of Social Obligation.* Christ and Culture Collection. London: Tyndale, 1960.

Keesmat, Sylvia C., and Brian J. Walsh. "'Outside of a Small Circle of Friends:' Jesus and the Justice of God." In *Jesus, Paul, and the People of God: A Theological Dialogue with N.T. Wright*, edited by Nicholas Perrin and Richard B. Hays, 66–88. Downers Grove, IL: IVP Academic, 2011.

Kloppenborg, John S. "Fiscal Aspects of Paul's Collection for Jerusalem." *Early Christianity* 8.2 (2017) 153–98.

Knapp, Robert C. *Invisible Romans.* Cambridge, MA: Harvard University Press, 2011.

Larsen, Mik Robert. "The Representation of Poverty in the Roman Empire." PhD diss., University of California Los Angeles, 2015.

Lewis, Naphtali, and Meyer Reinhold. *Roman Civilization: Selected Readings.* 2 vols. 3rd ed. New York: Columbia University Press, 1990.

Llewelyn, S.R. *A Review of the Greek Inscriptions and Papyrii Published 1984–85.* New Documents Illustrating Early Christianity. Grand Rapids: Eerdmans, 1998.

Longenecker, Bruce W. *Remember the Poor: Paul, Poverty, and the Greco-Roman World.* Grand Rapids: Eerdmans, 2010.

———. "Socio-Economic Profiling of the First Urban Christians." In *After the First Urban Christians: The Social-Scientific Study of Pauline Christianity Twenty-Five Years Later*, edited by Todd D. Still and David G. Horrell, 36–59. London: Continuum, 2009.

Lott, John Bertrand. "An Augustan Sculpture of August Justice." *Zeitschrift für Papyrologie und Epigraphik* 113 (1996) 263–70.

Malherbe, Abraham J. *Moral Exhortation: A Graeco-Roman Sourcebook.* Library of Early Christianity. Philadelphia: Westminster, 1986.

———. *Paul and the Popular Philosophers.* Minneapolis, MN: Fortress, 1989.

———. *Social Aspects of Early Christianity.* 2nd ed. Philadelphia: Fortress, 1983.

Martin, Ralph P. *2 Corinthians.* Word Biblical Commentary, 40. Waco, TX: Word, 1986.

Meeks, Wayne A. *The First Urban Christians: The Social World of the Apostle Paul.* New Haven, CT: Yale University Press, 1983.

Meggitt, Justin J. *Paul, Poverty and Survival.* Studies of the New Testament and Its World. Edinburgh: T. & T. Clark, 1998.

O'Brien, Peter T. *Colossians, Philemon.* Word Biblical Commentary, 44. Waco, TX: Word, 1982.

Ogereau, Julien M. "The Jerusalem Collection as Κοινωνία: Paul's Global Politics of Socio-Economic Equality and Solidarity." *New Testament Studies* 58.3 (2012) 360–78.

Onur, Fatih. "'The Monument of the Roads' at Patara." In *From Lukka to Lycia: The Land of Sarpedon and St. Nicholas*, edited by Havva İşkan and Erkan Dündar, 570–77. Istanbul: Tüpraş—Yapı Kredi, 2016.

Osborne, Robin. "Introduction: Roman Poverty in Context." In *Poverty in the Roman World*, edited by E.M. Atkins and Robin Osborne, 1–20. Cambridge: Cambridge University Press, 2006.

Rathbone, Dominic. "Poverty and Population in Roman Egypt." In *Poverty in the Roman World*, edited by E.M. Atkins and Robin Osborne, 100–114. Cambridge: Cambridge University Press, 2006.

Rowland, Robert J. "The 'Very Poor' and the Grain Dole at Rome and Oxyrhynchus." *Zeitschrift für Papyrologie und Epigraphik* 21 (1976) 69–73.

Scheidel, Walter, and Steven J. Friesen. "The Size of the Economy and the Distribution of Income in the Roman Empire." *Journal of Roman Studies* 99 (2009) 61–91.

Scramuzza, Vincent M. "The Personality of the Emperor." In *The Roman World*, edited by Donald Kagan, 327–36. Problems in Ancient History. New York: Macmillan, 1975.

Theissen, Gerd. *The Social Setting of Pauline Christianity: Essays on Corinth.* Trans. by John H. Schütz. Philadelphia: Fortress, 1982.

Tucker, J. Brian. "The Jerusalem Collection, Economic Inequality, and Human Flourishing: Is Paul's Concern the Redistribution of Wealth, or a Relationship of Mutuality (or Both)?" *Canadian Theological Review* 3.2 (2014) 52–70.

Vassiladis, Peter. "Equality and Justice in Classical Antiquity and in Paul: The Social Implications of the Pauline Collection." *St Vladimir's Theological Quarterly* 36.1–2 (1992) 51–59.

Vermote, Kristof. "The *Macula Servitutis* of Roman Freedmen. *Neque Enim Aboletur Turpitudo, Quae Postea Intermissa Est?*" *Revue Belge de Philologie et d'Histoire* 94.1 (2016) 131–64.

Welborn, L.L. "'That There May Be Equality': The Contexts and Consequences of a Pauline Ideal." *New Testament Studies* 59.1 (2013) 73–90.

Winter, Bruce W. *After Paul Left Corinth: The Influence of Secular Ethics and Social Change.* Grand Rapids: Eerdmans, 2001.

———. *Seek the Welfare of the City: Christians as Benefactors and Citizens.* First Century Christians in the Graeco-Roman World. Grand Rapids: Eerdmans, 1994.

World Bank. "Decline of Global Extreme Poverty Continues But Has Slowed: World Bank." http://www.worldbank.org/en/news/press-release/2018/09/19/decline-of-global-extreme-poverty-continues-but-has-slowed-world-bank.

Woolf, Greg. "Writing Poverty in Rome." In *Poverty in the Roman World*, edited by E.M. Atkins and Robin Osborne, 83–99. Cambridge: Cambridge University Press, 2006.

CHAPTER 11

# Martin Luther on Usury and the Divine Economy

Jonathan Lett

Martin Luther is often heralded for establishing what would become the central pillars of modernity: the individual's subjectivity, personal conscience, and freedom.[1] And yet, for all of Luther's revolutionary thinking, he appears to present a strikingly medieval rebuke of the nascent capitalism taking root in the soil of Europe.[2] Max Weber sums up this sentiment nicely when he judges the lifeblood of Luther's economics to be a "peasant's mistrust of capital."[3] One reason for categorizing Luther's economic thought as scholastic is his unrelenting condemnation of usury.[4] The prevalence of this view is in some part due to the editors of his collected works who state that Luther "held to the long scholastic tradition which, following Aristotle, taught that money does not produce money."[5] The newly published *Annotated Luther* reaffirms this perspective, noting that his "views of financial matters was [sic] thoroughly medieval" because he "echoed the Scholastics, who in turn had echoed Aristotle, with the cardinal dogma that *'nummus non paret nummum,'* meaning that money (being a dead thing) does not produce anything."[6] While it is true that Luther adheres to the Aristotelian notion of money's sterility,

---

[1] See Zachhuber, "Luther, Modernity, and Capitalism."

[2] For a summary of the prevalence of the view that Luther represents a retrenchment of the scholastic position on usury, see Singleton, "'Money Is a Sterile Thing'."

[3] Weber, *Protestant Ethic*, 166 n.11.

[4] This positioning of Luther's economic thought depends on the prior decision to define modernity by its penchant for a free capitalistic market, which reifies usury as the essence of backward premodern thought. Often such attempts to map Luther according to our valuations of modernity tend to reveal more about our thought than his.

[5] Pelikan and Lehman, eds., *Luther's Works*, 45:233. (Hereafter *LW*.)

[6] Hillerbrand, "Introduction" to *On Business and Usury* (1524), 134–35.

this idea plays only a negligible role in his economic thought in general and his condemnation of usury in particular.[7]

The judgment that Luther's view of usury does represent a scholastic line of thought is not entirely wrong. He deploys a version of a scholastic argument that usury contradicts the natural law, as epitomized by what we now call the "golden rule:" do to others what you would have them do to you. Here, Luther's ethic of the natural law breaks with the dominant scholastic habits of thought, offering an economic ethic grounded in a theology of creation that conceives of the world as a sheer gift of God. In what follows, I will argue that Luther's view of the world as *created*—that is, divinely blessed and abounding with the generosity of God—gives shape to his economic thought. Based on this theology of the world as divine gift, the goal of economic exchange is the flourishing of humans as neighbors in community. The Christian thus enacts practices of generosity to root out the besetting sin of greed and join in the divine economy. Before we turn to Luther's thought, I will briefly sketch the theological rationalization and social history of the scholastic discussions of usury that will highlight the distinctive shape of his thought.

## A Brief Social and Intellectual History of Usury

Luther's ethics of usury provide a glimpse into the radically different cosmology in place at the dawn of modernity. To understand his thought, historians must grapple with the profound differences between the social fabric of the premodern world and ours. The divergence is hard to overstate: rather than imagining the economy as a discrete, autonomous sphere, pre-capitalistic societies see economic relations intertwined with more fundamental social, political, and religious relations.[8] The economy is "embedded" in social, political, and religious relationships and institutions rather than embedding the social, political, and religious relations in the economic system.[9] As a consequence, pre-capitalistic Christian economic thought is explicitly moored by a commitment to the common good so that all economic achievements are measured against a standard of justice that, if met, promises to secure peace for a society. In short, discussions of usury presuppose a moral universe, one to which economic policies ought to conform to promote the flourishing of those human relationships and institutions that are fundamental to society.

The embedding of the economy in basic social, political, and religious relationships also blurs the lines between categories that are conceptually delimited for us today. The coalescing of the social, political, economic, and

---

[7] Singleton, "'Money Is a Sterile Thing';" Langholm, *Legacy of Scholasticism*.

[8] Armstrong, *Ideal of a Moral Economy*, 12.

[9] Polanyi, *Great Transformation*, 60.

religious is evident in the difficult problem of classification: Is usury a theological concept? A philosophical ideal? An economic policy? A civil or ecclesiastical law? As Lawrin Armstrong explains, "The economic was not conceived as a distinct analytical category or the economy as a sphere of human activity independent of—much less at odds with—the social and the political, as it usually is, for example, in neoliberal economics."[10] Given the religious matrix that undergirds all human activity in this period, this logic ought to be extended to include usury as a theologically embedded phenomenon. After all, the theory of usury is native to a time when "Once there was no 'secular,'" as John Milbank provocatively put it. According to Milbank, instead of a latent secularity waiting to fill the receding space of the sacred, "there was the single community of Christendom, with its dual aspects of *sacerdotium* and *regnum*. The *saeculum*, in the medieval era, was not a space, a domain, but a time—the interval between fall and eschaton where coercive justice, private property and impaired natural reason must make shift to cope with the unredeemed effects of sinful humanity."[11] The embedded economy can only be rendered intelligible within its "theo-cosmological" substrate. In God's creation, every aspect of life stands in intimate relation to God, deriving its being and meaning in reference to God. No realm exists independently of God or beyond theological description. Economic, political, and social spheres derive their intelligibility precisely in relation to God as created and fallen but redeemed.

In order to interpret Luther's economic thought, we must enter into his way of imagining the world. We must account for his way of seeing life on its own ontological terms.[12] Luther's ethics presuppose a doctrine of creation in which the world is a divine gift meant to be shared and enjoyed by humanity. This "theo-cosmological" view of the world can be captured by Charles Taylor's concept of a "social imaginary." A social imaginary is the way "people imagine their social existence, how they fit together with others, how things go on between them and their fellows, the expectations that are normally met, and the deeper normative notions and images that underlie these expectations."[13] It is these normative notions and images, funded by Luther's

---

[10] Armstrong, *Ideal of a Moral Economy*, 11. Armstrong reminds us that there is no "such thing as an autonomous discipline that studies 'human behavior as a relationship between ends and scarce means which have alternative uses' did not exist in the Middle Ages; it was an invention of the late eighteenth and nineteenth century."

[11] Milbank, *Theology and Social Theory*, 9.

[12] For an account of the deep-seated modernist ontology that makes the discipline of history an act of translation and thus distortion, see Anderson, *Realness of Things Past*.

[13] Taylor, *Secular Age*, 171. A social imaginary is constituted by a "common understanding which makes possible common practices, and a widely shared sense of

theology of creation, that underlie his economic thought. Therefore, an account of his position on usury must be articulated within its native cosmological habitat and in relation to its constituent dimensions—theological, ecclesiastical, social, political, and economic. It is my contention that attention to Luther's theology of creation is necessary to understand his ethical analysis of usury.

*Scholastic Habits of Thought*

The universal rejection of usury in medieval Europe has its roots in the church's interpretation of the Old Testament condemnation of lending with interest and Jesus' teaching to "lend hoping for nothing in return" (Luke 6.35).[14] But this biblical provenance of the prohibition is not identical to the scholastic position carried forward into Luther's day. The scholastic understanding of usury reflects the growing influence of Roman law on early medieval canonists and theologians. The influence of Roman law produces two shifts in the logic of usury.[15] First, the definition of usury is borrowed from the Roman idea of *mutuum* and refers to profit gained from a loan and fungible goods (food, wine, etc.), which can occur in other types of contracts as well.[16] Second, the sin of usury, once identified as avarice, is now catalogued as the sin of injustice under the sway of the Aristotelian underpinnings of Roman law.[17] With the importation of Aristotle, the canonists and theologians of the church analyzed usury within natural law constructions.

But this does not mean that natural law arguments are constructed independently of theological commitments and biblical interpretation. According to Jean Porter this is a common mistake for modern interpreters of scholastic natural law theory, who, unlike scholastic thinkers, have a voluntarist notion of the moral order.[18] John Noonan exemplifies this mistake when he charts the development of the church's view on usury as one that migrates from its theological basis to the universal foundation of reason. He writes,

---

legitimacy," 172. Importantly, Taylor notes that practices themselves shape and reshape social imaginaries, 176.

[14] Noonan, *Scholastic Analysis*, 20; Fontaine, *Moral Economy*, 185.

[15] Langholm, *Legacy of Scholasticism*, 31–32.

[16] Noonan, *Scholastic Analysis*, 39–41. See also Armstrong, "Law, Ethics, Economy," 42.

[17] Noonan, *Scholastic Analysis*, 14–20.

[18] Porter, *Natural and Divine Law*, 132–33.

far more important than its theological origin and direction is the fact that the theory does issue in this natural-law analysis. The scholastics do not depend on authority or revelation or Roman law alone. Increasingly, they make a determined effort to rest their case against usury on the nature of man and on the nature of things in themselves; similarly they try to determine what forms of credit are naturally lawful and just. Attempting to appeal to reason alone, they build the structure of the usury theory.[19]

Noonan correctly notes the shift to natural law reflection, but he wrongly separates claims about the nature of created things from the theo-cosmological view and doctrinal commitments that undergird natural law accounts. This misunderstanding shows the importance of paying heed to the metaphysical underpinnings of the pre-modern social imaginary. The grammar of usury is supplied by natural law, which depends on a picture of nature in which the moral order and the natural order are unified. For the scholastics and Luther alike, the doctrine of creation ensures a correspondence between the divine and natural law in the natural order. The revealed and natural law, therefore, do not differ in their basic content.

The scholastics had an arsenal of natural law repudiations of usury at their disposal, but three arguments in particular were marshalled most often in the discussion of usury. First, time belongs to God alone and thus cannot be sold in the lending of money. William of Auxerre declares that the usurer "acts against the universal natural law, because he sells time, which is common to all creatures."[20] This popular line of reasoning is deployed to condemn various forms of credit sales in which a good is sold for a future sum of money.[21] Second, usury violates the nature of money as a measure for exchange, which is fixed and independent of the goods being exchanged. Therefore, the value of money cannot be altered at different times without transgressing the teleological and formal nature of money. This is Aquinas's great Aristotelian innovation that every succeeding scholastic will ply to the issue.[22] The third natural law argument, also established by Aquinas, became the fundamental scholastic paradigm. Usury violates the nature of money as a consumptible good—that is, money, like wine, oil, and grain, is consumed as it is used. Essential to wine-drinking is the fact that wine is destroyed as it is consumed. The same is true for money—its value is identical with its use. And when money, like wine, oil, and grain, is loaned, ownership is transferred because its use lies in its consumption. As Aquinas argues, "if a man wanted to sell wine separately from the use of the wine, he would be selling the same thing twice,

---

[19] Noonan, *Scholastic Analysis*, 3.

[20] William of Auxerre, cited in Noonan, *Scholastic Analysis*, 43.

[21] Noonan, *Scholastic Analysis*, 81.

[22] Noonan, *Scholastic Analysis*, 52–53.

or he would be selling what does not exist, wherefore he would evidently commit a sin of injustice." Aquinas therefore concludes, "To take usury for money lent is unjust in itself, because this is to sell what does not exist, and this evidently leads to inequality which is contrary to justice."[23] These are the ontological underpinnings for the sterility of money objection to usury: money by its nature does not beget money. Hence, usury is a perversion of the natural order, an abomination of nature.[24] Flouting the natural order precipitates injustice and exploitation.

To these, we add a fourth type of natural law argument that was less prevalent in discussions of usury but is one that Luther would later employ. Lending at interest was deemed to contradict the "golden rule," as summed up in Christ's command "Do to others what you would have them do to you" (Luke 6.31).[25] In Aquinas, this command is paired with the injunction "Love your neighbor as yourself" (Luke 10.27).[26] For Aquinas, this master principle coheres with the ultimate common good to be pursued by humanity and to which our rational faculties are naturally oriented. For this reason, Christ's command functions as a natural law because it elucidates a first premise for moral reasoning that unites human communities according to their shared nature, and thus directs them toward a common good.[27] This strand of natural law reasoning reminds us that even Aristotelian-inflected natural law arguments against usury rest on a particular theological account of creation as divinely ordered. Usury disregards the golden rule because it subverts the justice necessary for the promotion of the common good. Lending at interest functions as a form of theft—the interest charge is money stolen from the pocketbook of the lender. When countering the objection that the borrower often freely and happily enters into a usurious agreement, William of Auxerre responds that this "freedom" is illusory. The ubiquity of unjust lending practices creates the conditions in which one is only too happy to suffer a little theft rather than a thorough pilfering.[28] These natural law debates highlight

---

[23] Aquinas, *Summa Theologica*, II.ii. Q. 78.1.

[24] Armstrong, *Ideal of a Moral Economy*, 3, notes that the unnatural nature of usury is compared to homosexuality in both Dante and Giotto.

[25] *LW* 45:292.

[26] Noonan, *Scholastic Analysis*, 23–24. Noonan considers this to be a confusion between divine and natural law that becomes entrenched in canon law through Gratian's *Decretum*. But the confusion is Noonan's alone. The divine law in general and the commands of Jesus in particular comport with the very essence and order of creation. This is the basic scholastic understanding of the natural and moral order, Porter, *Natural and Divine Law*, 134.

[27] Finnis, *Aquinas*, 126–29. See also Porter, *Natural and Divine Law*, 138.

[28] Langholm, *Legacy of Scholasticism*, 63.

the necessary interdependence between political relations and economic exchange for the just ordering of a community that is required for human flourishing.

### Discrepancies between Church Teaching and Social Practice

Although the church universally condemned usury, the rampant practice of usury went largely unchecked. Outlawing usury was one thing; enforcing its prohibition was another. In an attempt to curtail widespread usury, the Third Lateran Council (1179) barred unrepentant usurers from receiving the eucharist and Christian burial: "Nearly everywhere the crime of usury has become so firmly rooted that many, omitting other business, practice usury as if it were permitted."[29] Despite this and many other efforts to conform lending practices to church teaching, lending at interest would take root at the center of the medieval economy such that five or six percent per annum was deemed legal in the late fifteenth century.[30] The development of the bill of sale and cashless payments, both of which turned on interest-bearing credit, points to the dynamic, context-dependent nature of theological prescription in an evolving financial world.[31]

In addition to these permitted forms of interest, money-lenders and merchants devised creative methods by which to conceal illicit interest charges within contracts. These machinations circumvented the theological and casuistic discussions of the morality of usury. This allowed for an easy escape for lenders from prosecution at a time when the pursuit of legal action against usurers already faced an uphill battle in a decentralized juridical system that relied on local enforcement. These attempts to sidestep canon law pulled theologians into the intricacies of contracts, deepening their commitment to a casuistical approach to usury and lending. Many wealthy peasants could stay one step ahead of ecclesiastical law, while others were simply ignorant of the law.[32] Finally, Jews were permitted to lend in Europe, making them an object of scorn for performing a lending service in which Christians could not take part but very much desired.[33] In sum, there were no shortage of usurious lending practices despite the church's teaching. A distinction between lending at interest and usury became codified, and interest-bearing bills of sale regularly facilitated economic exchange. In addition to civil and canon

---

[29] First Council of Nicaea, Canon 17, in Tanner, ed., *Decrees of the Ecumenical Councils*, 1:200, cited in Jones, *Reforming the Morality of Usury*, 33.

[30] Geisst, *Beggar Thy Neighbor*, 58–96; Rössner, "Critical Introduction," 96.

[31] Rössner, "Critical Introduction," 97.

[32] Fontaine, *Moral Economy*, 184–94.

[33] Geisst, *Beggar Thy Neighbor*, 52–53.

approval of interest charges, clandestine measures concealed illegal usurious transactions within the terms of sale. This disjunction between ecclesiastical teaching and social practice continued into Luther's time and became an impetus for publicly stating his position on usury and commerce.

In Luther's day, the church had more than relaxed its position on usury, even participating in usurious lending practices itself to help cover the extensive costs of building St Peter's Basilica.[34] And yet, the church continued to issue bans and prohibit usury for the laity. These clear examples of hypocrisy would become clear signs of the church's Babylonian captivity and perversion of the gospel in the eyes of the Reformers. When Luther posted his Ninety-five Theses in Wittenberg, economic issues were on the forefront of the minds of many Germans as they suffered the hardships of a sagging economy. Once the main source of Europe's monetary stock, Germany's silver mines had begun to run dry, constricting the national economy.[35] Merchant families like the Fuggers, who specialized in bills of sale, cashless exchange and currency exchange, were thought to have compounded matters by creating a shortfall of credit in relation to demand, driving interest rates well beyond the legal interest rate of five percent.[36] As the son of a silver mine merchant, Luther had intimate knowledge of economic issues, including awareness of the practical inner workings of Germany's silver mines. This familiarity with economic realities enabled Luther to apply the gospel with precision to the particularities of buying, selling, and lending of his day.

### Luther's Theological Vision of Economic Exchange

Luther addressed the topic of usury three times between the short span of 1519 and 1524. He saw the need to redress the rising levels of poverty exacerbated by unsatisfactory church teaching on economic exchange. His final publication on the subject combined a new treatise on trade with his *Longer Sermon on Usury*, which first appeared in 1520. *On Trade and Usury* (1524) represents a summation of Luther's theology of economic exchange in something akin to a devotional manual.[37] This devotional manual marks a return to a pre-scholastic classification of the sin of usury as avarice over and against the later medieval view of usury as injustice. Luther begins with an apocalyptic decree that the "brilliant light" of the holy gospel reveals the stark

---

[34] Jones, *Reforming the Morality of Usury*, 35. Moreover, the church employed the financial instruments and banking houses of Italian merchants to move money across Europe to Rome. The church's financial practices perfected the system of cashless exchange that utilized interest-bearing capital, Rössner, "Critical Introduction," 95.

[35] Rössner, "Critical Introduction," 56.

[36] Rössner, "Critical Introduction," 68–69.

[37] Hillerbrand, "Introduction" to *On Business and Usury* (1524), 135.

reality of good and evil manifest in the two incommensurate economies of gift and greed. These rival economies are built on two diametrically opposed loves—the love of money and the love of God. The former is the root of all evil; the latter is the basis for the freedom to love neighbor.[38] "The gaping jaws of avarice" are so deadly that Luther must issue the call to repentance for the sake of those few merchants who "would rather be poor with God than rich with the Devil."[39] For Luther, God's economy and the world's economy have radically different origins, and thus radically different goals which produce alternative visions of the nature of exchange and trade. As we shall see, Luther exhorts merchants to practice commerce in the temporal realm in light of the ultimate reality of the divine economy. In what follows, I shall sketch the contours of this theological vision, first, by tracing Luther's understanding of the abundance of God's provision in creation and its perversion by the fall, and, second, by outlining his prescriptive practices that hedge against greed and prepare the Christian for God's eternal economy.

*Creation, Gift, Economy*

According to Luther, the exchange of goods exists to realize God's desire to distribute the gifts of creation among the human community. As Luther states, "buying and selling are necessary. They cannot be dispensed with, and can be practiced in a Christian manner, especially when the commodities serve a necessary and honorable purpose . . . These are the gifts of God, which he bestows out of the earth and distributes among mankind."[40] Although he only makes a passing reference to it here, the idea that God has created a world with an abundance of gifts for creatures to flourish runs throughout his thought. If we turn to Luther's *Commentary on Genesis*, we find a creation suffused with divine blessing by the God who lavishly gifts existence to human creatures. In fact, Luther goes so far as to suggest that

> God speaks after the custom of one who has become tired, as if he wanted to say, "Behold I have now prepared all things for man with all perfectness. I have prepared for him the heaven as his canopy and the earth as his floor. His possessions and his wealth are the animals with all the productions of the earth, the sea and the air. The seeds, the roots and the herbs of the garden are his food . . . Nothing is wanting. All things are created in the greatest abundance for the sustaining of animal life. Now therefore I will rest! I will enjoy a Sabbath!"[41]

---

[38] *LW*, 45:245.

[39] *LW* 45:245–46.

[40] *LW* 45:246.

[41] *LW* 1:73.

God "exhausts" himself by endowing the creation with more than humanity needs to flourish. Luther speaks of three overlapping "estates" that order the very structure of creation and constitute human life: church (*ecclesia*), economics, or literally "the household" (*oeconomia*), and politics (*politia*).[42] These fundamental forms are the means by which God's gifts are received and humans flourish. Buying and selling belong to the *oeconomia* and are the vehicles through which God's gifts are to be shared and enjoyed.

Although buying and selling belong to God's good creation, they are also distorted by sin. As a result, we now conceive of God's world in terms of its utility rather than as an exquisite creation that exists quite apart from our use of it. Our minds cannot begin to fathom the "utterly innumerable blessings, which are all irretrievably lost to us in our present state of life."[43] Reflecting on the pronounced difference between the prelapsarian world of Eden and his own, Luther writes, "But all things are quite the contrary now. For at the present time, all the creatures together scarcely suffice for the nourishment and gratification of man."[44] Sin alters the once abundant world, leaving it in a state of decay, marked by scarcity and human toil. Luther's claim here extends beyond the noetic effects of the fall to something bordering on ontological degradation. On the one hand, he can claim that "as man is no longer the same being, so the world is no longer the same world. Upon the fall of man followed corruption and upon this corruption the curse of the now corrupt creation."[45] But on the other hand, "In this manner [by the work of the Holy Spirit] does the image of God begin to be restored in us through the Gospel by this new creation in this life."[46] Despite the Spirit's work of new creation, sin continues to terrorize the world. In response to the power of sin, God institutes the third estate, the civil authority (*politia*), to curb corrupted human desire by wielding the sword to avenge evil and enforce the law.[47]

Despite the loss of a world teeming with divine blessing, we still reside in a place of divine benefit wherein God distributes gifts to his creatures and his

---

[42] *LW* 1:103–4. Lindberg, "Luther's Struggle," 167; Wannenwetsch, "Luther's Moral Theology," 130–31. See *LW* 37:365.

[43] *LW* 1:72.

[44] *LW* 1:71–72.

[45] *LW* 1:77.

[46] *LW* 1:65.

[47] Wannenwetsch, "Luther's Moral Theology," 130, notes that Luther's position on the third estate is "somewhat inconsistent." Luther emphasizes the political estate as God's response to check sin's power in the world. But he also "clearly entertains the existence of politics in a prelapsarian sense: namely as an ordered way of living together harmoniously under God's rule without the coercive feature that marks political authority after the fall."

creatures respond with gratitude and service. The market continues to serve its intended purpose to distribute God's gifts by the exchange of goods, but now it must do so by overcoming a lack of resources. In spite of the effects of the fall, Luther contends that God's generosity, not the scarcity of resources, remains the basis for exchange. In his exposition of Psalm 127, Luther exhorts Christians at Riga in Livonia to recognize that human labor depends on God's prior gifts. He writes,

> Tell me: who puts silver and gold in the mountains so that man might find them there? Who puts into the field that great wealth which issues in grain, wine, and all kinds of produce, from which all creatures live [sic] Does the labor of man do this? To be sure, labor no doubt finds it, but God has first to bestow it and put it there if labor is to find it. Who puts into the flesh the power to bring forth young and fill the earth with birds, beast, fish, etc.? Is this accomplished by our labor and care? By no means. God is there first, secretly laying his blessing therein; then all things are brought forth in abundance. And so we find that all labor is nothing more than the finding and collecting of God's gifts; it is quite unable to create or preserve anything.[48]

Here and in his Genesis commentary, human dominion rests on God's gratuitous blessing of creation with life-sustaining gifts. For this reason, Luther defines labor in relation to God's gift: "labor is nothing more than the finding and collecting of God's gifts." Likewise, buying and selling are nothing more than the distribution of God's gifts to one's neighbors. The economy derives its nature and purpose from God's ordering of creation to facilitate God's generosity.

Luther's theology of creation frames the scholastic categories that he uses to interrogate common trade and lending practices. He criticizes the idea that business ought to be conducted to maximize profit, striking at the foundational presupposition of commerce as it was practiced in Germany. Profit maximization inserts an objective that runs counter to the true *telos* of economic exchange in the divine economy, namely, to distribute the gifts of God among the human community. The transgression occurs when a price reflects the neighbor's need of that good. Luther writes, "When he has to buy his wares at a higher price because of his need, that is the same as having to buy his own need; for what is sold to him is not simply the wares as they are, but the wares plus the fact that he must have them."[49] Luther's moral reasoning reflects the common scholastic understanding of the natural law in which the usurer is guilty of breaking the eighth commandment. Since the neighbor has need of the good, she has no choice but to pay what the merchant demands. In taking more than the just price of a good, the merchant

---

[48] *LW* 45:325–26.

[49] *LW* 45:248.

steals the extra money he has coerced his neighbor to pay.[50] Luther applies this same line of thinking to the sale of a good on credit, rather than cash, to increase profit. This ploy exploits the neighbor's inability to pay up front for what she needs.[51] For this same reason, he condemns raising a price based on the scarcity of a good. Those who hoard goods or have a monopoly on the market also rob their neighbor by artificially increasing the need for a commodity by making it less available. In Luther's eyes, these merchants deny the economy's created nature by supposing that "God's goods were created and given for them alone, as if they could take them from others and set on them whatever price they chose."[52] This theo-cosmological view unites buying and selling with love for neighbor so that neglect of neighbor is a denial of the nature of being human.

### Character, Conscience, and the Natural Law

This reciprocal relation between God's generosity and human generosity sounds a common theme in Luther's work. The prodigality of God towards humanity is not only an example to follow but the inspiration for imitation: the Christian is to reciprocate this kind of prodigal generosity toward others. For instance, in *The Freedom of the Christian*, Luther explains that love for neighbor flows from the Father, "who has overwhelmed me with his inestimable riches." Moreover, this neighborly love ought to reflect the fact that the Father distributes all things to all people richly and freely.[53] Works, then, find their proper place as the response to the Father's generosity, especially the gift of Christ's righteousness. According to Luther, the chief maxim "I may sell my goods as dear as I can" as the basis of business violates both Christian love and natural law. For Luther, natural law refers to the golden rule expressed in Luke 6.31: "Do to others what you would have them do to you." This view of natural law, as we have seen, has precedent in scholastic thought as a first principle for moral reasoning. Lenders are acting contrary to nature by pretending that human nature is not oriented towards reciprocity, exchange, and communion. They are "acting contrary to nature, are guilty of mortal sin, are usurers, and are seeking in their own profit their neighbor's loss."[54] Greed thus stands at loggerheads with the very purpose of

---

[50] *LW* 45:248.

[51] *LW* 45:261.

[52] *LW* 45:262.

[53] Luther, "Freedom of the Christian," 51.

[54] *LW* 45:292.

buying and selling and leads to the exploitation and violation of others.[55] When human beings dismiss God's generosity, they see the world's resources as something to be grasped rather than received and others as competitors rather than neighbors. Greed puts down roots in the absence of gratitude. But gratitude recognizes the unbounded generosity of God's blessings bestowed upon creation and responds in kind with self-giving love.

If the sin of avarice is the taproot from which exploitative economic and social relations spring, then only an appeal to conscience and character goes deep enough to root out injustice. Participation in God's economy—that is, God's generous provision for communities through the exchange of creaturely goods—requires the cultivation of neighborly love and the mortification of avarice. Luther believes that conscience plays a pivotal role in proper economic practices for two reasons. First, avarice is a matter of character, involving an individual's subjective desires. Conscience is required to assess intent and regulate desire. Second, the complexity and particularity of each and every economic exchange precludes objective, universal regulations. Instead, conscience is required to adjudicate the just price for any given commodity because "costs, trouble, labor, and risk" vary each time a good is brought to the market to be sold. In addition to these outlays, the just price of a good also includes another variable: the amount of profit necessary to keep the business afloat and provide for the seller's family.[56] Luther wishes he could guarantee that the seller will arrive at the just price, but he concedes that

> here one can truly give you no instructions but only lay it on your conscience to be careful not to overcharge your neighbor, and to seek a modest living, not the goals of greed ... I would not have anyone's conscience be so overly scrupulous or so closely bound on this matter that he feels he must strike exactly the right measure of profit to the very heller. It is impossible for you to arrive at the exact amount that you have earned with your trouble and labor.[57]

Even if it were theoretically possible to set prices by a council or governing body, it would simply be too impractical to implement. Luther is thus content "to let goods be valued at the price for which they are bought and sold in the common market, or in the land generally." The market price reflects the subjective calculation by many individuals, and, therefore, can serve as a

---

[55] Langholm, "Martin Luther's Doctrine on Trade," 95, observes, "If there is one theme that runs through all Luther's works dealing with economic subjects, it is 'Geiz' (greed, avarice)."

[56] *LW* 45:249–50. Langholm, "Martin Luther's Doctrine on Trade," 96–97, identifies Conrad Summenhart's treatise on contracts and the work of the German nominalist Henry of Langenstein as the scholastic sources of Luther's definition of the just price.

[57] *LW* 45:250.

general approximation the just price.[58] For this reason, the character guiding one's conscience matters a great deal since the market price of a good will be inflated to the extent that sellers give in to avarice.

Luther's category of conscience aims to regulate the economy by addressing the individual's heart, which is a space that the law cannot target. To this end, he singles out two "erroneous principles" that, if instantiated in practice, function as "fountainheads of evil." If "breathing space and room" are afforded to them "opportunity and power is given them to practice unhindered all manner of wiles and trickery, and daily to think up more schemes, so that everything stinks of avarice, indeed, is submerged and steeped in avarice as in a great new Deluge."[59] The first of these erroneous principles is the maxim, "I may sell my goods as dear as I can." Avarice seizes upon this axiom and "every window and door to hell is opened."[60] With profit maximization as its goal, trade "can be nothing but robbing and stealing the property of others."[61] The second erroneous principle presumes usurping the place of God, as is the case in the practice of surety. In surety, the third party assumes full liability for the obligations of a debtor to their creditor. The person engaged in surety would often be literally penniless, leaving one's own body as the only capital that could serve as collateral.[62] Luther condemns this practice because of its un-Christian logic: surety requires trust in oneself to safeguard the loan by doing what only God can do, namely, upholding life and guaranteeing the future.[63] These two erroneous principles both exploit the need of the neighbor, and thus contradict the logic of creation as divine gift, which is the foundation of economic exchange.

Lending practices must correspond to the divine economy of grace to fulfill the natural law. Luther enumerates "three ways of dealing fairly and righteously with temporal goods" to combat the tentacles of avarice, which threaten to ensnare by enflaming love for temporal goods instead of God's eternal goods.[64] First, we are to live by the words of Jesus' in the Sermon on the Mount: "If anyone would sue you in court to take your coat, lend him your cloak as well" (Matt. 5.40). Luther rejects the interpretation of canon and civil

---

[58] *LW* 45:250.

[59] *LW* 45:261.

[60] *LW* 45:247.

[61] *LW* 45:248, 306.

[62] Rössner, "Critical Introduction," 138.

[63] *LW* 45:253–54. As Brecht notes, *Martin Luther*, 144, Luther did not always practice what he preached. On several occasions he found himself in trouble for standing as surety to help someone in great need.

[64] *LW* 45:273.

law that Christ's words are a recommendation for some.[65] He also rejects the scholastic use of Augustine to focus the meaning of the command on the inner disposition of the heart. The command stands for all Christians and requires literal obedience. Christ calls us to allow others to take, rob, and steal from us in order "to establish within us a peaceful, pure, and heavenly life."[66] Luther explains,

> It would also be impossible for us to become cleansed of our attachment to temporal goods if God did not ordain that we should suffer unjust losses, and thereby be trained to turn our hearts away from the false temporal goods of this world, letting them go in peace, and pinning our hopes on invisible and eternal goods ... In short, such commandments are intended to detach us from the world and make us desirous of heaven. Therefore, we ought freely and joyfully to accept God's faithful counsel, for if he did not give it, and did not let us experience injustice and trouble, the human heart could not maintain itself; it becomes too deeply enmeshed in temporal things and too firmly attached to them. The result is satiety, and disregard of the eternal goods in heaven.[67]

God commands that we practice radical generosity—allowing others to determine what we are willing to give away—with our temporal goods to combat greed, which threatens our salvation by orienting our love away from divine things to earthly things.

Luther employs this same logic in the two other ways to deal christianly in the economy. These are practices that fulfill the lower forms of Christ's command in Matthew 5.40: first, lend without expecting any return to whomever asks and, second, lend without interest. Both train Christians for the eternal economy by the enactment of practices that force them to trust God in this temporal economy. Luther declares that those who do not practice even the lesser degrees of the principal command "have more taste for temporal than eternal goods; they have not enough trust in God to believe that he can or will sustain them in this wretched life. They therefore fear that they would die of hunger or be ruined entirely if they were to obey God's command and give to everyone who asks of them. How then can they trust him to maintain them in eternity?"[68] In his treatise on trade, these three ways of exchanging goods (being robbed, giving away, and lending without interest) enact trust in God alone and avoid the temptation to control the future or

---

[65] *LW* 45:275.

[66] *LW* 45:279.

[67] *LW* 45:279–80.

[68] *LW* 45:280–81. Luther enumerates several specific lending practices that violate these commands, such as giving to friends and the rich rather than enemies and the poor, *LW* 45:282–83.

trust human ability.⁶⁹ These commands also reveal an even more stringent position on usury than the Old Testament prohibition. Christ has no need to teach that Christians are to lend without charge, because he commands that they give away goods, lend them without charge, and let them go when taken by force.⁷⁰ In other words, Christians do not lend; they give as God gives. The standard for Christian business dealings extends beyond lending without charge to the natural law's injunction to love neighbor as oneself through radical generosity.⁷¹

Luther's claim that Christian lending ought to conform to God's radical generosity is qualified by his account of sin. While this type of "lending" would be plausible if it were practiced between Christians, it remains imprudent at best in a world under the control of greed because only regenerate Christians are capable by the power of the Spirit to fulfill the natural law. The divinely instituted civil authority, with its vaunted sword, "must be red and bloody, for the world will and must be evil, and the sword is God's rod and vengeance upon it."⁷² As members of God's kingdom, Christians are called to enact Christ's commands to live by these practices but as members of the world to participate within the bounds set by the law.⁷³ In order to align one's life with the law of loving service to all, one must recognize the co-existence of these two realms or kingdoms. Christians, therefore, must be pragmatic in their buying and selling in the face of the abiding realities of corruption, abuse, greed, and injustice, which necessitate the existence of civil authority. Fulfilling Christ's command to lend without remuneration must not be separated from the Christian's obligations to love all within the three overlapping estates of creation, church, economy, and civil authority. The business person must decide if lending without the expectation of a return will result in harm for his or her family, for one has a duty to love and serve all. In a sinful world, Christians must negotiate a broken system because seeking the good of one's neighbor requires participation in the economic and political spheres.⁷⁴

It is an open question as to whether Luther's so-called "two kingdoms doctrine" fatally undercuts his ethical vision at this decisive point.⁷⁵ While

---

⁶⁹ *LW* 45:257.

⁷⁰ *LW* 45:291.

⁷¹ *LW* 45:297.

⁷² *LW* 45:258. Cf. 45:89–90.

⁷³ *LW* 45:97.

⁷⁴ *LW* 45:95–96.

⁷⁵ For two recent attempts that seek to uphold Luther's teaching about the two kingdoms by locating them within the more foundational concept of the three estates, see Bayer, *Martin Luther's Theology*; and Wannenwetsch, "Luther's Moral Theology."

space does not afford an exploration of this inquiry, it is worth noting that Luther's two kingdoms solution falls in line with the long list of scholastic attempts to reconcile discrepancies between enacting the literal sense of the biblical command and acknowledging the practical demands of civil law for a fallen world. It is Luther's attention to the practical demands of the reality of a sinful society that allows him to tolerate lending at usurious rates of up to six percent.[76] Despite Luther's hard line on the evils of usury, he knows that overturning the customary five or six percent lending charge that had been legal since the fifteenth century would greatly disrupt the economy.[77] To fulfill Christ's command to lend without charge would be at odds with the natural law, because a ban on usury would cripple the economy, and thus injure one's neighbor.[78] Luther summarizes the dual requirements that are necessary to fulfill Jesus command of Matthew 5.39–40 this way: "In what concerns you and yours, you govern yourself by the gospel and suffer injustice toward yourself as a true Christian; in what concerns the person or property of others, you govern yourself according to love and tolerate no injustice toward your neighbor. The gospel does not forbid this; in fact, in other places it actually commands it."[79] This also highlights the pivotal role conscience plays in fulfilling the command to love neighbor as oneself. The natural law must be fulfilled within a fallen context in which the Christian is simultaneously a citizen of the heavenly and earthly kingdom.

To sum up: Luther's economic ethics track his theo-cosmological view of the world as gift. The neglect of the divine economy of gift leads to exploitation of neighbor, which, in turn, destroys a society. First, when God's gift as the basis for commerce is forgotten, human beings reinterpret their labor as a means by which to control capital rather than disburse it equitably.[80] Second, when God's distributive purpose is lost, human beings reinterpret

---

Singleton, "Sterility of Money," 635, argues that Luther's notion of conscience introduced a subjective element into the medieval theological foundation upon which the rejection of usury was built. This had the unintended consequence of crumbling the coherent basis of the prohibition against usury.

[76] *LW* 45:305. See also Luther's *An Open Letter to the Christian Nobility* (1520); *Temporal Authority: To What Extent It Should Be Obeyed* (1523); and *Ordinance of a Common Chest* (1523). All three can be found in *LW* 45.

[77] On the historical development of the legalization of lending at interest, see Geisst, *Beggar Thy Neighbor*, 96.

[78] Luther's *On Trade and Usury* (1524) was published in response to Jakob Strauss, a preacher and disciple of Luther, who sought to reestablish Mosaic law and abolish all interest-bearing loans in Eisenach in 1523, Brecht, *Martin Luther*, 142–44.

[79] *LW* 45:96.

[80] *LW* 45:328.

their buying and selling as a vehicle for the accumulation of wealth and for the sake of self-satisfaction. Luther claims that greed has choked out generosity, and thus commerce is ruining the German lands rather than sustaining them. Germans are draining their land of life-sustaining goods in exchange for worthless accoutrements "which minister only to ostentation but serve no useful purpose."[81] As a result, rampant debt, usurious lending, and exploitative pricing hobble the economy as more and more people are dragged into grinding poverty.[82]

### Luther's Theological Social Imaginary and Our Disenchanted, Secular Economy

In Martin Luther's economic thought, we encounter a grand theo-cosmological vision of the world as creation—divinely blessed and abounding with the generosity of God. His economic ethics are only intelligible within this metaphysic of creation and the social imaginary of neighborly exchange that it entails. In this divine economy, economic exchange is one way that God enables Christians to participate in God's love for the world. By distributing the gifts of creation to their neighbors, Christians live according to their created nature. As a result, they and their neighbors flourish in communities of generous exchange, where justice and love ensure that the needs of the members of the community are met. For Luther, this theological vison of buying and selling is the *telos* of all economic activity. Accordingly, economic relations must be regulated by civil authority when human need is exploited to inflate profit on a good or loan. Given the ambiguity of calculating a good's cost to the seller, and given the seller's subjective judgment required in buying and selling, Christians ought to practice business according to the divine economy. This means giving away goods, lending them without charge, and letting them go when taken by force. Luther believes that nothing less than one's salvation is at stake: if the Christian cannot reciprocate the generosity of God toward one's neighbor with temporal goods, then she will not be the kind of person who will desire God's generosity in the eternal economy. Even though concessions are permissible in a world under the sway of sin and evil, the Christian still practices business for the good of the neighbor rather than for the sake of profit maximization. Their love of neighbor reflects the gracious activity of God that orders the world as a gift to be shared and enjoyed.

In light of this view, we can reformulate Weber's view that Luther's economics reflect a "peasant's mistrust of capital." Instead of a peasant's mistrust, might we not detect in a theologian's mistrust of profit the lifeblood

---

[81] *LW* 45:246.

[82] *LW* 45:247.

of his economics? Luther has no illusions about the heart's susceptibility to avarice. His pessimism lies with the market's inability to form people with the generosity necessary to live together in community as neighbors rather than as buyers and sellers. Although God created economic exchange for the flourishing of human communities, greed perverts the created order such that the market violates the natural law. Despite the rampant abuse in the market, Luther's conviction that God created buying and selling to unite the human community around the gifts of creation drives his economic thought. His theology of trade and usury foregrounds the extent to which this kind of economic rationale is embedded in a theo-cosmological world.

This social imaginary exposes the extent to which our conception of a self-regulating market of buyers and sellers is only intelligible in a "secular" world like our own. Luther's economic thought poses (at least) three questions for Christians living in a late-modern capitalistic society. First, what is the wider reality that grounds economic exchange, and do human practices of exchange coordinate with the divine economy? Second, what is lost when a human person is defined as a neutral, economic actor over and against the theocentric account of a person created and ordered for love of neighbor? The final question shifts our focus from the significance of creation for economic flourishing to the site of eschatology. How should economic activity in this life be subordinated to the economy of the next life? Or, in what ways does God's future economy determine the nature of economic relations and exchange in the present age? Luther would also remind us that answers to these questions must account for both the pernicious nature of sin that imperils flourishing within the created order and the political estate instituted by God to militate against sin's destructive power.

Christians who wish to promote flourishing today in our disenchanted, secularized economies must not settle for a simple translation of Luther's social imaginary into our own. Such a move disregards the fundamentally incommensurate metaphysical commitments that constitute these two social imaginaries. Instead, what is needed is a recovery of a Christian doctrine of creation that can re-embed all social, economic, and political relations within the divine economy of God. This is a critical first step because Christian communities cannot engender flourishing unless they are able to *see* their neighbors in the economy and *vice versa*. After all, Christians can only enact practices of love to the extent that Christians recognize who their neighbors are and their place in the divine economy.

## Bibliography

Anderson, Greg. *The Realness of Things Past: Ancient Greece and Ontological History*. Oxford: Oxford University Press, 2018.

Aquinas, Thomas. *The Summa Theologica of St. Thomas Aquinas*. Translated by Fathers of the English Dominican Province. New York: Benziger Brothers, 1947.

Armstrong, Lawrin. *The Ideal of a Moral Economy: Gerard of Sienna on Usury, Restitution, and Prescription*. Toronto: University of Toronto Press, 2016.

———. "Law, Ethics, Economy: Gerard of Siena and Giovanni D'Andrea on Usury." In *Money, Markets and Trade in Late Medieval Europe: Essays in Honour of John H.A. Munro*, edited by Lawrin Armstrong, Ivana Elbl, and Martin M. Elbl, 41–58. Leiden: Brill, 2007.

Bayer, Oswald. *Martin Luther's Theology: A Contemporary Interpretation*. Trans. by Thomas H. Trapp. Grand Rapids: Eerdmans, 2008.

Brecht, Martin. *Martin Luther: Shaping and Defining the Reformation 1521– 1532*. Translated by James L. Schaff. Minneapolis, MN: Fortress, 1990.

Finnis, John. *Aquinas: Moral, Political, and Legal Theory*. Oxford: Oxford University Press, 1998.

Fontaine, Laurence. *The Moral Economy: Poverty, Credit, and Trust in Early Modern Europe*. New York: Cambridge University Press, 2014.

Geisst, Charles R. *Beggar Thy Neighbor: A History of Usury and Debt*. Philadelphia: University of Pennsylvania Press, 2013.

Hillerbrand, Hans J. "Introduction to On Business and Usury." In *The Annotated Luther: The Christian Life in the World*. Volume 5, edited by Hans J. Hillerbrand, Kirsi I. Stjerna, and Timothy J. Wengert, 131–35. Minneapolis, MN: Augsburg Fortress, 2017.

Jones, David W. *Reforming the Morality of Usury: A Study of Differences That Separated the Protestant Reformers*. Lanham, MD: University Press of America, 2004.

Langholm, Odd. *The Legacy of Scholasticism in Economic Thought: Antecedents of Choice and Power*. Cambridge: Cambridge University Press, 1998.

———. "Martin Luther's Doctrine on Trade and Price in Its Literary Context." *History of Political Economy* 41.1 (2009) 89–106.

Lindberg, Carter. "Luther's Struggle with Social-Ethical Issues." In *The Cambridge Companion to Martin Luther*, edited by Donald K. McKim, 165–78. Cambridge: Cambridge University Press, 2003.

Luther, Martin. "The Freedom of the Christian." In *The Protestant Reformation*, edited by Hans J. Hillerbrand, 31–58. New York: Harper Perennial, 2009.

Milbank, John. *Theology and Social Theory: Beyond Secular Reason*. 2$^{nd}$ ed. Oxford: Blackwell, 2001.

Noonan, John. *The Scholastic Analysis of Usury*. Cambridge, MA: Harvard University Press, 1957.

Pelikan, Jaroslav, and Helmut T. Lehman, eds. *Luther's Works*. 55 vols. Philadelphia: Muhlenberg Press and Fortress Press; and St Louis, MO: Concordia, 1955–86.

Porter, Jean. *Natural and Divine Law: Reclaiming the Tradition for Christian Ethics*. Grand Rapids: Eerdmans, 1999.
Polanyi, Karl. *The Great Transformation: The Political and Economic Origins of Our Time*. Boston: Beacon, 1957.
Rössner, Philipp Robinson. "Critical Introduction." In *On Commerce and Unity (1524)*, edited by Philipp Robinson Rösser, 1–166. London: Anthem, 2015.
Singleton, John D. "'Money Is a Sterile Thing': Martin Luther on the Immorality of Money Revisited." *History of Political Economy* 43.4 (2011) 683–98.
Tanner, Norman P., ed. *Decrees of the Ecumenical Councils*. Volume 1. Washington, DC: Georgetown University Press, 1990.
Taylor, Charles. *A Secular Age*. Cambridge, MA: Harvard University Press, 2007.
Wannenwetsch, Bernd. "Luther's Moral Theology." In *The Cambridge Companion to Martin Luther*, edited by Donald K. McKim, 120–35. Cambridge: Cambridge University Press, 2003.
Weber, Max. *Protestant Ethic and the Spirit of Capitalism*. Translated by Talcott Parsons. London: Routledge, 2001.
Zachhuber, Johannes. "Martin Luther and Modernity, Capitalism, and Liberalism." *Oxford Research Encyclopedias: Religion*, edited by John Barton, 1–29. Oxford: Oxford University Press, 2017. https://oxfordre.com/religion/view/10.1093/acrefore/9780199340378.001.0001/acrefore-9780199340378-e-301.

CHAPTER 12

# Capitalism, Socialism, and Karl Barth's Pragmatism: Lessons from a Disillusioned Socialist for Christian Economic Engagement

Kimlyn J. Bender

It is safe to say that current political discourse in the United States (with analogous patterns in Europe) is marked by an ever-shrinking center pushed out by the margins. Such political movements are strangely wedded to a growing plurality of economic policies. Former commitments among conservative political affiliates in the US to a global free market have given way in recent times to national protectionist policies and tariffs in the current Republican presidential administration, while moderate progressive positions of recent Democratic platforms are being challenged with candidates promoting avowedly social-democratic programs. In this paper, I examine the case of Karl Barth as a resource for thinking about how Christians in this time might eschew ideological commitments in favor of creative economic solutions, a position perhaps surprising given Barth's apparent socialist sympathies.

### Karl Barth—The Complex Case of a Disillusioned Socialist

Karl Barth is widely considered the most significant Protestant theologian of the twentieth century. He is understood to have had democratic–socialist commitments, and, while rooted in fact, Barth's own political and economic convictions are not so easily summarized. During his first pastorate in the Aargau region of Switzerland, Barth grew increasingly disillusioned with the liberal theological and political commitments of his former teachers and education. His tenure in the small village of Safenwil introduced him to the harsh working conditions of factory workers at first hand, and he became involved in the socialist movement of his time.[1] His famous December 1911

---

[1] For Barth's socialist writings during the period of the First World War and its aftermath, as well as his contemporary reflections on the Russian revolution of 1917, see the essays in Barth, *Vorträge und kleinere Arbeiten 1914–1921*.

address, "Jesus Christ and the Movement for Social Justice," presented distinct religious socialist commitments.[2] There Barth echoed classic socialist positions such as an opposition to private ownership of the means of production and private profits unshared by labor which received only wages.[3] Yet Barth's position was truly a religious socialist one, for his theological and political convictions were closely wedded, evidenced in his famous assertion in his address, "Jesus is the movement for social justice, and the movement for social justice is Jesus in the present."[4]

Barth's speech was seen as provocative and dangerous enough that a response was published in the paper *Zofinger Tagblatt* by the regional factory owner Walter Hüssy, who attacked Barth's radicalism and attempted to school Barth in basic capitalist principles.[5] Barth would have none of this. He in turn responded with a fiery letter that affirmed his socialist convictions. Against Hüssy's claim that all of the risk of enterprise was assumed by the factory owner, and that the workers contributed "not in the least" to its profits and therefore had no claim to any share of them, Barth responded, "Even a child can see that an industrial enterprise would have neither net profits nor profits in general without the participation of the worker."[6]

In but a short time, however, Barth's admiration for the socialist movement soured. Two primary reasons might be given for this, and these were noted by Helmut Gollwitzer in his essay, "Kingdom of God and Socialism in the Theology of Karl Barth."[7] Gollwitzer claimed that Barth became disillusioned with socialism because of "the participation of the European socialist parties in the wholesale slaughter of the First World War and rise of Leninist centralism after the Soviet revolution."[8] Indeed, Barth's disillusionment with socialism as a movement was in no small part due to the failure of the socialists to stand against war and their breaking up along national lines in support for their respective warring nations. Barth's turn from his Protestant liberal inheritance was followed by a loss of confidence in what he had earlier called in his letter

---

[2] This address is published in Hunsinger, *Karl Barth and Radical Politics*. Hereafter *KBRP*.

[3] Barth, "Jesus Christ and the Movement for Social Justice," in *KBRP*, 9.

[4] Barth, "Jesus Christ and the Movement for Social Justice," 1.

[5] These contentious letters between Walter Hüssy, a local factory owner, and Barth are published in *KBRP*. For an account of this exchange, see Busch, *Karl Barth: His Life*, 68–72.

[6] Barth, *KBRP*, 22.

[7] Gollwitzer, "Kingdom of God and Socialism," *KBRP*, 50–85.

[8] Gollwitzer, "Kingdom of God and Socialism," 52.

to Hüssy the belief in "the moral progress of humanity."[9] Such naïve liberal optimism and straightforward identification of the kingdom of God with socialism evidenced in his 1911 lecture was replaced with a radical judgment of God upon all human programs of culture and politics, as expounded in the famous second edition of his Romans commentary of 1922.[10] Because his early socialism had been predicated on a sanguine view of human nature, it was therefore impossible for his socialist commitments to remain unchanged in light of his new theological viewpoint. In a late biographical sketch, Barth reflected back on the revolutionary time of the Great War:

> A change came only with the outbreak of World War I. This brought concretely to light two aberrations: first in the teaching of my theological mentors in Germany, who seemed to me to be hopelessly compromised by their submission to the ideology of war; and second in socialism. I had credulously enough expected socialism, more than I had the Christian church, to avoid the ideology of war, but to my horror I saw it doing the very opposite in every land.[11]

Nearing the end of his life, Barth therefore remarked in comments too often overlooked in considering his socialist proclivities, "Once I was a religious socialist. I discarded it because I believed I saw that religious socialism failed to take as serious and profound a view of man's misery, and of the help for him, as do the Holy Scriptures."[12]

In truth, Barth never was and could not be an ideological socialist, though he aligned himself with its goals of justice and fairness for all workers. Even after his disillusionment with religious socialism, he could turn to socialist movements as an avenue of resistance to political triumphalism preceding the First World War and to the rise of German nationalism leading up to the second, which was itself a kind of socialism, hence the Nationalsozialismus of the National Socialist German Worker's Party (Nationalsozialistische Deutsche Arbeiterpartei, i.e., NSDAP).[13] Moreover, while the mature Barth would not equate the kingdom of God, or the church, with a political program, including that of socialism, neither would he isolate dogmatic and

---

[9] See Barth, *KBRP*, 21.

[10] Barth grew to reject immanent identifications of culture with the kingdom of God, see Gollwitzer in *KBRP*, 70. Gollwitzer states, 71, "In the infinite distance of the creature from the Creator, increased by the distance of the sinner—even the justified sinner—from divine righteousness, our immanent realizations *follow* God's kingdom always as mere imitations, always pervaded by sin, always without claim to identification, always dependent upon the grace of forgiveness and election."

[11] Barth, *Karl Barth–Rudolf Bultmann Letters 1922–1966*, 154.

[12] Barth, *Final Testimonies*, 39; cf. also Barth, *God in Action*, 125.

[13] Gollwitzer, *KBRP*, 62–63.

theological commitments from ethical and political ones, though his mature thought was much more circumspect and nuanced than his early socialist position. Writing in the *Church Dogmatics* on the relation of the church and the political and economic order, Barth stated,

> The Christian community can and must also espouse various forms of social progress or even of socialism—always the form most helpful in its specific time and place and in its specific situation. Yet her decisive word cannot consist in the proclamation of social progress or socialism. It can only consist in the proclamation of God's revolution against all "ungodliness and wickedness of men" (Rom. 1:18). That means, however, that it consists in the proclamation of his kingdom as it has already come and comes.[14]

George Hunsinger, in an essay entitled "Toward a Radical Barth," concluded that Barth's position was one of a non-authoritarian socialism. More importantly, it was predicated upon a distinction between theology and politics that saw the second as implicated by the first but not identified with it, nor the first collapsed into the second. As Hunsinger stated, "Theology must not be politicized, nor politics theologized. Theology can make its contribution to politics only by remaining theology, and vice versa."[15] Barth could put this point quite succinctly late in life: "God is not identical with any ideology, and is not to be confused with such."[16]

Barth's relationship to socialism was thus quite complicated, and not nearly as straightforward as both his detractors and admirers grasped. On the one hand, Barth gave up on the political hopes he had for a transnational socialist movement (as well as for any form of religious socialism), and he increasingly saw the church as God's chosen instrument for the announcement of God's kingdom and transcendent action. Yet Barth also held that the church could not hold itself aloft from the concrete concerns of its neighbors, and this implied action and involvement in secular political activity, evidenced in Barth's own membership in the Social Democratic Party. The most accurate way to state Barth's own position is to designate it as a kind of pragmatic socialism that embraced socialism's concerns for the welfare of workers while maintaining a critical distance from its ideology and its methods.[17] It also was

---

[14] Barth, *Church Dogmatics* III/4, 545 rev., quoted in *KBRP*, 56 (emphasis added). Hereafter *CD* followed by volume number.

[15] Hunsinger, "Toward a Radical Barth," *KBRP*, 135.

[16] Barth, *CD* IV/4, 140.

[17] Barth's appreciative yet critical espousal of socialism is already evident in his lecture "Religion and Socialism," given in 1915, see Marquardt, "Erster Bericht" in Marquardt, *Verwegenheiten*, 472–73; for a discussion, see Chung, *Karl Barth*, 98–99. Chung rightly states, 102, that in his work in Safenwil "Barth had less interest in

entirely different from communism, which Barth strongly rejected. Barth's socialism was always a democratic one focused on the concerns of labor, not a state sponsored program. In sum, Barth never was, by his own admission, an ideological socialist, and even if it might be argued that he was so in those years of his first pastorate, he certainly was not following the First World War, and not a dogmatic one at any time.[18]

### Lessons from Barth's Principled Political and Economic Pragmatism

Having surveyed the complex example of Karl Barth's non-ideological socialist commitment, what might we glean from his example? Three initial lessons might be proffered.

First, Barth's commitment to siding with the workers of his village and against capitalistic owners and management was based upon a true concern for the concrete welfare of such workers in a specific location and from there extended from this specific concern to more general ones for labor throughout Europe. Barth's time as a pastor in the early twentieth century was marked by real social and economic stratification in Switzerland and in Europe generally, and the conditions of workers were marked by a lack of social safety nets and protections. Barth embraced the socialist movement as the most pragmatic option for addressing such issues. As he later commented on his time in the Aargau, "The aspect of socialism which interested me most in Safenwil was the problem of the trade union movement. I studied it for years and also helped to form three flourishing trade unions in Safenwil (where there had been none before). They remained when I left. That was my modest involvement in the workers' question and my very limited interest in socialism. For the most part it was only practical."[19] No small part of this practical

---

Marxist principles and ideology as a worldview than in practical social questions associated with the life of workers."

[18] So, Barth wrote in 1917 that the real task of the day was not to become socialists but new and right Christians, see Barth, "Die Zukunft des Christentums und der Sozialismus (1917)," in *Vorträge*, 407. One of the real weaknesses of Hunsinger's generally incisive account of Barth's political views in *KBRP* is that it never defined socialism or "radical politics" with precision, at times conflating Barth's concern for the poor with socialism itself (see *KBRP*, 177–78). Socialism is, in truth, an umbrella term used for numerous positions, some of which favor, and some of which oppose, a market economy. What can safely be said is that Barth's socialism was focused upon the welfare of workers, and he had no time for state communism. Socialism also was secondary to theology. For an insightful analysis of Barth's socialist commitments on this score, see Baranowski, "Primacy of Theology."

[19] Busch, *Karl Barth*, 103–4.

involvement stemmed from his opposition to the (mis)use of child labor in the local factories.[20]

Second, Barth's commitment remained non-ideological in its orientation and was certainly so by the completion of The Great War.[21] His mature theological position which allowed for no direct identification of the divine reality of the kingdom of God with the contemporary political or economic order or any such program entailed that there could be no moniker of "Christian" placed upon any worldly program, including that of a political party or economic system.[22] Barth remained adamant that no direct line could be drawn from the kingdom of God to current political or economic realities, with the latter serving at best as "analogies" or "parables" of the kingdom of God. The task of the church is to witness to the kingdom of God (though the church is not the kingdom), and in its life in the world it should side with those political and economic options that most reflect the kingdom's concerns. As Barth stated with regard to political life, but which fully reflects his thought regarding economic life as well, the church is called to a specific public position: "Among the political possibilities open at any particular moment it will choose those which most suggest a correspondence to, and analogy and a reflection of, the content of its own faith and gospel."[23] With regard to economic interests in particular, Barth insisted on the church's concern for the poor and vulnerable:

> The Church is witness of the fact that the Son of man came to seek and to save the lost. And this implies that—casting all false impartiality aside—the Church must concentrate first on the lower and lowest levels of human society. The poor, the socially and economically weak and threatened, will always be the object of its primary and particular concern, and it will always insist on the State's special responsibility for these weaker members of society.[24]

This concern for the disadvantaged leads to the third and final point. Barth was always more occupied with the concerns of socialism than committed to its methods or principled economic theories and convictions. He had no penchant for Eastern communism and rejected it as an answer to any question the workers may have, and as noted, he was distressed, as were many, by the

---

[20] See Chung, *Karl Barth*, 102–3.

[21] Barth's final break with religious socialism, and one might add, with sympathy for ideology of any kind, is clear in the second edition of the Romans commentary and already in place by 1919, see Hunsinger, "Toward a Radical Barth," *KBRP*, 165.

[22] See Barth, "The Christian Community," in *Community, State, and Church*, 182–84.

[23] Barth, "Christian Community," 170.

[24] Barth, "Christian Community," 173.

authoritarianism and violent excesses of the Soviet revolution and its aftermath, even though he had earlier read and studied Marxist theory.[25] Yet, regardless of this opposition to communism in the East, he nevertheless remained critical of capitalism in the West to the end of his life as well, and especially of its propensity to social and economic stratification with its growing disparities of wealth between rich and poor and its disenfranchisement of common labor. His mature position was marked by a realism toward a fallen political order that in various instantiations was comprised of tribal constituencies where, in his context of democratic Europe, the West naively overlooked its own problems in its principled and persistent opposition to Eastern communism, or optimistically overestimated the scope and possibilities of its own free market solutions. This realism seemingly had the effect of turning Barth to a slight pessimism later in life, so that by the mid-1960s when the Cold War was firmly entrenched, he could attest that he had lost faith in both capitalist and socialist (or communist) systems: "Today there are really no longer any genuine alternatives. No great fundamental ideas seem to clash. I often feel at a loss about which party to vote for, if at all."[26]

Again, such despair did not entail that Barth believed the church and Christians should abandon political and cultural engagement for quietism. But such engagement could not track directly with current political and economic programs and solutions. And if this is so, then one might question Barth's own form of socialist commitments and ask if another way forward is in order for Christian economic reflection today. For it may be valid to ask whether Barth's concern for the conditions of labor as well as for the underclass and those in poverty might be distinguished and even separated from his socialist commitments.

Such an observation might easily lead one to expect that this essay will hereafter move into an ideological defense of capitalism as currently practiced, but such binary forms of thought wherein to point out the problems of communism or even socialism is taken to entail a commitment to contemporary capitalism, or *vice versa*, is itself part of the current problem of reflection upon economic and political questions for both Christians and others. Barth's rejection of ideological socialism did not entail an abandonment of his criticisms of capitalism, criticisms which he quite consistently embraced throughout his life.[27] Rather, it led to a more *ad hoc* approach to political and economic engagement for Christians, one that complemented his eclectic approach to borrowing from philosophy in the work of theology. He outlined such pragmatic and christologically-grounded

---

[25] Gollwitzer, *KBRP*, 75.

[26] Quoted in Hunsinger, "Preface to the Second Edition," *KBRP*, xvii; original in Barth, *Gespräche 1964–1968*, 551.

[27] See Barth's discussion in *CD* III/4, 534–45.

engagement in the earlier-mentioned essay, "The Christian Community and the Civil Community." While his christological reasoning of analogical and indirect relations between the kingdom of God and the political order have themselves been criticized, it is nevertheless true that Barth's attempt to find limited analogies and parables of the kingdom of God in the world that the church could in turn support was an attempt in the political and economic areas of the world to steer between what in the framework of theological language might be identified as positions of parity or univocity on one side, and disparity or equivocity on the other.

Just as Barth insisted that theological language that spoke of God could neither be equated with language pertaining to human and created realities nor seen as having nothing to do with them, but instead had to be considered under the form of analogy that preserved both similarity and difference, so also the church was not only allowed but required to make relative judgments of earthly systems and thus to side with those that more closely reflected the kingdom of God.[28] Such political and economic programs were at best echoes of the kingdom, not instantiations of the kingdom. For this reason, the church and Christians must neither identify the kingdom with such programs nor eschew the responsibility to support them for the benefit of the world which stood under the Lordship of Christ. As noted above, Barth identified these analogical reflections as parables of the kingdom of God, instances of indirect correspondence to the kingdom rather than an identification with it.[29] Hence, Barth's theological understanding of divine freedom and God's concern for the oppressed revealed in scripture led him to uphold political freedom and social programs in the present that sided with the poor and disenfranchised, and thus his preference for a kind of non-authoritarian, democratic socialism.

Barth did not, however, think that the church could simply adopt a political, cultural, or economic program in principle. Such would embrace an ideological commitment that the freedom of obedience to the command of God would not allow. The church could only make relative, rather than absolute, judgments of current systems. In favoring one over others, the only

---

[28] For Barth's description of analogy pertaining to theological language in contrast to parity (univocity) and imparity (equivocity), see *CD* II/1, 224–36.

[29] For the importance of "parable" (*Gleichnis*) and "correspondence" (*Entsprechung*) in Barth's political thought, see Gollwitzer in *KBRP*, 69–72. Negatively, Gollwitzer posits, 71, parable signified for Barth that there could be no identification of God's socialism of the kingdom and our socialism. Positively, 71, it signified that what takes place in social affairs is capable of reflecting the kingdom of God. As he concludes, 71, "Eschatology does not brake, but propels, our activity." Gollwitzer, 80, thus pushes back on the first negative principle when he asks, "Do socialist groups have *a priori* no possibility of being 'a provisional representation' of the 'the salvation already taken place in Christ for all persons,' especially if 'provisional' means 'in a broken form, imperfect, endangered and questionable'?"

absolute commitment of the church and the Christian is to Christ and the kingdom of God, and no earthly program of whatever type could claim such allegiance. For the church to give absolute allegiance to such a thing would be no less than the confusion of the kingdom of God with contemporary politics, and this is nothing less for Barth than idolatry.

George Hunsinger in the introduction to *Karl Barth and Radical Politics* has argued, nevertheless, that Barth supported both political democracy ("parliamentary democracy") and "economic democracy," each marked by an opposition to both concentrations of power and wealth in a small minority, for democracy requires opposition to a wealthy class that unduly influences or controls government.[30] As Hunsinger observed, "Throughout his life Barth favored a 'practical,' non-authoritarian socialism, essentially because he believed in democracy."[31] Hunsinger thus seemed to draw quite a direct line from such democratic commitments to the necessity of economic socialism. Yet it is here that we might raise some critical questions. For one, what Hunsinger did not consider is whether other options than those of Barth's day might now be at hand; certainly, the rise of mixed economies makes appeals to "capitalism" and "socialism" as static and self-contained economic philosophies far too simple. In truth, capitalism and socialism are terms that themselves require precise definition and cover a variety of positions regarding markets, state regulation, private ownership, and social safety nets. In addition, Hunsinger did not consider the possibility that certain forms of capitalism (whether free market or mercantilist/protectionist) can create not only disparities of wealth but can also, in certain cases, be shown to create wealth itself and lift persons out of poverty—which has indeed been the case.[32] Nevertheless, there remains the enduring problem of rising inequality that unmitigated capitalism can foster.

---

[30] Hunsinger, "Preface to the Second Edition," *KBRP*, xiv.

[31] Hunsinger, "Preface to the Second Edition," xiv. Hunsinger, xxi, states that for Barth "Socialism was a predicate of the gospel." This is too strong, for Barth's socialist commitments were more pragmatic than directly derived. As Baronowski, "Primacy of Theology," 455, rightfully states, "Barth avoided programmatic socialist platforms beyond the goals of peace and justice. No ideology, be it Marxism, pacifism, reformist socialism or the like could become the norm for Christian political behavior."

[32] This has been argued by Max Stackhouse, who takes a much more optimistic view of global capitalism, see Stackhouse, *Globalization and Grace*, 27–33. According to United Nations' reports, global poverty rates have been cut in half since 2000, in no small part due to economic development, see United Nations, "Ending Poverty;" and also Barnes, *Redeeming Capitalism*, 69. For a nuanced argument that global trade and providing widespread access to market economies is the best way to take a preferential option for the poor with real seriousness, see Waters, *Just Capitalism*. For an unvarnished appraisal of both the achievements and failures of modern capitalism, see Barnes, *Redeeming Capitalism*, 69–77; also Milanovic, *Capitalism, Alone*.

The more important question we might ask, however, is whether state (i.e., federal) socialism does not simply mirror, rather than alleviate, the very problems that both Barth and Hunsinger saw in modern forms of capitalism, namely, the concentration of power and wealth in a limited number of political and economic central authorities, the particular outcome of a distinctively modern project of the intensification of power under a hegemonic center of control. Certainly this is true for many forms of corporate capitalism, but it is questionable if such economic democracy as Hunsinger described is really achieved when market decisions, if not the means of production, are increasingly concentrated in a centralized economy, and when the political and the economic spheres of life are so closely merged. Is this really economic democracy—or is it in truth economic monarchy? Hunsinger espouses a radical politics that questions the centralized power of bureaucracies of government and its managerial class (evidenced in his criticisms of the conduct of the US government in the Vietnam War). It is thus unclear why he should then argue that the solution to economic plight is to invest more and more economic decisions and power in a centralized bureaucratic federal government. It is perfectly valid to ask whether the excesses of corporate capitalism and its concentrations of wealth among the few is really to be answered with the concentration of wealth and economic power in the state.

## Mapping the Current Economic and Political Landscape

Such concerns are not simply theoretical of course. James Scott's work *Seeing Like a State: How Certain Schemes to Improve the Human Condition Have Failed* has incisively revealed the true problems of concentrated power in both unaccountable and powerful large multi-national corporations and the utopian socialist projects of powerful nation states.[33] Scott's work is a defense of local knowledge, local control, and heterogeneity, as well as the decentering of both political and economic power and decision-making against the high modern project of universal knowledge and centralized decision-making and control. In a manner consistent with Catholic and secular arguments for subsidiarity, Scott reveals the tremendous tragedies of large political revolutions enforced by centralized power in the former Soviet Union, China, and Cambodia, but also argues that "large-scale capitalism is just as much an agency of homogenization, uniformity, grids, and heroic simplification as the state is, with the difference being that, for capitalists, simplification must pay."[34] Such homogenous structures can thus be the product of both state and corporate power and overreach. Certainly, such overreach is seen in the failed communist experiments of the twentieth century, failures that are now entirely

---

[33] Scott, *Seeing Like a State*. Hereafter *SLAS*.

[34] Scott, *SLAS*, 8.

indefensible. But Scott also contends that such centralized dangers exist in areas where free markets are ascendant: "Today, global capitalism is perhaps the most powerful force for homogenization, whereas the state may in some instances be the defender of local difference and variety." He notes that "the conclusions that can be drawn from the failures of modern projects of social engineering are as applicable to market-driven standardization as they are to bureaucratic homogeneity."[35]

While Scott does not entirely reject political and social planning, including that on a large, federal scale, nor argues against every form of international free trade, he states that his work's purpose is "making a case against an imperial or hegemonic planning mentality that excludes the necessary role of local knowledge and know-how." His goal throughout the book is to "make the case for the indispensable role of practical knowledge, informal processes, and improvisation in the face of unpredictability."[36] In effect, Scott highlights the deeply problematic results of the centralization of political and economic power in a diminishing number of corporate players or in a centralized federal government, each which through the use of utilitarian visions of human betterment end up stripping persons of freedom and local communities of vibrancy and empowerment. As but one example, he recounts that what American capitalism and Soviet collectivism share in common is "the belief in huge, mechanized, industrial farms."[37] His picture of centralized bureaucratic programs of social betterment is quite sobering. As he writes,

> Authoritarian social engineering is apt to display the full range of standard bureaucratic pathologies. The transformations it wishes to effect cannot generally be brought about without applying force or without treating nature and human subjects as if they were functions in a few administrative routines. Far from being regrettable anomalies, these behavioral by-products are inherent in high-modernist campaigns of this kind. I am purposely ignoring here the more obvious inhumanities that are inevitable whenever great power is placed in the

---

[35] Scott, *SLAS*, 8.

[36] Scott, *SLAS*, 6.

[37] Scott, *SLAS*, 193. Indeed, it is not lost on Scott, 164, that while a contingent of the radical left hangs on to a wistful admiration for a communistic system, it was Lenin and the Russian revolution that in fact gave us a "condemnation of small-scale family farming and a celebration of the gigantic, highly mechanized forms of modern agriculture." Moreover, 166, Lenin was, in fact, the exemplar of high modernism with its belief that technology and science could be our savior, and certainly this is a conviction shared by modern Western capitalism with its own form of consumerist (if not communistic) materialism. Yet Scott moreover concludes with regard to the Soviet project, 217, "What must strike even a casual student of [communist] collectivization, however, is how it largely failed in *each* of its high-modernist aims, despite huge investments in machinery, infrastructure, and agronomic research."

hands of largely unaccountable state authorities who are under pressure from above to produce results despite popular resistance.[38]

Such elimination of local knowledge and concerns is then coupled with an even more insidious form of dehumanization. William Schweiker notes that at the root of the dangers of economic commerce of any type is the danger of depersonalization and commercialism, where everything is open to commodification and sale.[39] As he writes, "The loss of 'persons' is a pervasive threat in systems of commodification that reduce value to one system of measurement (say, money) and feed human vice, especially greed. The inability to articulate a robust sense of the worth of persons is a fact in most commercial cultures." He adds that this is not, contrary to common opinion, a feature only of modern capitalist societies, but is rather a perennial factor of all economic exchange from time immemorial in which the poor are driven to sell not only their labor but "their bodies, children, and futures."[40] Indeed, income inequality long predates the rise of capitalistic societies.

Of course, even with a recognition of such dangers and pathologies, Christians and churches may well disagree on the solutions, and, more specifically, upon the tactics and even strategies by which they attempt to live out and support matters of political well-being and economic fairness, but the modest argument of the current proposal here given is the call for Christians to reject a binary capitalist or socialist imagination and all ideological thinking which embraces one pure system to the exclusion of complexity and pragmatic creativity, accompanied by a blindness to the deep problems of every system as it has been practiced in the modern world.[41] Alasdair MacIntyre, in his seminal work *After Virtue*, reminds us that such arguments of binary options are often staged as those between individual liberties and communal bureaucratic authority but in effect hide the fact that both are forms of centralized power exercised by means of managerial control.[42] In this, for all their differences of project and perspective, MacIntyre and Scott echo one

---

[38] Scott, *SLAS*, 243–44.

[39] Schweiker, "Responsibility in the World of Mammon," 118; cf. 122.

[40] Schweiker, "Responsibility in the World of Mammon," 108–9. He adds, 109, "Grinding poverty means that everything can (must?) become a 'commodity' for sale, trade, or negotiation. To demonize capitalism is to miss the deeper problem inherent in economic life as such."

[41] This problem is a general one in the contemporary world. As Barnes, *Reforming Capitalism*, 138, notes, "it would not be an exaggeration to suggest that doctrinaire positions on both sides of the political spectrum have hijacked political discourse, especially in the United States. Entrenched political views are polarizing people without actually contributing to the discussion in a reasoned and logical manner."

[42] MacIntyre, *After Virtue*, 26. Hereafter *AV*.

another. Similar to Scott, MacIntyre argues that debates of modern societies that appear as focused upon two radically different alternatives are in fact debates about positions that in fact share much in common.

> Those debates are often staged in terms of a supposed opposition between individualism and collectivism, each appearing in a variety of doctrinal forms. On the one side there appear the self-defined protagonists of individual liberty, on the other the self-defined protagonists of planning and regulation, of the goods which are available through bureaucratic organization. But in fact what is crucial is that on which the contending parties agree, namely that there are only two alternative modes of social life open to us, one in which the free and arbitrary choices of individuals are sovereign and one in which the bureaucracy is sovereign, precisely so that it may limit the free and arbitrary choices of individuals. Given this deep cultural agreement, it is unsurprising that the politics of modern societies oscillate between a freedom which is nothing but a lack of regulation of individual behavior and forms of collectivist control designed only to limit the anarchy of self-interest.[43]

MacIntyre states that both of these are "in the long run intolerable." He continues, "Thus the society in which we live is one in which bureaucracy and individualism are partners as well as antagonists. And it is in the cultural climate of this bureaucratic individualism that the emotivist self is naturally at home."[44] What MacIntryre frames in terms of the inadequacies of the prevalent options of ethical, moral, and political realities is just as true of economic ones that oscillate between the pure types of an absolute and unregulated free market catering to individual materialist desire and a regulated and centralized state-controlled economy that dissolves the individual into a collectivist whole.[45] Here terms like "capitalism" and "socialism" not only become too simple but are debased to the level of epithets that hide deeper and more serious issues.

Like Scott, MacIntrye also notes that bureaucratic structures can be those of "private corporations or of government agencies."[46] And MacIntyre, like Scott, also sees the problem as not only one of centralized power but the

---

[43] MacIntyre, *AV*, 34–35.

[44] MacIntyre, *AV*, 35.

[45] As Scott, *SLAS*, 349, notes, "The point is simply that high-modernist designs for life and production tend to diminish the skills, agility, initiative, and morale of their intended beneficiaries." Moreover, the state with its centralized institutions "undermines individuals' capacities for autonomous self-governance." Of course, MacIntyre and Christians at large might consider the very notion of "autonomous self-governance," when shorn of theological definition and moral character, as itself part of the problem.

[46] MacIntyre, *AV*, 25.

depersonalization of decision-making among an unaccountable technocratic managerial class far removed from those impacted by their actions: "Government itself becomes a hierarchy of bureaucratic managers, and the major justification advanced for the intervention of government in society is the contention that government has resources of competence which most citizens do not possess."[47] As we have seen, Scott has called much of this into question, and he presents numerous failed large-scale projects that in the end caused devastation to traditional and historic communities and local ecosystems.[48] Such arguments are augmented by MacIntyre's own that the intractable unpredictability of complex systems and the contingencies of history put to lie the claims of "bureaucratic managerial expertise."[49] The large-scale intentions of the social managerial class are thus betrayed to be not only politically and economically problematic, but emblematic of the theological conviction that humanity attempts to plan and build towers that reach to heaven in a stark attempt to overcome not only our historical contingency but our created finitude in claims of omniscience and omnipotence. Centralization goes back at least as far as the tower of Babel. Yet it betrays the locality of knowledge mirrored in the plurality of languages. Such bureaucratic centralization when conducted without such realist restraints and humility in the face of finitude, complexity, unpredictability, and contingency, displays the attempt to regulate all through an omnicompetence of planning undergirded through an unspoken but assumed omnipotence and omniscience. And so as MacIntyre succinctly concludes, "Since organizational success and organizational predictability exclude one another, the project of creating a wholly or largely predictable organization committed to creating a wholly or largely predictable society is doomed and doomed by the facts about social life."[50] Again, this position does not deny that some large-scale planning is necessary, but it greatly chastens such ambitions and places them into subservience to the ends of local communities.

---

[47] MacIntyre, *AV*, 85. Scott, *SLAS*, 346, similarly notes, "What is perhaps most striking about high-modernist schemes, despite their quite genuine egalitarian and often socialist impulses, is how little confidence they repose in the skills, intelligence, and experience of ordinary people."

[48] Scott, *SLAS*, 340, contends, "What has proved to be truly dangerous to us and to our environment, I think, is the *combination* of the universalist pretensions of epistemic knowledge and authoritarian social engineering."

[49] MacIntyre, *AV*, 106. MacIntrye thus provides a sobering perspective that qualifies more optimistic understandings of the task of management. For such a theological account and example of this latter optimistic type, see Stackhouse, "Spheres of Management," 243–58.

[50] MacIntyre, *AV*, 106.

### Christian Pragmatic Engagement without Commitment to Ideology

If the particular problems of such political and economic matters cannot be simplistically played off between capitalism and socialism but are instead tied intrinsically to the concentration and limitation of power to but a few centers of effective authority, then Christians who oppose corporate irresponsibility and the exploitation of labor need not be seen as advocates of state socialism, nor are Christians who oppose state socialism necessarily defenders of entirely unregulated international corporate capitalism.[51] These are not the only alternatives, and what are contrasted as opposites are in fact similar projects of high modernism that result in intensifying power in central authorities (corporations or the state) that in the end undermine the democratic and economic interests of persons and local communities, and lead to the depersonalization, and in some cases the denigration, of work and labor.

In contrast to such dualistic ideological commitments to systems of capitalism or socialism with ensuing purity tests, Christians are to begin with theological convictions brought to economic reflection which are categorically and qualitatively more foundational than economic convictions themselves. Certainly, the first is that, in light of the gospel and the teachings of Jesus, the church is to function according to its own practices of grace and generosity that stand in contrast to all worldly systems of exchange and thus serve as a sign of the kingdom to come. Yet it is also the case that, second, the church lives within the world and is called to share the burdens of those within it. The church, therefore, must uplift its neighbors in the world not only in its direct action of witness, charity, and generosity, but also in giving support to the political and economic life of the state that best reflects the church's own theological convictions of the identity and dignity of persons and the church's witness to the kingdom of God.

---

[51] Both capitalism and state socialism can lend themselves to the disenfranchisement of persons through the intensification of power and wealth, though the latter in its communistic variety has been especially coercive in nature. If capitalism has an advantage in this regard over state socialism, it is that the state does not become the center of both political power and of the economy and production. Capitalism thus diffuses this intensification among various corporations with limited ability to regulate any individual human life. Scott, *SLAS*, 101–2, in turn buttresses this skepticism about large scale political oversight of the complexities of the economy: "The point of liberal political economy was not only that a free market protected property and created wealth but also that the economy was far too complex for it ever to be managed in detail by a hierarchical administration." If socialism has an advantage, and socialism *not* as state-sponsored ownership of the means of production but as a more general (if imprecise) term designating generous social policies practiced in strong market economies, it is that it keeps (at least in principle) the question of those at the bottom of the social and economic ladder constantly in view, and reminds society of its obligations to them and of their welfare in a world of increasing disparities.

One of the most fundamental of these convictions is the inalienable value of the human person as one for whom Christ lived and died and who bears this image of Christ, who himself is the singular image of God. Each person bears this image in an embodied form set within a matrix of needs, obligations, and duties, yet the value of each person is not predicated solely on the fulfillment of such responsibilities, for each person re-presents Christ to us in his or her lived and embodied existence.[52] Moreover, the conviction of Christ's work of reconciliation and the Spirit's promised redemption entails also a sober understanding of sin, and one of the first implicates of such a conviction regarding sin and salvation should be a wariness of the potential and often real corruption of complex institutions that amass concentrations of wealth and power and that de-humanize persons through increasing forms of bureaucracy, managerial excess, and technocracy. It must be stated that such things can be found as readily in an oppressive state as they may be found in corporations that wield ever-growing global economic and indeed political power. It must also be said that such sinfulness is found not only in the current systems of the world, but in the hubris of thinking any current system can simply be overthrown by "innocent" revolutionaries to form a utopian one, ignoring not only MacIntyre's observation of the unpredictability of social complexity, but also, more problematically, the intractability of human depravity and limitations of even good intentions.[53] In turn, there is no logical reason to accept that the answer to the excesses of global capitalism is state socialism or even socialism at all, nor is the answer to wasteful state bureaucracy an unfettered corporate capitalism that maximizes profits at the expense of local exploitation of labor. Part of the answer may well be both to decouple political power from the life and influence of corporations, and to decenter economic power from the state, even as the state may and must in certain limited areas provide a necessary regulatory check upon economic markets and perform a limited range of fiscal responsibilities. Even here, the actual application of these regulations, apart from a select number of fundamental moral commitments, cannot be predicted and standardized but must be examined as needs arise in each case.

This argument against any form of economic ideological purity is not an argument for economic anarchy, or against relative and even strong arguments for the relative superiority of one economic system over another, or against the leverage of capital for growth and human benefit. It is, however, an argument

---

[52] See Barth, *CD* I/2, 428–29.

[53] As Barnes, *Redeeming Capitalism*, 88, rightly notes regarding such unpredictability, "Whether driven by political will or economic theory, well-meaning people creating an economic utopia are destined for disappointment from the first, beginning with the obvious hurdle of the mere size and complexity of the global economy." See also 88–89. For Christians, such is all the truer due to the theological conviction of the realities of a fallen world.

for the practice of a separation of powers not only between the branches of government but between government and the economic sphere where each is set as a check on the other. If anything, this political principle of the separation of powers which is central to the US Constitution is best seen not only as a principle within the political realm, but as a pragmatic principle that may be extended to apply across society so that political and economic areas may serve as mutual checks upon the power of the other (though these checks themselves must be carefully circumscribed).[54] The political realm must not be given undue and unchecked powers of economic regulation and certainly not the reins of the means of production—if the twentieth century has taught anything, it is the complete failure of such centralized economic programs—and the economic sphere must not be left to its own devices for the maximization of profit at the expense of other non-economic cultural and common values that must be protected from the overwhelming forces of a global free market. Moreover, the interests of corporations must not be allowed to sway unduly and dictate the political process through the targeted infusion of vast means of capital for the purchase of influence, such that capital is traded and exchanged for political power, undermining the democratic process. Most important of all may well be the recognition and designation of areas of human life that transcend and must be shielded from market forces and the reduction of all of life to commerce.[55] For Christians, the basis for this recognition and protection lies in deep theological convictions, and these theological convictions transcend, but may find their own analogies in, secular ones that entail safeguarding the welfare of persons against the onslaught of pure market and bureaucratic forces.

Certainly what is here offered is but a broad proposal, and arguments can be brought up against the decentralization described. Perhaps the one immediate argument against this is that large corporate capitalism has provided the engine for much that has bettered human life especially in the realms of medicine and the development of life-saving drugs administered world-wide. Moreover, an argument against local authority and sovereignty can be made by pointing to the corresponding importance of the regulatory functions of federal agencies such as the American Food and Drug Administration, which provide national standardized protection for the populace. For a political parallel, one might think of the American Civil Rights movement which made its greatest gains through the power of the

---

[54] See Waters, *Just Capitalism*, 165–66.

[55] Schweiker, "Responsibility in the Word of Mammon," 131–32, comments, "Economic justice is, of course, about fairness of exchange, distribution of goods and services, or the creation of wealth. Yet justice, substantively defined, is the demand that within each of the social spheres the moral standing of persons as such be respected and enhanced. And this requires some way to conceive of the worth of persons *outside* or *prior to* their worth in social practices."

federal government which brought change to bear upon resistant segregationist state and local authorities.

Yet these examples may themselves serve the larger argument that Christian approaches must in the end be pragmatic rather than ideological. At the very least, the complexity of economic systems is akin to the complexity of all sustained areas of human development and interaction, and thus a level of humility and minimalism in planning and social engineering is not only in order but necessary. This complexity also requires a recognition that decentralization provides not only a mitigation of the harmful effects of the corruption that attends the concentration of human power, but also a respect for the reality that the resilience of diversity pertains not only to natural habitats but to economic systems.[56] Starkly put: it is one thing for a company to fail; it is entirely something different for a state to fail. This truth argues for the vibrancy and adaptability of market economies over centrally planned ones. It also provides warrant for the separation of the political and economic centers of a society and for the legitimate and necessary place for antitrust regulation and laws.

For Christians, this recognition of both the fallen nature of the powers and their nevertheless inevitable presence in a shared civil life entails a rejection of dogmatic commitments to economic systems or programs *carte blanche*. In contrast, it warrants an intensive examination of actual practices on the ground. Christians, therefore, should hold economic convictions much more loosely than they often do and insist on their revisability in light of further knowledge and changing conditions. In short, they should take up economic reflection without unquestioned attachments to an ideological economic theory.[57] Here Barth is a true resource for Christians even today. A careful reading of Barth must push beyond the socialist commitments that he held to their underlying foundation, which was a commitment to a concern for persons and his assertion that the church must always favor those forms of social progress that are "most helpful in its specific time and place and in its specific situation."[58] If this is true, it is Barth's economic pragmatism, not his

---

[56] Scott, *SLAS*, 281.

[57] See Scott, *SLAS*, 345. Stanley Hauerwas is often accused of Christian sectarianism, though his position is more accurately understood when considering the following: "Am I therefore suggesting the Christians must 'withdraw' from the social, political, and legal life of America? I am certainly not arguing that; rather, I am trying to suggest that in order to answer questions of 'why' or 'how' Christians participate in the life of this country we do not need a theory about the Christian character of democracy." See Hauerwas, "A Christian Critique," 477. I would argue that Hauerwas' conviction that Christians can make pragmatic use of the democratic forms of government under which they live for the betterment of others without a settled final "theory" of political life can be extended to matters of economic policy as well.

[58] Barth, *CD* III/4, 545.

socialism, that is his most basic economic philosophy, just as eclecticism marked his *ad hoc* borrowing from philosophy in the theological task. It might do the church well to escape the dualism of a static binary form of economic thinking and explore other more nuanced alternatives as well as the most creative solutions of the time for the betterment of persons. Just as theology must not become irrevocably identified with a particular philosophical school, so also it must not become unquestionably wedded to a single economic philosophy. This pragmatism is not an argument for a crass utilitarianism; it is, rather, the realization that the theologically-determined end may require a non-ideological flexibility and creativity as to the means taken to pursue it.

At the very least, an economic pragmatism which follows from principled theological convictions argues for a preference for a limitation of powers in the political and economic sphere (as Barth himself argued for the relative benefits of democracy and the church's partiality for it).[59] Such practical political and economic entailments may mean a preference for Christian action in politics and economics that are "bottom up" rather than "top-down," and thus an emphasis upon local and municipal action and solutions rather than state and federal ones. This may include, for instance, support for local community initiatives that refuse to allow predatory businesses free reign (such as certain payday and auto-title loan and lending agencies that prey upon the poor) or for those that resist other national companies that drive off local businesses that embody communal goods that extend beyond economic ones (such as small grocery stores in rural areas that provide fresh produce and thus indirectly serve the health of the community's residents).[60] Christians may advocate for local governmental and economic decisions that themselves are inclusive of factors beyond those of economic considerations alone. Further examples may include the embrace of certain forms of (reasoned) regulation and even (carefully considered and limited) forms of protectionism (i.e., mercantilism).[61] Should some argue that such regulation might suppress markets, it might be rejoined that: a) certain regulatory decisions and legal strictures already suppress or prohibit certain forms of commerce for which markets are readily available (i.e., prostitution, et al.); and b) all markets require forms of regulation that provide for fairness within them and that exist to protect larger civic values from pure commercialization, as well as from

---

[59] Barth, "Christian Community and Civil Community," 181–82.

[60] For one example of local resistance to the danger of rural food deserts created by the disappearance of local grocery stores in the light of large corporate companies, see McGreal, "Where even Walmart won't go."

[61] For the necessity of market regulation, see Waters, *Just Capitalism*, 173–77. For the limitations of protectionism and mercantilism of this type, with an argument that they in the end harm, rather than help, workers, see Waters, *Just Capitalism*, 8–9, 53–54, 149.

being marginalized by the market.[62] In sum, Christians should find their commitments to the gospel and a distinctive ecclesial ethic more foundational and determinative for what they accept and argue for in the society in which they participate than they do any economic theory or practice.

Again, such pragmatic strategies may entail that Christians begin to focus their civic engagement not on national and even state areas of political and economic activity but on those of local counties and municipalities, and thus upon matters defined by immediate human need rather than party affiliation, platform, or programs. This embrace of local action is further justified by acknowledging the alienation that comes simply from the scale of the nation state and its intrinsic depersonalization. As Scott notes, "Officials of the modern state are, of necessity, at least one step—and often several steps— removed from the society they are charged with governing."[63] For Christians and churches, such local action reflects their own theological commitments related to the humanization and dignity of persons and the radical particularity of the gospel and its revelation. At the very least, they should be driven by the preservation and furtherance of such dignity in concrete forms of local political and economic activity. As Barth stated,

> The church is based on the knowledge of the one eternal God, who as such became man and thereby proved Himself a neighbor to man, treating him with compassion (Luke 10:36f.). The inevitable consequence is that in the political sphere the church will always and in all circumstances be interested primarily in human beings and not in some abstract cause or other, whether it be anonymous capital or the State as such.[64]

---

[62] Max Stackhouse and Dennis McCann, themselves quite optimistic about market capitalism and critical of socialism, nevertheless write in their essay "A Post-Communist Manifesto," 222, "If we can no longer affirm the socialist decision, must we now become enthusiastic neoconservatives? The answer is No, for questions of social justice are a necessary part of modern economics, not an intrusion into it." They continue, "Whenever capitalism rapes the earth or becomes a pillar of racism, sexism, classicism, or nationalism, it must be resisted." Of course, "social justice" requires definition and is a contested and often vague notion. This too is a matter of Christian reflection, criticism, and discernment. Moreover, it is unclear that Stackhouse and McCann have a thick enough theological account to provide the opposition to the injustices that they identify. The limitations of their position can be seen in their subjugation of christology to anthropology, and in a parallel way, of theology to sociology, accompanied by a seeming parallel regard for church and corporation in which the second seems in places more significant than the first. For such criticisms, see Long, *Divine Economy*, 50–56.

[63] Scott, *SLAS*, 76.

[64] Barth, "Christian Community and Civil Community," 171.

Such must be true not only for the church's political but also its economic commitments, which must be driven not by ideological adherence but by theological conviction wedded to a policy of pragmatism that embraces and fosters analogies and parables of the kingdom where they may be found. The church (as the Christian) has no final commitment to capitalism or socialism but to the adoption of an ever-refined and ever-revisable economic policy that meets the particular goals of ensuring the well-being of persons. This principled pragmatism in favor of the well-being of persons must be considered paramount, rather than first considering what is most beneficial for either the corporation or the state. Of course, these need not be set in opposition but should ultimately be at one.

This section must be brought to a close. The utopian but tragic and horrendous results of twentieth-century state socialism projects (communism) need not be reargued but do need to be constantly remembered, even if such arguments are often unfairly applied to current chastened social welfare programs within vibrant market economies. More important for Christians in the West is the necessity of highlighting the dangers of a global market freed from the consideration of a larger matrix of cultural and common goods and devoid of ethical and moral reflection and practice. This recognition, of course, should not ignore the true benefits that capitalism has produced, but one need not embrace a socialist economic program to highlight the fact that contemporary capitalism is often marked by the reward of reckless financial speculation in the pursuit of material gain. It is also predicated upon the fulfillment of material desire, for supply seeks to meet demand, and it is this demand that is created and encouraged. Modern capitalism enhances and drives our basest desires of pleasure (because they are the most addictive and thus easiest to exploit) for monetary and material reward, and, therefore, modern capitalism, as the maximalization of our materialistic and consumerist proclivities, often works against any conceptions of deeper moral or spiritual questions and is ever at the door to overwhelm them. In reality, the free market, as it currently exists, often undermines the very deep convictions Christians uphold regarding the unchecked desires of pleasure and materialism and the dangers of greed and evaluating societal health in purely monetary terms. This is again not simply due to the fact that large industries revolve around meeting the basest desires because they are the most addictive, but also because of the naivety of thinking of the market in purely neutral terms and the mistaken premise that matters of ultimate concern and moral character are irrelevant to a consumerist society in which health is measured almost exclusively in terms of GDP (often accompanied with a complete disregard of personal and collective deficit spending and debt leveraged against future generations). For the church and for Christians, what is needed is deep reflection upon the truth of the gospel, and this will in fact entail a much more critical account of both capitalist and socialist forms of economic life, and the need for the church to witness beyond and against them.

## Conclusion

If Christians in the end favor a form of capitalism over state socialism in their public witness, and compelling arguments can be made for this position, such arguments cannot be based upon a belief in capitalism's absolute intrinsic superiority without remainder, but rather for the pragmatic reasons of capitalism's dissipation of the authoritarian power that a centralized economy possesses, as well as for the benefits a market economy produces with its ability to move beyond zero-sum conceptions of wealth in meeting the needs of persons over time.[65] The past demonstrates the dangers of centralized and collectivist failures, not only for economic reasons, but for more serious threats to the dignity and freedom of persons. Ideological socialism fails to realize that the drive for efficiency and equity of outcome in the end undercuts the very value, dignity, and freedom of the individual person.[66] At the same time, principled capitalists in the end gauge social health through the same materialist grid, though one predicated on consumerism rather than collectivism. Christians must be much more critical of both than they have been, and Barth's dialectical and principled rejection of any equation of the kingdom of God with current political or economic programs is a protection not only against naïve forms of economic optimism but, more importantly, against economic ideology and idolatry. In sum, Christians should, in economics and politics, as in all things, have a rich and vibrant dialectical imagination disciplined by the gospel which proceeds and exceeds all things. Such an imagination requires that all positions be open to re-visitation and revision in light of changing circumstances and human need. There is no timeless system.

Barth's understanding of the church may in the end provide a key for such thinking that exceeds his political and economic observations. His ecclesiology, in which authority and decision-making was never centralized in a universal magisterium or denominational structure, but was vested in the realm of the local congregation and regional synods, would point against overly-vested centralized governmental and economic authorities. If Barth's socialist convictions were not ideological but based, as Hunsinger states, upon socialism being "a series of concrete goals with strong affinities to the kingdom of God," then we are justified to ask if socialism is in fact the best current form for such commitments to be addressed.[67] It may, in fact, be argued that distributivism is a more worthy form of inquiry—here, it is not the state (nor is it corporations) that should be the center of economic policy, but persons themselves. This preserves the decentralization of capitalism, but also

---

[65] See Waters, *Just Capitalism*, 4.

[66] As but one historic example, the very (local) agrarian visions some socialists often uphold stand in opposition to the very (state) collectivist forms they espouse.

[67] Hunsinger, "Preface to the First Edition," *KBRP*, ix.

the equality of access (though not outcome) of socialism. Hints of this are already evident in recent returns to agrarian discussions, as well as in Catholic arguments for subsidiarity, such as those articulated in the 1931 encyclical *Quadragesimo Anno* and those prefigured earlier in *Rerum Novarum*. Indeed, an ecumenical project for both Catholic and Protestant Christians may be a reexamination of the possibilities of distributivism as an economic alternative to current forms of both corporate capitalism and state socialism, or at least as a regulatory principle and aspiration within the current global market economy.[68] That project would of course also have to be predicated upon a non-ideological and pragmatic examination of the strengths and weaknesses of such distributivism. But its consideration would require an investigation that must go beyond the current essay. What in the end must be said is that the church does indeed live within the world, but it should explore and point to answers that are not constrained by it. With creativity and courage, the church with humility is called to embrace the analogies and parables of the kingdom it finds within the world in this time between the times, while never confusing them for the kingdom itself, or even its own distinctive life and witness.

## Bibliography

Baranowski, Shelley. "The Primacy of Theology: Karl Barth and Socialism." *Studies in Religion* 10 (1981) 451–461.

Barnes, Kenneth J. *Redeeming Capitalism*. Grand Rapids: Eerdmans, 2018.

Barth, Karl. *Church Dogmatics*. Edited by G.W. Bromiley and T.F. Torrance, translated by G.W. Bromiley et al. Four volumes in 13 parts. Edinburgh: T. & T. Clark, 1936–77.

———. *Community, State, and Church: Three Essays*. Gloucester, MA: Smith, 1968.

———. *Final Testimonies*. Edited by Eberhard Busch, tranlated by Geoffrey W. Bromiley. Grand Rapids: Eerdmans, 1977.

———. *Gespräche 1964–1968*. Zürich: Theologischer Verlag Zürich, 1997.

———. *God in Action: Theological Addresses*. Translated by E.G. Homrighausen and Karl J. Ernst. New York: Roundtable, 1936.

---

[68] In such distributivism, workers might, therefore, receive stock in companies or businesses as well as wages as a form of payment, in effect one form of distributing capital ownership and not simply increasing wages (i.e., employee stock ownership plans—ESOPS). Such would entail that all persons in a company or corporation would share in both the wealth produced and the risk ventured by and in their common investment of labor as well as capital. As the persons of oversight and primary ownership draw salaries and stock, so should all persons within a company, though here, too, justice might be understood not in terms of equitable payment but of proportion in line with risk and investment ventured. Such a form of ownership and participation entails that risk and reward of the company is shared among all.

———. "Jesus Christ and the Movement for Social Justice." In *Karl Barth and Radical Politics*, 2nd ed., edited and translated by George Hunsinger, 1–23. Eugene, OR: Cascade, 2017.

———. *Karl Barth-Rudolf Bultmann Letters 1922–1966*. Edited by Bernd Jaspert and Geoffrey Bromiley. Edinburgh: T. & T. Clark, 1982.

———. *Vorträge und kleinere Arbeiten 1914–1921*. Edited by Hans-Anton Drewes. Zürich: Theologischer Verlag Zürich, 2012.

———. "Die Zunkunft des Christentums und der Sozialismus (1917). In *Vorträge und kleinere Arbeiten 1914–1921*, edited by Hans-Anton Drewes, 390–407. Zürich: Theologischer Verlag Zürich, 2012.

Busch, Eberhard. *Karl Barth: His Life from Letters and Autobiographical Texts*. Translated by John Bowden. Grand Rapids: Eerdmans, 1994.

Chung, Paul S. *Karl Barth: God's Word in Action*. Cambridge: James Clarke, 2008.

Gollwitzer, Helmut. "Kingdom of God and Socialism in the Theology of Karl Barth." In *Karl Barth and Radical Politics*, 2nd ed., edited and translated by George Hunsinger, 50–85. Eugene, OR: Cascade, 2017.

Hauerwas, Stanley. "A Christian Critique of Christian America." In *The Hauerwas Reader*, edited by John Berkman and Michael Cartwright, 459–80. Durham, NC: Duke University Press, 2003.

Hunsinger, George, ed. and trans. *Karl Barth and Radical Politics*, 2nd ed. Eugene, OR: Cascade, 2017.

———. "Toward a Radical Barth." In *Karl Barth and Radical Politics*, 2nd ed., 135–80. Eugene, OR: Cascade, 2017.

———. "Preface to the First Edition." In *Karl Barth and Radical Politics*, 2nd ed., ix–x. Eugene, OR: Cascade, 2017.

———. "Preface to the Second Edition." In *Karl Barth and Radical Politics*, 2nd ed., xi–xvii. Eugene, OR: Cascade, 2017.

Long, D. Stephen. *Divine Economy: Theology and the Market*. London: Routledge, 2000.

MacIntyre, Alasdair. *After Virtue*. 2nd ed. Notre Dame, IN: University of Notre Dame Press, 1984.

Marquardt, Friedrich-Wilhelm. "Erster Bericht über Karl Barths 'Sozialistisches Reden.'" In Friedrich-Wilhelm Marquardt, *Verwegenheiten: Theologische Stücke aus Berlin*. München: Kaiser, 1981, 470–88.

McGreal, Chris. "Where even Walmart won't go: How Dollar General took over rural America." https://www.theguardian.com/business/2018/aug/13/dollar-general-walmart-buhlerhaven-kansas.

Milanovic, Branko. *Capitalism, Alone: The Future of the System That Rules the World*. Cambridge, MA: Belknap/Harvard University Press, 2019.

Schweiker, William. "Responsibility in the World of Mammon." In *Religion and the Powers of the Common Life: God and Globalization Volume 1*, edited by Max Stackhouse and Peter Paris. Harrisburg, PA: Trinity Press, 2000.

Stackhouse, Max L. *Globalization and Grace: God and Globalization Volume 4*, 105–39. New York: Continuum, 2007.

———. "Spheres of Management: Social, Ethical, and Theological Reflections." In *Shaping Public Theology: Selections from the Writings of Max L. Stackhouse*, edited by Scott Paeth et al., 243–58. Grand Rapids: Eerdmans, 2014.

Stackhouse, Max L., and Dennis McCann. "A Post-Communist Manifesto: Public Theology after the Collapse of Communism." In *Shaping Public Theology: Selections from the Writings of Max L. Stackhouse*, edited by Scott Paeth et al., 221–29. Grand Rapids: Eerdmans, 2014.

Stackhouse, Max L., and Peter Paris, eds. *Religion and the Powers of the Common Life: God and Globalization Volume 1*. Harrisburg, PA: Trinity, 2000.

Scott, James. *Seeing Like a State: How Certain Schemes to Improve the Human Condition Have Failed*. New Haven, CT: Yale University Press, 1998.

United Nations. "Ending Poverty." https://www.un.org/en/sections/issues-depth/poverty/

Waters, Brent. *Just Capitalism: A Christian Ethic of Economic Globalization*. Louisville, KY: Westminster John Knox, 2016.

# General Index

Abelard, Peter 93
absolution 97 n.28
*adiaphora* 32
Albertus Magnus 92
Alexander of Hales 92
almsgiving 91
Ambrose 68
Anglican church 102
Anselm of Canterbury 79, 80, 81
anthropology 61, 70, 71, 195 n.62
Antony, Mark 148 n.58
Aquila 31
Aquinas, Thomas 91, 159, 160
Aristotelianism 155, 158, 160
Aristotle 155, 158
Armstrong, Chris xiv
Armstrong, Lawrin 157
Arzt-Grabner, Peter 33, 35
Asbury, Francis 112
asceticism 33, 40
aseity 46 n.2
assault 5
Augustine xxvii, 61–72, 169
  Augustinianism 70
Augustus 138, 139, 140, 142, 147
authoritarianism 182

Bacote, Vincent xiv
Baldwin, James xvi
Bale, John 74
banks/banking 91, 92, 93, 94, 98, 99, 108
bankruptcy 102
Barclay, John M.G. 29, 150
Barnabas 150
Barth, Karl xxiii, xxvi, xxviii, 176–98
  Barth's pragmatism 176–98
Beale, Greg K. 8, 9
Bell, Adrian 76
Bender, Kimlyn J. xxvii
Biggs, Robert D. 13
Blanco, Kathleen 41
Blanton IV, Thomas R. 31
Bloch, Ruth 107
Bonaventure 91
Breshears, Gerry xiv
Breu, Jörg the Elder 98 n.35
Brookins, Timothy 32
Brown, Peter 40

Buckingham, James Silk 107
Burton, Janet 77
Buschart, David xiii
Bush, George W. 41
Bysted, Ane 91, 94

capitalism xxvi, xxvii, 123, 132, 137, 176–98
  capital ownership 198 n.68
  capitalistic society 173
  corporate capitalism 185
  global capitalism 186, 191
Carey, Matthew 113
Carmelites 105
centralization 189
chantries 82–83, 84
character 166–72
charity(–ies) 91, 103, 104, 105, 106, 109, 110, 111, 113, 115, 190
Christendom 70, 157
Chrysostom, John 35 n.33, 41 n.52
church(es) xviii, xix, xx, xxiii, xxiv, xxv, 17, 22, 23, 25, 28, 29, 66, 70, 76, 77, 80, 81, 88, 89, 90, 91, 92, 98, 99, 102, 103, 104, 112, 117, 145, 147, 158, 162, 170, 178, 179, 181, 182, 184, 190, 195, 196, 198
  ecclesial body xviii, xix, xx
  ecclesial communities 69, 70
  ecclesial home xix
  ecclesio-economics 98
  ecclesiology 197
  house churches 29
  medieval church 74
  mystical body of Christ 91
  Philippian church 32
  redeemed community 25
  redemptive community 17
  regenerate community 64, 65
  unregenerate community 64, 65
Cicero 66, 67, 138, 141
civil rights 108
civilization 3
classicism 195 n.62
Claudius 140
Cohen, A. 129
coherence xxiv, xxv, xxvi
Cohick, Lynn H. xxvii
collectivism 186, 188

Colvin, Howard 84
commerce xxv, 194
　commercialism 187
　commercialization 90, 194
commodification 51, 187
common good, the 40
commonwealth(s) 67, 68, 69
communism 180, 181, 182, 196
community(–ies) 11, 12, 13, 16, 52,
　144, 156, 165, 167, 183
　Christian community 29
　civil communities 69
　communal merit 98
compartmentalization 61
complacency xxiv
confession 89, 90, 96
　penance 88
conflict(s) 63, 64
conscience 166–72
　personal conscience 155
consumerism 196, 197
contracts 167 n.56
　contract rights xxv
conversion 36, 68
Cornuelle, Richard 105, 117
corporation(s) 102, 103, 104, 105,
　106, 108, 115, 116, 195 n.62, 197,
　198 n.68
covenant(s) 22, 46
　Abrahamic covenant 21
　divine-national covenant 23
　Mosaic covenant 17, 21
　new covenant 21, 22
　old covenant 22
Cranmer, Thomas 82
creation xx, xxvi, xxvii, 3, 4, 10, 11,
　17, 18, 19, 45, 46, 47, 48, 49, 50,
　53, 54, 55, 56, 128 n.23, 156, 157,
　158, 160 n.26, 163–66, 170, 172,
　173, 192 n.55
　creation mandate 4, 5, 9, 10, 11–
　　12, 13
credit 93, 166
Croasmun, Matthew xiii, xv n.1, xx,
　xxiii
Cross, Anthony R. xxvii
cross, the 21, 47, 49, 80 n.31
Cummean 89
Cynics (Roman) 67 n.5, 138, 145

Dale, Richard 76
Damian, Peter 89
De Tocqueville, Alexis 105

Deane, Herbert 67, 69
Debs, Eugene V. 114
decentralization 192, 193, 197
Deibert, Ronald 87
Deism 112
Deissman, Adolf 135, 136
democracy xxv, 40, 184, 185, 192, 193
　n.57
depersonalization 190
discipleship 16, 21, 23, 26, 55
disenfranchisement 182, 190 n.51
distributivism 197, 198
doctrine of merits 79, 81
domestic home(s)/household xvi, xviii,
　xix
Donatists 68
Donkin, R.A. 77
dualism 70, 71, 194
Duffy, Eamon 75, 76
Dunne, John Anthony xxvii

eclecticism 194
ecology xv, xvi, xvii, xix, 51 n.12, 55
　n.21
　climate change 52 n.16
　ecojustice 52 n.15
　ecological collapse/challenge xv,
　　xx
　ecological home(s) xvii, xix, xx
　ecosystem degradation 54 n.17
economics xv, xvi, xx, xxiv–xxv, xxvii,
　12, 31, 40, 41, 123, 156, 157, 158,
　161, 162, 164, 167, 168, 172, 173,
　179, 181, 182, 183, 190, 193, 194,
　195, 196, 197, 198
　economic activity 78
　economic democracy 185
　economic development xxiv, xxv,
　　62
　economic engagement 176–98
　economic equality 41
　economic flourishing 123
　economic freedom 104
　economic inequality 137
　economic justice 135–51, 192
　　n.55
　economic life xxv
　economic philosophy 194
　economic policies 176
　economic regulation 192
　medieval economics 77–78
economy, the 51 n.13, 76, 77, 104,
　108, 135, 137, 156, 157, 161, 162,

# General Index

163–66, 168, 169, 170, 171, 172, 188, 198
market economies 196
secularized economies 173
Eisermann, Falk 88
Ekelund, Robert B. 30
Epaphroditus 29
Epictetus 138
Epicureans 145
equality 148, 149, 150
  egalitarianism xxv, 189 n.47
  inequality 187
  spiritual equality 66
equity 149
eschatology xix, xxi, 18, 24, 31, 36, 37, 38, 39, 40, 41, 45, 47, 48, 55, 56, 65, 66, 68, 69, 71, 144, 151, 157, 173
Essenes 142, 144, 145
Estes, Daniel J. xxvii
eternal good 65, 69
ethics xxiv, xxvii, 28 n.5, 61, 156, 170, 179, 188, 196
  ethic(s) of care xvi, xvii, xix, xx
  theological ethics 16
ethnicity 17
  ethnic cohesion 22, 23
  ethnic diversity 18, 19, 20
  ethnic reconciliation 22
  ethnic unity 19
eudemonism 64
Euodia 32
Evagrius 41 n.52
evangelicals 132, 133
exploitation 28, 51, 126 n.16
  overexploitation 54
extinction(s) 54 n.17

faith, the xxvi, xxvii, 31, 70, 90, 110, 131
Finley, Moses I. 135
forgiveness 13, 21, 80, 81, 87, 89
formal associations 108
Forster, Greg xiv, xxvii
Fox, Michael V. 128
Foxe, John 74, 75
fragmentation xxiv–xxv, xxvi
Francis I, King 97
free market 176
freedom 160
  liberty 188
  personal freedom 155
Friesen, Steven J. 136

Gardner, Gregg E. 144 n.46
Geffken, Johannes 96
Geiler, Johann 97
generosity 22, 166, 167, 190
gift(s) 163–66
  giving practices 135
Gill, Deborah xiv
Ginzburg, Lori 108
globalization xv
Golden Rule, the 109, 156, 160
Goldingay, John 6, 9
Goldsworthy, Graeme xxiii
Goldwater, Barry 116, 117
Gollwitzer, Helmut 177
gospel, the 13, 16–27, 29, 33, 47, 68, 145, 146, 162, 164, 181, 196, 197
government(s) 109, 115
Graham, Billy 114 n.67
Grandin, Mary Temple 51 n.13
greed 42, 51, 125, 156, 167, 170
Gregory of Nyssa 40, 41 n.52
Gregory, Eric 64, 72
Gutenberg, Johannes 94, 95
Guthrie, Donald xiv

Hadrian 148 n.58
Hamilton, Victor P. 5
Hamm, Bernd 88
Hansmann, Henry 103
Hauerwas, Stanley 193 n.57
Henry of Langenstein 167 n.56
Henry of Susa 90, 91
Herod Archelaus 142
Hill, P.J. xiv
Hitchcock, Nathan xiii, xiv, xxvii
Hock, Ronald F. 135
holiness 72
home xvi, xvii, xix, xx, xxi
  civic home(s) xvii, xix, xx
  cosmological home(s) xix
  household code(s) xviii, xix
  physiological home xvii
  private home xvii
  public homes xvii
  somatic home(s) xix
homogenization 186
Hoover, Herbert 116
hope xxvi, xxvii, 56, 131
Horsley, Richard 137
Hugh of Saint-Cher 90, 91
human flourishing/flourishing life xv, xx, xxi, xxiii, xxiv, xxv, xxvi, xxvii,

3–14, 45–56, 123, 124, 133, 156, 173
flourishing of all creation 45–56
human rights xxiv, xxv, 40
humanism 87 n.4
humanization 195
    dehumanization 187
humiliation 42
humility 130 n.35
Hunsinger, George 179, 184, 185, 197
Hus, Jan 74
Hüssy, Walter 177, 178

identity 16, 17, 22
ideology 190–96
individualism 26, 188
indulgences 87–99
inflation 93
interdependence/interdependency xv, xvi, xvii

James, Apostle 150
Jannsen, Johannes 96
Jefferson, Thomas 115
Jesus Christ 11, 16, 21, 23, 24, 25, 26, 30, 33, 41, 47, 48, 56, 65, 71, 72, 75, 79, 90, 93, 114, 145, 146, 149, 158, 160, 166, 177, 184, 190, 191
    Christ's suffering and death 79
    christology xix, 182, 195 n.62
    death and resurrection of Christ 80, 146
    incarnation 47, 48 n.7, 79, 146
    merit of Christ 99
    resurrection of Jesus Christ 21, 24, 26, 47, 48
    sacrificial death of Christ 80
    Suffering Servant, the 38
    sufferings of Christ 79, 146
    vicarious satisfaction 98
Jindal, Bobby 41
John, Apostle 150
John the Baptist 72
Josephus 142, 144
jubilee 52
Judge, Edwin A. 135, 137
judgment 39, 71, 124 n.5, 143
Julius Caesar 138
just war 65, 71
justice 3–14, 40, 68, 71, 72, 144, 148, 150, 184 n.31, 192 n.55

injustice xxiv, 41 n.52, 143, 145–50, 151, 162
    environmental injustices 52 n.16
    public justice 67
    social justice 40, 137, 177, 195 n.62
justification 39, 81

Karam Forum xiii
Keesmat, Sylvia 137
Kern Family Foundation xiv
kingdom of God xx, 12, 23, 33, 41, 42, 56, 61, 67, 69, 70, 71, 72, 177, 178, 179, 181, 183, 184, 190, 196, 197, 198
Kinney, Hannah 108
Kitchen, John A. 130
Kloppenborg, John S. 147, 149
knowledge xxiii, xxiv, xxvi, xxvii
Knox, John 37
Koch, Klaus 123, 129
Kuyper, Abraham 132
Kuyperianism 67, 70

labor xvi, 190
Lamoreaux, Naomi 107
law 62, 63, 65, 66
    criminal law 62
    legal judgment 62, 63, 65, 66
    modern natural law 70
    Mosaic law 23, 144
    natural law 156, 159, 160, 165, 166–72
Le Goff, Jacques 87
Lenin 186 n.37
Lett, Jonathan xxvii
Lewis, C.S. 71
liberation theology 67, 70
Lieber, Francis 106
Locke, John 104
Lollards 82
Lombard, Peter 82
Longenecker, Bruce 136
love xxvi, xxvii, 26, 46, 67, 131, 146, 163, 170, 172
Luschner, Johann 95
Luther, Martin xxvii, 87, 88, 98, 155–73
Lydia 31

MacCulloch, Diarmaid 97
MacIntyre, Alasdair 187, 188, 189, 191

Macrina 40, 41
Marxism 180 n.17, 182, 184 n.31
materialism xxiv, 196
  material prosperity 115
Mather, Cotton 104
McCann, Dennis 195 n.62
McDonald, Suzanne xxvii
McKane, William 130
means of production 177
media history 88
medieval superstition 82
Meeks, Wayne A. 135
Meggitt, Justin 136
Meir, Rabbi 142 n.41
mercantilism 194
merit 98
Methodists 111, 112
Middleton, Richard 7
migration xv
Milbank, John 157
Miller, Patrick 124
mission 16, 21, 22, 23, 28, 30, 31, 37,
  80 n.31
  evangelism 16, 26, 31
modernism 186 n.37, 190
  modernity xxiv, 16, 155, 156
  premodernity xxv
modernization xxvi
Moenjak, Thammarak 93
money xxiv, 155, 159, 160, 163
  monetary depreciation 96 n.26
  monetary theory 88
  money surplus 94
monopoly(-ies) 115
morals 196
  moral formation xxiv
  morality 188
Mouw, Richard xxiii, xxiv, 24
Murphy, Roland E. 127, 131

narcissism xxiv
nations 16–27
  national identity 23
  nationalism 26, 195 n.62
  nationality 17
  nationhood 23
  nation-state(s) 16
Nelson, Tom xiv
neo-Anabaptism 67
neoconservatives 195 n.62
Nero 141
new consensus 135
Newbigin, Lesslie xxiii

nominalists 167 n.56
Noonan, John 158
Nuth, Joan 79

O'Donovan, Oliver xxiii, xxiv, 68
obligation(s) 150, 191
  lamentable obligation 61–72
Ogereau, Julien M. 148
*oikology* xvi, xviii, xix, xx
Oikonomia Network, the xiii, xiv, xxvi
*oikonomia* xvii, xix
Onesimus 29, 30, 32, 33, 34, 35, 36,
  41
Oppenheim, A. Leo 13
Origen 41 n.52
Otis, James 106
Ovid 139, 140

pacifism 63, 184 n.31
pacifists 71
pandemic xv, xvi
*parousia* 30, 36, 37, 39, 40, 69
Pastafarianism 112
Paul, Apostle xvii, xviii, xix, xx, xxiii,
  xxvi, xxvii, 23, 28–42, 123, 135–
  51
Paula 41 n.52
peace 22, 26, 62, 63, 65, 66, 67, 71,
  72, 184 n.31
Pennington, Jonathan xxiii
Peraudi, Raymund 95, 96
personalization 187
Peter, Apostle 23, 80 n.31, 81, 150
Peters, Greg xxvii
philanthropy 110, 117
Philemon 29, 33, 34, 35, 36, 41
Philo 142, 143, 144
philosophy xv, 64, 68, 194
  pagan philosophies 64
Phoebe 31, 32
Pickman, C. Gayton 107
piety 76, 83 n.43, 96
pilgrim(s)/pilgrimage(s) 76, 77, 91
Plato 64
Pleins, J. David 128
pluralization 69
Plutarch 138
politics xxv, 23, 24, 62, 63, 67, 164,
  178, 180 n.18, 181, 182, 183, 184,
  186, 188, 190, 192, 194, 195, 197
  anti-political theologies 67, 68,
    69, 70, 71, 72
  political activity 65

political conflict 62
political structures xxv
political theology 61–72
social politics 111
Pope, the 74, 75, 91
   Clement VI 80 n.31
   Francis I xv
   Leo X 97
   Sixtus IV 97
   Urban II 90
population shifts xv
Porphyry 66
Porter, Jean 158
Porterfield, Amanda 102
   Porterfield thesis 102–17
poverty 41, 123–33, 135–51, 162, 172, 187 n.40
   apostolic poverty 146
   poverty of Christ 146
   voluntary poverty 138, 145
Presbyterian churches 112
priesthood of all believers xxv
printing press, the 87–99
Priscilla 31
privatization 137
   privatization of faith 25
profit(s) 165, 166, 167
   for-profit business(es) 102, 103, 107
   nonprofit business(es)/companies xxvii, 102–17
   private profits 177
property xxv
protectionism 194
Protestantism 98, 109, 112, 177
   Protestant church 75
   Protestant denominations 111
Protestants 88, 198
Proverbs, Book of xxiii, xxvii, 123–33
providence 47, 75, 131 n.38
Ptolemy 142
punishment 92
purgatory 82, 84, 92, 98
   purgatorial rules 98

Quakers 104
quantity theory of money 94
quietism 182

racism 195 n.62
Rae, Scott xiv
Ramelli, Ilaria 40
Rastafarianism 112

reason 158, 159
reconciliation 22, 26
   reconciliation of nations 16
redemption 2, 3, 21, 16–27, 191
Reformation, the 74, 75, 133
   Protestant Reformation 87, 88, 97
reformers 99
   Protestant reformers 74
regeneration 64, 65, 68
regulation 194
Reiner, Erica 13
religious freedom xxiv, xxv, 69, 103
religious houses/monasteries 77, 78, 81, 82, 83, 84, 92
   medieval monasticism 74–84
   medieval monks 77–78
   medieval soteriology 84
   religious orders
      Benedictines 77 n.17, 78
      Cistercians, the 77, 78, 79
      Cluniacs 92
      Dominicans 90
      Sisters of Our Lady of Mercy 105
religious structures xxv
retribution 124
righteousness 80, 92, 93, 98, 129, 130, 131, 166, 178 n.10
Robbins, Mary 110
Roberts, Jonathan 108
Roman Catholic Church 87, 88, 94
   Roman Catholicism 185, 198
   medieval Catholicism 75
Roman Catholics 103, 105, 111, 198
Ross, Allen P. 125
Roth, Ulrike 28–42
Rubin, Miri 82

sabbath(s) 52, 163
   sabbath command 50
sacrament 80
   baptism 35, 38 n.41
   eucharist, the 79, 80, 81, 82, 84
   Lord's supper 135
   mass, the 81–82, 83, 84
   masses for the dead 82, 83
sacred, the 35
   sacred work 31, 41
salvation 13, 14, 17, 23, 25 n.17, 47, 88, 90, 183 n.29, 191
   cosmic salvation 25 n.17
   divine economy, the 155–73

## General Index

economies of salvation xxvii, 74–84
sanctification 68, 71, 72
Saucy, Mark 8, 9
Schiedel, Walter 136
Schleiermacher, Friedrich xxvi
scholasticism 155, 156, 158–61, 169, 171
Scholastics 155, 159
Schweiker, William 187
Schwinges, Rainer Christoph 90
Scott, James 185, 186, 187, 188, 189, 195
secular work/job 31, 41
secular, the 35
secularization 69, 113
Self, Charlie xiv
Seneca 32, 33, 138
Seneca the Elder 140
Sermon on the Mount, the 11–12, 168
sexism 195 n.62
Shaner, Katherine 32
shrines 30, 76
simony 89
sin 3, 5, 6, 9, 10, 12, 13, 14, 17, 18–21, 22, 23, 24, 45, 46, 47, 50, 55, 64, 80, 89, 90, 98, 164, 166, 167, 172, 178 n.10, 191
slave(s) 28–42, 150
slavery 5, 28–42, 115, 141, 143
  abolition of slavery 108
  economics of slavery 28–42
  manumission 36 n.33, 40, 139
  masters (of slaves) 150
Smith, Adam 112
social coherence xxv
social conflict xxv
social engineering 186, 189 n.48
social life xxv
social networks 108
social problems/ills 114, 115, 116
social structures 61
socialism xxvi, xxvii, 114 n.68, 123, 176–98
  democratic socialism 183
  ideological socialism 197
  pragmatic socialism 179
  religious socialism 179, 181
socialists 114 n.68, 197 n.66
socioeconomics xvii, xviii, xx
sociology 195 n.62
soteriology 18, 47, 64, 70, 79, 92

soteriological universalism 47
spiritual discipline 77
spiritual freedom 66
Stackhouse, Max 184 n.32, 195 n.62
Staupitz, Johann 97
Stearns, Jonathan 107
stewardship 49
stewardship of the world's resources 3
Stillman, Hannah 108
Stoicism 138
Stoics 145
Strauss, Jakob 171 n.78
subduing the earth 3–14
subjectivity 155
subsidiarity 185, 198
Suetonius 147
suffering 68, 108, 136, 138, 145, 146
Summenhart, Conrad 167 n.56
sustainability 54
Swanson, R.N. 81
Sylla, Richard 103
Syntyche 32

Tacitus 138
tax(es)/taxation/taxpayers 107, 114, 115, 116, 141
Taylor, Charles 157
Taylor, John W. xxvii
technology xxvii
technological development xxiv, xxv
technological innovation 76
temporal good 65, 69
temporal punishment(s) 90, 91, 92
Tertius 29, 31
Tetzel, Johann 97
theo-cosmological view of the world 157, 159, 166, 171, 172, 173
theology xiii, xvi, xx, xxiii, xxiv, xxv, xxvi, xxvii, 23, 36, 41, 54, 61, 64, 65, 66, 67, 68, 69, 70, 72, 84, 88, 179, 180 n.18, 182, 194, 195 n.62
Thiessen, Gerd 135
Thigpen, J. Michael xiii, xxvii
Tiberius Caesar 139, 140
Ticciati, Susannah xvi
Timothy 31
Titus 31
Tollison, Robert D. 30
Trajan 147
treasury of merit 79, 80, 81, 91, 93
triune God, the 46, 55

Tucker, Brian 149
Tuckerman, Joseph 111
Tychicus 31

Unitarians 111
usury xxvii, 155–73
utilitarianism 186, 194

Vander Hart, Mark D. 8
VanDrunen, David, xxiii, xxiv
Vanhoozer, Kevin xxiii
Varro 66
Vassiliadis, Peter 149
violence 7, 62, 64, 65, 67, 130
Volf, Miroslav xiii, xv n.1, xvi, xx, xxiii
voluntary associations 102, 103, 104, 105, 106, 115
voluntary collection for the poor 147, 149

Walsh, Brian 137
Waltke, Bruce K. 129, 131
Washington, Harold C. 126

water technologies 76 n.9
wealth 42, 129, 131, 142, 151, 163, 172, 182, 190 n.51, 192 n.55
wealth creation xxv
Weber, Max 155, 172
Welborn, L.L. 148
White, Michael 35
widows 147, 150, 151
Willard, Dallas xxiii, 26
William of Auxerre 159, 160
Wink, Walter xxiii
Winterhager, Wilhelm Ernst 97
women 29, 41 n.52, 108
Wong, Fook-Kong 127
work xxv, 190
works (good and bad) 70
World Wildlife Fund 54
worship 3, 23, 25
Wright, Christopher xxiii
Wright, Robert E. xxvii
Wycliffe, John 74, 93

Yoder, John Howard xxiii, xxiv

www.ingramcontent.com/pod-product-compliance
Lightning Source LLC
Chambersburg PA
CBHW051641230426
43669CB00013B/2391